Lets be better !

ETHICS @ WORK

ISBN: 9788797284100 (print)
ISBN: 9788797284117 (e-book)

Date of publishing: February 2022

ETHICS @ WORK

DILEMMAS OF THE NEAR FUTURE AND HOW YOUR ORGANIZATION CAN SOLVE THEM

EDITED BY KRIS ØSTERGAARD

To my children Aya, Zoey, Louise, Emilie & Izabella
who need an ethics revolution

CONTENTS

INTRODUCTION: IMAGINE A NEAR FUTURE

KRIS ØSTERGAARD

Imagine a near future. Recent leapfrogs within deep learning have enabled your company to develop an "objective computer system" that can analyze massive data sets from a variety of sources at a far greater capacity than, probably, any other organization in the world. Amongst many opportunities to leverage this advantage, the executive team is considering installing the computer system as Head of Department and make it the de facto boss of a team of 25 people. Considerations are that this is a large enough department to create true learnings before a bigger rollout and also small enough that risks are acceptable. Not surprisingly, it is a controversial project, which raises a host of ethical questions. Will an AI be able to manage the not-so-rational behaviors of human beings? Is it ethical to give AI power over humans? If yes, then how to hold AI accountable? Are humans willing to be managed by AI? Can it be guaranteed that there are no hidden biases in the algorithms, etc?

This scenario may sound far-fetched until you consider that hundreds of thousands of people, in effect, already work for AI. Think about the Amazon warehouse worker or the driver for a ride-hailing service like Uber or Lyft, who are assigned tasks and monitored algorithmically. Even penalized and fired algorithmically. So, to put you on the spot: if you were a key decision-maker in this scenario, would you choose to install the "objective computer system" as manager? The fact is that due to exponential and converging technologies, we are rapidly heading into a world where we will have to make many decisions like this that are without precedent and where prior experience, or common sense don't apply. The mentioned dilemma is one of several that we have been debating with both senior executives, graduates and students in our education programs over the last couple of years. It turns out that people, regardless of seniority, find this and other near-future dilemmas really hard to navigate. (One interesting finding from our debates on the mentioned scenario is that senior leaders who vote to install the computer system as Head of Department often wouldn't want to work for it themselves).

It is also a clear learning that even in the biggest, most successful companies of the world, most professionals are not accustomed to discussing neither current nor near-future ethical dilemmas. They lack awareness of the increasing need to do so. They lack a language and the analytical tools to identify important dilemmas. And they have a very limited toolbox to create the principles to guide their decision-making as well as operational frameworks to turn those principles into concrete actions. In short, when it comes to ethics in an organizational context, it is early days. Most organizations are too ethically illiterate. And the clock is ticking.

That is the motivation for publishing this book. It is our ambition to support professionals in identifying important ethical dilemmas they may already be facing—but that they certainly will face in the near future—and explore which thinking and tools might help solve those dilemmas. An important caveat here: there are no easy answers. "Seven Steps to Successful Ethics" is not a thing. Ethics is complicated. Ethical dilemmas are complicated. Future ethical dilemmas even more so. So, exploring solutions takes time, effort and a lot of heavy thinking, debating and acting. That is why, in this anthology we have asked some of the world's foremost thinkers and doers to examine a variety of ethical dilemmas they find to be the most important, taking their own domain expertise and experiences as the starting point.

The anthology has been designed to provide you with the opportunity to shop around and read whatever essay you find most compelling in the order that makes the most sense to you. Some topics covered here you have probably never thought about; some may lay a good step into your future; some you may be knee-deep into. But all are important for our future and, hopefully, you will experience learnings, provocations and food for thought in all of them. Given the nature of an anthology, each essay could easily demand an entire book's worth of focus. So, it is also our hope that you will use this anthology as a shortcut to explore many important ethical topics and then specifically identify where you need to deep dive further to learn even more about the dilemmas and solutions than what each essay here can provide.

Despite the intent of enabling you to shop around in the anthology, there is some method to the madness and, thus, the book is divided into three parts: "System," "Organization" and "Human." Essays collected under "System" have a wide lens perspective and explore ethics at a macro angle. Essays under "Organization" move into the machine room of running an organization and essays under "Human" take the human beings who are at the core of any organization as their primary center of attention.

A final important point to highlight about this anthology—it is a non-profit project. This means that all essayists as well as project owners behind the scenes have been working pro-bono and do not receive payment for their efforts. All profits made from book sales will be channeled into other awareness-providing activities around ethics at work such as virtual and physical events, conferences, workshops. etc. By following the activities on www.rehumanize institute.org you can see whenever there are new activities. Also, we have chosen to publish under our own imprint Re:humanize Publishing to be able to keep the project non-profit and, equally important, to allow all essayists to maintain all rights to their own work. If you are familiar with the publishing world, you will know that this is otherwise rarely a possibility. We cannot thank the contributors, both on and off stage enough for believing so much in the importance of putting out this anthology to which they have contributed their most valuable resources—time and brainpower. We are in awe of your skills and grateful for your dedication!

Below you will find a short introduction to each of the essays in the anthology. We hope they will make you reflect, learn, enjoy, share and act.

SYSTEM – THE BIG PICTURE

The anthology kicks off with an essay by biomedical and electrical engineer Adam Pantanowitz who sets the scene by exploring the three existential layers of the world—natural, conceptual and digital—and the responsibilities we must take as we couple ourselves more closely to the digital world while the digital world simultaneously has started to decouple from us. In the following essay Margarita Quihuis, Co-Director of Stanford's Peace Innovation Lab and I discuss the relationship between peace and business. Margarita argues why we must start by asking ourselves the fundamental question: "How good can we be to each other?" Dr. David Bray, Founder and Inaugural Director of the Atlantic Council's GeoTech Center dives into *Why a More People-Centered Approach to Data Science Can Help Societies Thrive* given that "future historians may conclude modern human brains weren't ready for the sheer scale of data that we will produce in the next decade." Nell Watson, a researcher of emerging technologies who, amongst many other initiatives, has started the platform Pacha.org—which connects service providers to help enable the automated accounting of externalities—discusses why we must stop sending the bill of our organizations' current negative impacts to future generations and how we can do this to create what she calls a *Eucatastrophal Phoenix*. Sheila Jasanoff, Pforzheimer Professor of Science and Technology Studies at the Harvard Kennedy School and author of *The Ethics of Invention* explores the transformation our societies are in the midst of where the private sector increasingly takes over responsibilities that used to be reserved for the public sector in *When Public Goes Private: Ethics for Workers in the Digital Economy*. This shift in responsibilities has profound implications for the private sector, which needs to "align their ethical thinking more closely with principles of good governance," Sheila argues. In *The Ethical Paradox of Business Modernization*, Valter Adão, Chief Executive for Cadena Growth Partners argues why digitization, which up until the COVID-19 pandemic, to a very large extent was perceived as the enemy of the lucrative status quo, has become our best ally to not only conquer the pandemic, but also enable organizations to create a better future. Finally, futurist and Director of Arizona State University's Threatcasting Lab, Brian David Johnson discusses *Autonomous Sentient Technologies and the Future of Ethical Business*. The big question that organizations need to answer, according to Brian, is not how to develop ethical AI but how to make their future multitude of AIs ethically compliant to the "rules, culture, regulation, business practices and laws that govern" an organization.

ORGANIZATION – INSIDE THE MACHINE ROOM

Part two of the anthology moves from part one's big picture perspective and zones in on crucial dilemmas that are or will be experienced in the machine room of all organizations—and how to possibly solve them.

Dr. Tiffany Vora, who holds a PhD in Molecular Biology from Princeton and is the current Faculty and Vice Chair of Medicine and Digital Biology at Singularity University, opens the investigation by exploring how other industries can apply learnings and methods from biomedicine, which is a field with a long history of applied ethics in *Infusing Ethics into Your Business – Insights from Biomedical Ethics*. Benjamin Rosman, Associate Professor in the School of Computer Science and Applied Mathematics at the University of the Witwatersrand then explores the fundamentals to *Making Effective and Ethical Business Decisions*. As Benjamin states: "We know from research into behavioral economics that the human brain discounts future rewards." Nevertheless, there lies not only tremendous reward but also tremendous need in figuring out how to think of and calculate value in the future to truly make the right decisions.

Then follows three essays that have a distinct focus on artificial intelligence. Firstly, Elaine Weidman-Grunewald & Anna Felländer, Co-Founders of the AI Sustainability Center look into *Managing the Ethics of Data-Driven Solutions* by identifying three areas in particular where this is crucial: recruitment, delivery of products and services, and process optimizations for tailored client relationships. Secondly, Guendalina Dondé, Head of Research at the Institute of Business Ethics shares their interactive framework of fundamental values and principles for the use of AI in *Understanding Human Values to Develop Values-Led Technologies*. Thirdly, Ray Eitel-Porter, Managing Director at Accenture and Global Lead for Responsible AI closes off the AI section with *The Ethics of Artificial Intelligence* where he suggests practical steps for ethical leaders to ensure organizations actually live up to their principles. Jaya Baloo, Chief Information Security Officer of software company Avast, then turns the focus but keeps us in the digital realm by taking us down the ethical rabbit holes of cybersecurity and privacy in her aptly titled essay *Don't Destroy Security and Privacy to Save It*.

The next several essays of part two all take different starting points to uncover how organizations can identify, avoid and eliminate ethical dilemmas as well as make a bigger positive, future-oriented impact in society by applying specific lenses and tools: Arash Aazami shares his own journey of turning established business models upside down by building an energy company that earned more as it sold less energy. In the essay *Seeking Wisdom in Business*, he challenges us to consider how we can base our businesses and business models on wisdom rather than just on intelligence.

An important set of tools to move ethically into the future come from the design world since "a rule of thumb says that 85 percent of a new product's environmental impact is defined in the design phase," according to the two authors of *Ethical Design – The Competitive Edge of the 21ˢᵗ Century?* Christian Villum & Christian Bason, respectively Director of Digital & Future Thinking and CEO of the Danish Design Centre. One of the tools is an ethical compass they are developing and sharing the exciting prospects of. Mic Mann, Co-CEO of SingularityU South Africa and Mann Made explores the increased present and future merge between humans and machines in the workplace in *The Exponential Professional – Ethics in An Age of Human-Machine Convergence*. In her provocatively titled essay *The Ethics of Blowing Up Your Job Description*, Carin Ism, Co-Founder of the Future of Governance Agency examines the responsibilities you as a business leader should consider taking on as a consequence of your digitization efforts. Even possibly offering a form of Universal Basic Income to the people your automations will make unemployed. Alex Gladstein, Chief Strategy Officer of the Human Rights Foundation continues in setting the bar high for organizations by making the argument for *Investing with Democratic Values in Mind* given that "the kind of investments we make today will determine the society of the future. And, unfortunately, that future is headed in the wrong direction unless we make a drastic change." The final two essays in the organizational machine room discuss corporate activism as a tool to build more ethical companies and societies. Nille Skalts, who is a corporate activist and founder of the Nordic B Corp Movement, conducts an analysis of activist pioneers Ben & Jerry's in *Corporate Activism – Corporations Ready to Fight – And Die – For Their Beliefs*. And Patagonia's HR Director, EMEA, Evelyn Doyle shares how their organization embeds activism into its DNA and literally works off a purpose to "save our home planet" in *The Art of Unlearning: Why Organizations Need to Rethink Business as Usual.*

HUMAN – AT THE CORE

The third part of the anthology takes the final step into the core and examines ethics with the human at the core.

Divya Chander, who is an anesthesiologist, neuroscientist and serial entrepreneur, starts us off by examining what you might argue is the very core of human beings: the brain.

She brings us into a future, which you might find to be surprisingly, and shockingly near where we have to figure out how we can protect our own brain prints and digital twins from misuse in the essay *I Think, Therefore I am – Neural Sovereignty and Neural Rights in the 21*st *Century.*

Mei Lin Fung, Chair and Co-Founder with Vint Cerf of People-Centered Internet turns our focus from the brain to the heart with *Human Relationships – The Ethical Heart of Resilient Organizations and Communities*. Mei Lin delivers a strong critique of how organizational systems negatively impact human relationships: "Technology is obedient – doing only what you program it to do. When we incentivize CEOs to increase the stock price, to grow profits, they no longer prioritize measuring what matters to humans," and rhetorically asks: "Should we be surprised to suffer deteriorating customer relationships, employee relationships, community relationships, neighborhood relationships and family relationships?" She also proposes a way forward by creating Networked Leadership Competencies.

Nathaniel Calhoun, who has guided hundreds of impact-driven startups to leverage technology to solve the world's biggest problems, then shares concrete tools on how to build human-centered ethical cultures from the ground up in *Business Ethics – Every Employee, Every Quarter*. Isabelle Ringnes, Co-Founder and Chief Evangelist of Equalitycheck.it—a platform for anonymous reviews about equality and diversity in the workplace—continues that conversation by sharing her insights on the importance, pitfalls and potentials of diversity in *Effectively Managing a Diverse Organization Relies on Ethical Leadership*. Then Roger Courage Matthisen dives further into that field in *Embodying Anti-racism Work in Business* before the final three essays double down on why it is crucial to put the human at the core. Yngvar Ugland, Executive Vice President at Norway's biggest bank DNB, head of its NewTechLab and the country's first consumer technologist, argues why *We Owe It to Our Grandchildren to Fix the Bugs in the Human Algorithm* in a world where computers are becoming better than us in more and more domains. Daisy Løvendahl, who is a therapist, speaker and author of the trilogy Live, Love and Die, dares us to consider *Why Companies Should Care about Everyone's Love Life*. And finally, Laila Pawlak, Co-Founder and CEO of Re:humanize Institute, explores the inner workings of human motivation and values in relationship to the paradox, which we find fitting to end this anthology's many reflections with: *Rehumanize - The More Technological We Become the More Human We Need to Become*.

Enjoy!

KRIS ØSTERGAARD

Besides being the editor of this anthology, Kris has more than two decades of experience as a behavioural researcher. He has authored or co-authored several books including *Transforming Legacy Organizations*, where he thoroughly investigated innovation in large, complex systems. He is Co-Founder of the educational institution SingularityU Nordic and has previously co-founded and run accelerators, incubators and co-working spaces. He is also a GeoTech Center Action Council Member at the Atlantic Council (a nonpartisan organization that works towards shaping a stronger future together). When Kris is not writing, researching or teaching he keynotes globally on innovation, ethics and technological development.

SYSTEM –
THE BIG PICTURE

WITH GREAT APES COMES GREAT RESPONSIBILITY

ADAM PANTANOWITZ

Why do we expect so much from one another? We are simply Great Apes of an approximately 200,000-year vintage era. There is no manual to our existence: we make it all up as we go along. Moreover, this moment in time is like all the moments before: it is the first time the world is in its current state. It is the first time it is all being done. Why are we so hard on ourselves? There is no playbook, no guideline rules to navigate this frontier that marches us forward through each small action collectively cascading into this planetary forge.

We've been aware of our conscious selves for a moment of those 200,000 years and reached a pinnacle for this in the era of the instantly connected world. We now observe ourselves and one another with remarkable precision in stories told instantaneously over a great distance.

Consider that ethics is having an awareness that our thoughts and actions have consequences. These thoughts and actions are informed by individual values, but they have a downstream impact on other conscious beings. The impact may be over a great distance, in time and space.

We, humans, arrange ourselves into interesting structures and organizations together. These are living organisms consisting of human brains and machines, which go out and perform actions in the world. As a corollary, we can as individual actors come up with a new concept, go out into the world, and act.

We can build something from an idea that persists beyond the confines of us—art, a business model, words on a page, a piece of software. This becomes, in fact, an extension of us. It is born of our own neurological selves. It persists and exists outside us, free to disperse itself in the world—like electrical seeds that give rise to waves of intellectual stimulation. These propagate and influence other brains without our direct intervention or knowledge.

The Internet and globalization have boosted this in decrees of magnitude, and our present paradigm imbues us with vast neurological reach. Our nervous systems have become interwoven, connected, and will be more intertwined in our technological future.

This manifests from the reality that we are increasingly heading toward digitization of ourselves: we are moving ourselves into digital spaces. This is obvious in terms of online meetings, emails, and the rest. However, it is far more subtle and profound: our devices have become extensions of our consciousness.

We are now delocalized and distributed into networks. Consider that when we have certain thoughts, we are compelled to capture them online (we may post them to social media)—these are outputs from us to the network.

Similarly, when the state of the network changes (and we receive that red banner notification), we are compelled to deliver that information into our brains (these are inputs from the network to us).

This flow is reciprocal: from the network's perspective, we create its inputs, and it delivers outputs to us. We are thus now cyborgs, and we have been for a considerable time.

Thus, we have elements of our conscious mind (our neurology) entangled with a network. This entangled mind has far more reach than ever before. In an instant, we can influence the life of a stranger vastly disconnected from our propinquity, and without our knowledge, by posting an idea from one nervous system to another. This idea vector can spread again, without our knowledge. Our nervous systems, our neurology, have a profound extent.

As we move outward, we grow our neurology from our biology into digital spaces. Through existing and emergent technology, we continue extending ourselves into this digital frontier. Human-computer interfaces improve and ease the friction between ourselves and machines. Brain-computer interfaces promise the most intimate of connections between our minds and our builds.

As we grow into this world, let us consider briefly the existential layers of our world:

1. We have the physical and biological world from which we emerged (an example of this world is the Amazon rainforest)—this is the "natural world";

2. Then, we have the constructed world which overlays nature, a world of concepts and ideas that exist in our collective knowledge/perceptions (an example of this world is the concept created in your mind when you hear the word "Stonehenge"). This exists partially in nature, but it abstracts in our collective consciousness and our writing—this is the "conceptual world"; and

3. Now we have this digital frontier into which we extend ourselves, which exists as a layer in nature (hardware). It embeds and extends the conceptual world. This is the "digital world."

We have become de facto custodians of the natural world, having manipulated it to bring about the conceptual and digital worlds. Much of this creation is done while at work.

What is remarkable, is that we created these "new worlds" from our neurological selves. Every single one of the creations in these worlds is a concept born of neurological thought, transmitted concept, observation, and neurological action. While we more closely couple ourselves to the digital world, it is itself now starting to decouple from us in its creation. We are in a time when we set up the initial conditions and parameters, and that world self-creates. Decoupled from the neurological systems of these Great Apes. This self-creating world is through robots ushering in the next generation of themselves, through code creating virtual worlds, through advanced machine learning making decisions on our behalf—and a variety of other tangible technological phenomena. As we enter the digital world, we gain much more neurological reach. Paradoxically, we tend to feel more decoupled from ourselves, and this makes us lose touch with the consequences of our actions.

This is a complex domain, and it is growing more complex as we hurtle ourselves into our technological future. But underlying everything is us humans: technology must serve us. Used correctly it can be the biggest enabler of our species and can be a socioeconomic panacea.

We now have all the tools on hand to build the best future we can imagine—anything we envision can be made in a more affordable, accessible way than ever before. Catalyzed by technological prowess, our species can reach frontiers unexplored in space and time.

However, we impede ourselves.

Fermi's Paradox explains how a species faces extinction events at each point in their growth and development, as a species extends its reach, it finds a potential barrier which may filter the species out if it is not able to conquer the demons of its former technological self (the one we face now is climate change). How can we battle the demons of our former technological selves if we do not learn from our mistakes? If we ignore scientific progress and reason, we are dooming ourselves to a miserable species filter. One that we have seen coming for a hundred years or more. It is a chugging train, and we stand staring at it like intoxicated koalas bewitched by the profits of the technologies that got us here.

But we can choose to avoid it, to do better, and to be more—to allow ourselves to propagate forward, and for our ideas to persist another day. To do so, we need to stop favoring our constructs from which we gained in the past over the scientific reason of the present. This is how we impede ourselves.

It is frustrating to imagine that we have the ability to be better, and yet we bewilder ourselves in political quagmires and invisible complexities, instead of coming together to fight the species filter that we bring upon ourselves: it must be said of our species right now that Frankenstein is the monster here.

If indeed we accept that our individual choices have meaning and impact: the things that we do on a day-to-day basis genuinely do resonate at a planetary level, through the simple cause-and-effect cascade that scales to massive numbers, we must acknowledge that we, then, are directly accountable for that which happens at scale—even if we cannot directly observe it.

Chaos theory sets forth that there is great sensitivity to initial conditions. This is intuitive to understand: think about pointing a boat in a specific direction. If we point it differently by one degree, after a few days we will find ourselves colossally off-course.

Similarly, we build our future in time through the thoughts we produce, and the actions we perform now, in the world(s): our neurological selves build the future states. When we act, we create that world.

Entropy is the concept that a system tends toward a state of disorder. There is a window in which the future world we define can be what we collectively vision and hope. There are few states and configurations which result in us flourishing. We have to work at it to create these flourishing states. At this juncture in our species, we are about to bring forth astounding creations and technologies that will forge our futures. The clock grows later each moment for us not to let ourselves down with great splendor.

The world we create in our work is a direct manifestation of our neurological selves. We directly imprint ourselves onto this world. Our work is where we are impactful. Our professional lives are where we expend our effort, deciding how we will build the worlds around us, and construct our future selves in our self-made future world. Everything around us in the future manifests and is constructed by our present neurological selves. Everything in our present world was created by our former selves.

Ethics is personal, and it is grounded in the conceptual world. It does, however, greatly influence the other worlds we are jointly influencing and building, and sometimes destroying.

By imprinting something on another's neurology, or imparting to the world something destructive, the damage goes beyond the self, and what is done may resonate into time and space in the future.

The world is growing more complex, more multidimensional, and we may not even have the language to describe the future state of the world, let alone the abstract issues that emerge from it. Thus, having a framework of collective empathy is crucial. The time urgency we have with which to imbue our future is palpable right now, as we usher in the most substantial changes our species has ever seen. And each day brings even more significant change. It is an ever-growing tidal wave, and the longer we wait to construct that future, the more challenging it may become to deconstruct it—should we need to.

It, therefore, follows that if we do not hold ourselves to the highest standard and cultivate our framework of collective empathy, we soon may face our great filter.

When something is said or done, it is an extension of our neurology. It persists with greater stickiness than ever before in the digital world. Our neurological domain grows every day as a result of the conceptual and digital worlds. We thus must use our influence wisely, as we extend, create, and build the world. As we directly make choices to influence others, and to build these future worlds.

The natural world is under great threat as a result of the inception of the other worlds, and they cannot continue independently of the natural world (with current science). Our existence depends on this, and every decision we make (in our work, and our lives) needs to be underpinned by the cascade to world 1.

We need to forge a future world mindfully, as the initial conditions we set in our thoughts, set the parameters for our daily actions, which builds our collective future. We are bound by this in our reality.

Our species is forging worlds. How can we thus not hold ourselves to the highest standards imaginable? We are changing and creating worlds: ours for now, and if we get it right, even other worlds.

It starts in our minds, at the point of choice: considering, or not considering, the downstream consequences.

ADAM PANTANOWITZ

Adam is an electrical and biomedical engineer, expert and enthusiast of artificial intelligence, serial entrepreneur, technologist, motivational speaker, researcher, and philanthropist. Projects he has been involved in include developing a real-time brain internet link; an eye-controlled wheelchair; a noncognitive brain transmission channel using light to network two computers through the human brain; and a thought-controlled robotic arm.

His work has been featured in publications such as Forbes, Ozy, Futurism together with producing a number of academic journals and patents. Adam regularly speaks on the future of tech at Singularity University and lectures

Engineering and Medicine at the University of the Witwatersrand, Johannesburg. From a young age, Adam has pursued the act of deconstructing technology in order to build a better and brighter future.

ON ETHICS AND PEACE INNOVATION

MARGARITA QUIHUIS

The following is an edited transcript comprised of two conversations between Margarita Quihuis and Kris Østergaard. This discussion focuses on the relationship between ethics and innovation and how organizations can ensure that they move ethically into the future.

What is the Peace Innovation Lab and why does it exist?

The Peace Innovation Lab started as a project in BJ Fogg's Persuasive Technology Lab at Stanford in the late 2000s. In 2007 we had this "aha" moment when we realized students that wrote a tiny app over the weekend could launch it on Facebook, influencing millions of people.

BJ Fogg wondered: if an app could trigger millions of people to send a 'poke,' could we get people to develop positive behaviors? Instead of building peace through policy, diplomacy or humanitarian actions, could we use behavioral psychology and technology to foster world peace?

What is the Peace Innovation Institute?

Launched in 2018 through a collaboration between the Peace Innovation Lab at Stanford University and the City of The Hague, the Peace Innovation Institute sits at the intersection of behavior design, technology, innovation, and business.

We specialize in creating a culture of innovation and teaching collaboration across different boundaries. Our goal is to catalyze a thriving peace technology industry by making peace profitable.

What is Peace Technology?

If we look at information technology over the last 50 years, it was about arithmetic, logistics and accounting. In the 1980s, the breakthrough software products were Lotus 123, simple databases, and word processing. Managers kept track of the number and location of objects and bills of material.

With the rise of the Internet, software innovation shifted from tracking objects to connecting people.

Today, technology mediates the interactions between individuals. As technology as a whole becomes social, it has become another actor. We start interacting with technology as if it was a person. It shapes our behavior as if it was a person. Between two individuals, mediating technologies are screens, laptops, cellphones, Zoom, chat, and email. These technologies influence and define how we interact with each other.

Peace technology instigates pro-social behavior between individuals or groups of people that are different from each other. In business, enterprise software governs how we work together across space and time. We communicate, coordinate, and collaborate through email, chat, video conference, and shared documents. Sophisticated software can enhance the quality of the interaction between individuals and increase our opportunities to create value for each other. When we create mutual value for each other we are creating positive peace.

What is the role of ethics in businesses?

In our work at the Peace Innovation Lab, ethics is central to what we do. Our lab research question is "How good can we be to each other?" The question is simple but rich with opportunity.

Asking the question "How good can I be to someone different

than myself?" or "How good can I be to a counterparty in business?" lets us think expansively about creating extraordinary customer experiences and strong vendor relationships.

If you want to create a great customer experience, how might you realize that? Is it in the product design? Delivery? Disposal of the product? How do you treat someone with respect? What are the different ways you demonstrate respect for your customers? Partners? How do you treat someone with empathy? How flexible is your product or service for the diverse needs of customers? Companies exist to provide a service that is a benefit to the customer. Customers don't exist to serve the company; the company exists to serve the customer. How you deliver a service matters. The emotional tone in which you deliver the service, product quality, and the details that make up the experience can influence the customer to prefer you over the competitor.

The difference between two competing services often lies in how you treat people. That intangible is the difference. Ethical values are expressed through the design and delivery of the service. We're not talking about Aristotle and Kant. We're not talking about college seminar ethics. The ethics we're focused on is very practical at a business level.

If I treat people well, they will come back and they will be loyal. And what invokes loyalty? Reciprocity and consideration of needs and feelings, a consideration of a person's circumstance. The ability to not merely solve the customer's problem but to do it in an emotionally intelligent and responsible manner. A few years ago, the staff at United Airlines determined that the best way to deal with an overbooked airplane was to forcibly remove a passenger from his seat, breaking his teeth in the process. Could there have been a kinder way to deal with this scenario? What if the staff looked at the situation as an opportunity to create a delightful outcome for a passenger who would find an advantage in taking a different flight?

What ethical challenges do technology businesses face?

There are a couple of challenges. First, software developers haven't coded mediating technology with the explicit intention of increasing the quality of engagement between individuals or groups. Second, technology products have been launched in the marketplace with insufficient safeguards to minimize harm to the end-user. The industry as a whole has lacked a working set of ethical frameworks for product design and development.

As we know, companies cannot put an ethical framework in place after a crisis emerges. When a crisis hits, it's too late; you don't have the strategic headspace to think about what to do and how to respond because you're reacting. In the business sphere, ethics often centers around product safety. How do you monitor your product to make sure that it has the intended effect that you want in the marketplace? I don't believe the developers of Twitter intended the platform to be used for wide-scale harassment and cyberbullying.

We've entered an age where any technology can and will be weaponized. It's imperative that software engineers incorporate safety and security into the design of any new technology. This includes detection tools on how the technology is used and circuit breakers to slow or halt misuse. Similar to a pilot's flight control plan, engineers need to have a safety and ethics flight plan for their products with appropriate plans of action to safely shut down features that may cause harm.

You need to design automated safety controls because if you leave it to human decision-making at the point of crisis, their ethical decision-making will be highly unreliable.

Is it possible to map out the unintended effects of a product or service?

Developers can put processes into place to catch and anticipate many but not all instances of misuse or abuse. The cybersecurity world has practices where red teams and blue teams intentionally hack systems and respond to threats as part of the design protocol. We need to test that our product is safe before it reaches the public.

Pharmaceutical companies conduct randomized controlled clinical trials to test the efficacy and safety of new drugs. They learn which populations experience negative side effects and under what circumstances. In other industries, we have product recalls, where unsafe products are pulled from the market.

Many industries have customs, procedures, and regulations in place to enhance product safety. We do not have commonly used industry safety and ethical practices for software. Because software touches so many people, often in exponential numbers, negative impacts can be much more harmful. That said, Microsoft's Responsible Innovation Group has developed a comprehensive Harms Modeling[1] framework designed expressly for AI; Institute for the Future has their EthicalOS[2] framework for technology innovators to anticipate and mitigate future harms.

There's no way that you can catch all the bad uses, but there's going to be a common threshold of bad use. This is about probabilities and managing risk. When we have interconnected systems, we have no firewalls. One of the challenges of being in this interconnected world is that there's no friction. Because we want our systems to interconnect seamlessly, we optimize for efficiency and not risk.

That makes companies and customers very vulnerable because if something gets away from you, the problem moves very quickly through all your systems with no firewalls. If you're thinking about giving yourself enough time to respond and having enough friction, then yes, inefficient interconnected systems make it awkward for customers to do good things, but it also makes it difficult for customers to do harm.

You need to think about safety and security at the point of inception and the point of innovation. Companies like Facebook have demonstrated how difficult it is to incorporate adequate safeguards after network-scale harm has been done. For digital products, in particular, harm detection should be incorporated as part of the data analytics. Engineers should instrument products to detect if it's being used in the way that it was intended. Is the product preserving the safety and security of your customers? If it is not, we've got to fix it. Now, not a billion people later, but now.

How are business ethics affected by the COVID-19 pandemic?
In a moment of crisis, you will not make the same ethical decision as you would in advance of the crisis, because you're going to be in a very reactive mode. During this pandemic, leaders were at a loss of what to do. This has to do with human psychology and social cognition. Everyone else is looking for someone to set the direction, and then everyone can follow suit. Often, when we're not in a global crisis like this pandemic, it turns out that leadership doesn't matter all that much when things are going well. We can get by with mediocre leaders.

In times of crisis, superior leaders matter, and leaders with a strong ethical compass matter the most.

If you don't have a compass, then you're waiting for someone else to tell you what the right thing to do is. If you have an internal compass, you can assess the situation and make sure that people are safe and secure. It's Maslow's hierarchy of needs: we need to make sure that people feel safe and secure and that their basic needs are met. Everything else follows from that foundation, so take care of that first. I'm fascinated by how people are confused or reluctant to take care of people, thinking, "Yeah. But I still want to hang on to my profits or I still want to hang on to business as usual."

There's this lack of clarity of what the situation is, and how you may need to drop those old stories. But if you have an internal ethical compass, it keeps you calibrated; you know where your true North is. To operate in an ethical way is to stay grounded in terms of what your role is as a leader, a member of society, what your contribution is, and to do it in a way that's mutually beneficial to the other stakeholders in your business and society.

What are the shortcomings of CSR?

Many large global companies think they can offset harm through corporate social responsibility (CSR) PR activities. When you look at capital markets, there's a fundamental flaw: global capital markets control trillions of dollars. Governments get a percentage of that capital, say it's 30%. Philanthropy and charities receive a tiny percentage of the overall money available. CSR budgets are smaller. You have this tiny amount of money trying to fix the problems that this large amount of money in capital markets has created.

There's no amount of philanthropy or CSR that can fix the issues caused by second-order effects in capital markets. Instead of CSR which addresses band-aid solutions to harms, how might we integrate ethics into our product development? How do we integrate these values into our products? This way, companies can avoid or minimize the harm in the first place, rather than spend CSR pennies to offset the damage.

How do you ladder up from ethics in business and innovation to focus on peace?

We define peace as episodes of engagement between humans that are mutually beneficial. The political philosopher Montesquieu said, "Peace is the natural effect of trade. Two nations who traffic with each other become reciprocally dependent... their union is founded on their mutual necessities." From the Enlightenment on, this idea of trade as a force for peaceful relations between countries took hold.

Within the Peace Innovation Lab, we go back to the notion that value creation is a mutually beneficial exchange that is not exploitative. If it's exploitative, it's not sustainable. Exploitative capitalism and value creation come to a dead end. If you deplete me, then we can't trade anymore. On the other hand, if we are trading partners and we're looking out for each other's interests, we are engaged in sustainable capitalism. By the way, it's not just human to human trade. Humans engage in value creation with other species as well. We want to bring healthy, ethical, and sustainable capitalism back into people's awareness.

If you want to have a system that is healthy for both the natural world, the natural ecology, and also the human ecology, it needs to be mutually beneficial. Conflict and mutual value creation are incompatible.

What are the important domains and insights for businesses to promote peace?

The first insight is that most people spend the bulk of their lives interacting with others different from themselves in the workplace. Positive interactions such as communication, cooperation, coordination and innovation with others dominate our day.

Businesses create the context and the opportunity for us to engage in these everyday positive peace activities.

Because the world organizes itself around work, we've built extensive IT platforms that continuously gather data about those work activities. Global supply chains are certainly important for peace promotion. Supply chains cross geographies, time zones, nations, and cultures.

Apple outsources the manufacturing of its iPhones to Foxconn in China. US-based fast fashion brands hire clothing manufacturing in Bangladesh, Pakistan and Guatemala.

We can examine business enterprise supply chain data and ask, what are the wages? What are the hours? Are contractors being overworked? Are they getting enough breaks? It's a different lens on the same data. You can begin to create a scorecard to figure out: how good am I being to my suppliers? How good am I being to my stakeholders? Businesses have a unique opportunity to enforce humane practices through their procurement and outsourcing practices.

Positive peace is an everyday activity. When people typically think about peace, they think Nelson Mandela or Nobel peace prize winners, doing something very lofty. Or diplomats working on peace in the Middle East. Peacekeeping happens in some remote part of the world.

Most people don't live in those places and spaces. We live in Copenhagen, we live in Palo Alto. We think about, how does the grocer treat me? If I'm going to the coffee shop and I'm African American, do they serve me or not?

Even a small business can promote positive peace in its local community.

How do you measure positive peace?
We measure positive peace through episodes of engagement between individuals or groups that are different from each other. In particular, we're looking at the quality of interaction—be it awareness, attention, communication, cooperation, collaboration or innovation.

When people are interacting with each other at work, the activities are often captured in software. We look at enterprise software platforms because the world also organizes itself around enterprise software and software tools. By looking at the metadata on these platforms, we are able to do a social network analysis of the patterns of communication.

While this kind of work has been done in the past, we are

looking at it from the lens of positive engagement. You can get insights into the social health of organizations by examining communications across a boundary like gender or position. Based on interaction metrics you could give people feedback and concrete data on their communication patterns in the workplace. You can measure connectedness in an organization, which can then give you signals on organizational efficiency and effectiveness.

We can also go deeper and look at natural language processing and examine the qualitative nature of the communication. At a higher level, you can get a snapshot of communication flows and assess how well people are communicating and collaborating across different boundaries.

How do organizations know when wages are fair beyond their own perceptions of fairness?

You know that the wages aren't fair if people can't get their fundamental needs met. We have an enormous problem with homelessness in the United States. We have an enormous problem with people who are working in multiple jobs but are homeless.

One of the ironic things that happened in the Bay area because of Silicon Valley is that we have wage inflation. The poverty level in Silicon Valley is approximately $114,000 a year. If you were making $114,000 anywhere else, you would be wealthy. You could live in a mansion. In California, in the Bay area, that puts you at the poverty level because the rents are so high.

What these technology companies have done is create hyper-local inflation, because we have these young technology workers who earn a huge amount of money and non-technology workers' wages are much lower.

Those high earners can afford to pay a lot of rent, and we have limited housing stock, and so we get inflated rents. Teachers and police officers, through no fault of their own, can't afford to live in the communities they serve. In the quest to attract top talent, technology companies created new problems for society without consideration of the consequences.

Business leaders and businesses need to be integrated into the communities they operate in. It's easy to lose sight of the real-world consequences of business actions if you only live in the boardroom.

What advice do you have for entrepreneurs beginning to design for an ethical future, or companies doubling down on it?
The companies that will survive during this pandemic are the ones that actually walk their values in a way that their customers and their ecosystem can feel and recognize.

If you don't, you will not be trusted, and you won't survive. There is a reckoning right now as people shelter in place and think about what is essential. What we are discovering is that our market signals are broken; we have valued things that turned out are not essential, and the things that are essential have been undervalued, and thus they've been under-invested in. We have a fragile social foundation.

If you own a company, you need to be part of the solution. You need to demonstrate how you're going to strengthen the social foundation which is built around people and relationships. The relationship is the essential underlying asset of any economy: how well we treat each other, how well we take care of each other. If we fail to do that, it falls like a house of cards. So if you're playing a long game, you need to figure out how to show up as an ally.

MARGARITA QUIHUIS

Margarita is a researcher and behavior designer at Stanford's Behavior Design Lab and directs the Peace Innovation Lab where she applies behavior design, wide-scale innovation, persuasive technology, and the potential of technology to shape social behavior at scale.

She was the founding director of Astia, a tech incubator for women entre-preneurs; venture partner for NewVista Capital, a seed fund focused on women and POC tech founders; Reuters Fellow at Stanford; Director of RI Labs for Ricoh Innovations; Head, New Media at IDEO; and Director for venture fund of funds Horsley Bridge Partners. She is a recognized thought leader and public speaker in the areas of innovation, emergent social behavior, and technology.

WHY A MORE PEOPLE-CENTERED APPROACH TO DATA SCIENCE CAN HELP SOCIETIES THRIVE

DR. DAVID BRAY

It was the best of times, it was the worst of times,
it was the age of wisdom, it was the age of foolishness,
it was the epoch of belief, it was the epoch of incredulity,
it was the season of Light, it was the season of Darkness,
it was the spring of hope, it was the winter of despair...

So begins Charles Dickens' A Tale of Two Cities—with the narrator later noting that this characterization of contrasting superlatives represents a common thread throughout history. Nowadays, the same characterization could be said about societies debating the benefits and drawbacks of two important data science trends:

1. We are instrumenting the planet in a way that's unprecedented for human species. With an increasing number of industrial and commercial Internet of Things devices, as well as an increasing number of low-earth orbit (LEO) small and cube satellites, we will have sensors scattered around the planet. This translates into an unprecedented capability for individuals and organizations to access raw data associated with activities going on around the world.

2. We are producing ever-increasing volumes of digital data on the Internet. IDC's "Data Age 2025" white paper estimates 175 zettabytes (one zettabyte is a trillion gigabytes) of world-wide data by 2025, compared to an estimated 33 zettabytes on the planet as of 2018. That's a significant increase. To give a sense of scale, consider most new smartphones ship with 64 gigabytes of capacity. For just 1 zettabyte, we would need more than 15.6 trillion 64GB smartphones. Assuming the Earth's circumference around the equator is 40,075 km and the width of an iPhone X is 70.9 mm, these 15.6 trillion 64GB smartphones would circle the equator more than 27 times just for 1 zettabyte—or more than 4,800 laps for 175 zettabytes.

These two trends represent an unprecedented scale of data-related changes for our world. These trends also collide with the reality that for most of our history as a species, humans lived in nomadic groups and everyone in that nomadic group both knew each other and knew what was going on in that nomadic group. Now, an estimated 7.6 billion people are living on Earth, potentially more than 8 billion by 2025, with the potential, in terms of data science, to know nearly all that is occurring for the entire planet on an on-going basis.

Challenges will abound. The volume and immediacy of data will challenge pulling together the right data sets to make sense of new opportunities to pursue and new threats to avoid. The abstracted nature of global data will challenge sense-making of different contexts, exacerbated again by the reality that for most of human evolution, immediate visual and auditory environments signaled opportunities and risks. We will be challenged by an environment both physically and digitally more distant than the selection pressures of either three thousand or thirty thousand years ago. Future historians may conclude modern human brains weren't ready for the sheer scale of data that we will produce in the next decade.

Addressing such challenges will presumably include the use of semi-autonomous and autonomous methods of making sense of the data, including the "third wave" of artificial intelligence (AI) embodied in deep learning advances. Such data techniques spur important questions about how to ensure organizations employing such efforts effectively govern such endeavors appropriately.

WHY OUR RAPIDLY CHANGING WORLD CHALLENGES SOCIAL FOUNDATIONS

While lots of discussions have occurred about the ethics of AI, these well-intended conversations often miss two important elements:

First, AI ethics depends on a solid data ethics foundation; to date, data ethics have not received as much emphasis so far.

Second, ethics are socially defined, meaning ethics are normative and represent what the collective believes to be "right." This changes over time. In contrast, morals are internally defined. Morals are what a person individually believes is right to do.

The depths of human conflict between social ethics and individual morals have been plumbed by more than 3,000 years of human philosophy. To think that we modern humans will reach consensus on a global set of data science ethics by 2025 is probably unrealistic. However, we humans can consider where we—as organizations, communities, and societies—do want to go for the decade ahead.

Through shared narratives, the enforcement of laws, and through use of technologies, humans have shaped social norms and reshaped how power—defined as the capability to compel or oblige someone to take a certain course of action—has been distributed in our communities. Now with the beginning of the

21st century, we are facing big questions of "Quo Vadis?"—where do we want communities and human societies to go, especially given the recent rate of new data science capabilities challenging the distribution of power?

There is both huge opportunity for improving our communities with more people-centered approaches, as well as significant challenges where our digital future may not be as hopeful as we would like it to be.

For open, pluralistic societies that separate their private sector from their public sector, at least three potential doors present themselves as possible destinations.

Door number one includes employing the increasing instrumentation of the planet to create a state of always-on surveillance, a modern panopticon that protects stability and safety by always monitoring where everyone is and what they are doing.

Door number two includes much the same as the first door, with a market-based twist that employs the growing volumes of data and global instrumentation to create industries fueled by what some call surveillance capitalism—producing value by creating tailored insights about preferences, intentions, and how best to influence people based on their digital data.

Both doors pose challenges for open, pluralistic societies which require collective belief in the freedom to choose and free will. For either door number one or two, societies receive increased safety, stability, or market value at the expense of erosion in choices and free will.

To some degree, open, pluralistic societies have always tolerated some influence on free choice, to include marketing advertisements or political rhetoric. Both activities employ human biases to influence behaviors.

As one example, all humans have confirmation biases. Once we accept a belief, our brains discount additional data sets counter to our beliefs and overly inflate data sets reinforcing our beliefs. Now we have disparate data sets bombarding us daily and confirmation bias makes us less open to considering additional data.

As a second example, all humans also encounter cognitive ease. The more something is repeated, the more we are likely to believe it because it seems familiar, even if that's not necessarily what is true. Even saying "X is not true" repeats the element X in the minds of people and introduces the risk of cognitive ease swaying our beliefs.

As a third example, any data set, taken out of context, can be misinterpreted or misconstrued. We now face a world of growing data abundance at the same time as social forces have flattened historical gatekeepers who previously provided contexts. In the past, there were only a handful of radio or television outlets to convey data and narratives. While individuals may not have agreed with the contexts that the limited number of gatekeepers put out, they at least served as the conduits for data and narratives. Now the challenge is anyone can digitally "print" and view whatever they want—raising important questions about data sets and narratives taken out of context.

We would like to encourage a third door for open, pluralistic societies to consider for the decade ahead. This door will take hard work and investment, both in terms of developing new data science techniques and work to improve the understanding of what's possible between the interplay of data science, laws, narratives, and new technologies.

DOOR NUMBER THREE: SIGNPOSTS TOWARDS A HUMAN NOOSPHERE

The idea of a human noosphere—a global collective consciousness on the planet or interconnected 'mind space'—arose with the second decade of the 20th century. The idea arose first from geologists, who suggested there were three phases of life on Earth, starting first with inanimate matter (the geosphere), then the arrival of animated life (the biosphere), and an ultimate phase where humans transcend their individual thoughts of self, internal motivations, and thought to achieve a collective consciousness that surpasses ourselves (the noosphere). Some philosophers, notably Teilhard de Chardin, suggested that evolution's natural selection tended towards increasing the complexity of lifeforms and consciousness among lifeforms.

During the latter part of the 20th century, there were online chat room discussions expressing hopes that the World Wide Web could help achieve such a vision of global consciousness or noosphere. A lot of the idealism for the Web included this hope for the future. Yet looking back at the last few recent decades we now see some of the signposts along the way that include some cautionary signs towards such an ideal. In attempting to work towards greater human, global consciousness we've discovered that our human natures, both as individuals and as collective organizations, introduce speed bumps to such a vision. We also have seen recent cases where the Internet and related technologies may be creating more of a homogeneity of thought—producing echo chambers online or (worse) surveillance states with either direct or indirect pressures for the conforming of thought, behavior, and public shaming of those who act or see differently. In considering either potential future, neither a highly polarized world full of acrimonious thoughts on the Internet or a homogeneous, highly restrictive world only containing conforming thoughts sounds like hopeful aspirations for 2030.

Europe's General Data Protection Regulation (GDPR) has received a lot of praise for its intended outcomes and has also raised questions about whether the United States or other nations will do something similar or different. Questions about long-term impacts on Europe have also arisen. For the United States, the terms and conditions associated with online services mostly come with voluminous "terms and conditions" full of legalization that a majority of individuals don't read through fully before they click accept. Even for those who do read through them fully, individuals receive only a binary proposition of "accept or reject" what the conditions offer.

As alternative to the current voluminous "terms and conditions" provided for online services, I'd like to suggest a simple 2x2 table. This simple table is intended to take up no more than half a page, where entities—to include corporations, startups, communities, NGOs, and more—that provide services in the world can provide short bullets of four important elements; namely:

Top-left: Obligations in this Context – what principles the entity believes about its relationship with its stakeholders

Top-right: Acknowledgments in this Context – what "known unknowns" may exist tied to transactions and relationships

Bottom-left: Responses to Obligations – what the entity will do based on expressed Obligations

Bottom-right: Safeguards to Acknowledgments – what the entity will do based on expressed Acknowledgments

Obligations in this Context	Acknowledgments in this Context
What principles the entity believes about its relationship with its stakeholders	What "known unknowns" may exist to transactions and relationships
Responses to Obligations	Safeguards to Acknowledgments
What the entity will do based on expressed Obligations	What the entity will do based on expressed Acknowledgments

This "OARS" framework seeks to provide a visible signal that, while different for each individual or organization, both inform others of the intentions of an entity and encourages that entity to consider their shared connections to a larger, people-centered community.

Imagine if the public started to expect it could find a short, concise 2x2 table showing this for every website and app? This OARS framework enables any entity to acknowledge some perceived biases exist for any human endeavor because of our experiences, training, background, and more. For example, an organization sponsored by a certain group may receive subtle nudges by that sponsor and should acknowledge that sponsor. An engineering firm will probably be great at engineering efforts yet may not necessarily see other perspectives outside their expertise. There may also simply be acknowledging that the organization will "do their best" when it comes to an endeavor, yet for several endeavors, there will still be unknown factors that impact its delivery.

Achieving this door number three—that is neither surveillance states nor surveillance capitalism—will require the data science community to work across multiple fields to help both private and public organizations identify what obligations matter most. These obligations could include responsibilities to keep health or proprietary data confidential unless consent is given. Obligations could also include responsibilities to provide either transparency on what data analytics are performed or how data sets are employed.

The data science community will also need to work with private and public organizations to educate all members of society about human perceptual biases. This acknowledgment may include developing analytic "data mirrors" that help each of us know more about our biases innately present with all our decisions over time.

From this foundation, both individuals and organizations operating in open, pluralistic societies can make intentional choices regarding what responses to pursue as part of their data-illuminated obligations to members of the public, customers, shareholders, employees, boards of directors or other groups.

Individuals and organizations can also make intentional choices about what safeguards they deem necessary to make sure data sets are not misused in the digital future ahead. Such safeguards could include ombudsman-like functions responsible for ensuring data sets are both sufficiently diverse and sufficiently representative enough of different populations to ensure whatever deep learning occurs does not result in overt biases toward or away from different groups in society. Safeguards could include not letting emotionally laden headlines or articles that reinforce our existing biases be the sole motivator of our actions. Safeguards could also include ensuring whatever correlations or conclusions data analytics reveal, individuals as well as organizations, still have a chance to reflect upon, and consciously choose whether what the data shows represents a direction or action that the purposeful entity is willing to pursue.

As the last few decades have shown, for almost any tool or technology, there will be unintended uses both helpful and harmful. In an increasingly connected world, we need more rapid mechanisms to identify third-order or fourth-order unintended uses and adjust appropriately. As such, this updated OARS framework asks any entity to think about what safeguards it might implement should a well-intended service being provided start to be used in third-order or fourth-order unintended ways. For example, an organization might perceive an unintended use of their services would be the use of online advertisements to trigger violent radicalization of certain groups to harm others. In this example, a potential safeguard that could be listed is an "ombuds" group where early identification of such concerns can be shared and the organization can rapidly learn, adjust, and respond accordingly.

Only by such an approach—linking data science to reflect human Obligations, Acknowledged biases, Responses to obligations, and Safeguards relative to potential biases (OARS)—can open, pluralistic societies thrive in the era of growing data abundance. Here's to working to help make a more positive, inclusive future for all.

DR. DAVID BRAY

David has served in a variety of leadership roles in turbulent environments, including bioterrorism preparedness and response from 2000–2005, time on the ground in Afghanistan in 2009, serving as the nonpartisan Executive Director for a bipartisan National Commission on R&D, and providing leadership as a nonpartisan federal agency Senior Executive. *Business Insider* named him one of the top "24 Americans Who Are Changing the World" under 40 and he was named a Young Global Leader by the World Economic Forum. David served as Executive Director for the People-Centered Internet coalition chaired by Internet co-originator Vint Cerf. Later he was invited to work with the U.S. Navy and Marines on improving organizational adaptability and to work with U.S. Special Operation Command's J5 Directorate on the challenges of countering misinformation and disinformation online. He accepted a leadership role in December 2019 to incubate a new global Center with the Atlantic Council focused on how new technologies and data capabilities are transforming geopolitics and great power dynamics.

Photo Credit: The Atlantic Council

EUCATASTROPHAL PHOENIX

NELL WATSON

When the Black Death swept through Europe in the mid-14th century, serfdom and villeinage were prevalent. Common people lived as thralls, tied to their manor by law, as they had been since the Colonial edicts of Diocletian, a millennium prior.

The plague changed this long-held balance. It attacked indiscriminately, thinning out a proportion of every echelon. The loss in population led to an increase in the value of labor, and increased bargaining power, whilst creating gaps and loopholes that enabled bold and lucky folk to gain in social rank. Nouveau Riche burghers applied their wealth and influence to advance culture and learning, founding universities, boosting the nascent renaissance and encouraging the Age of Discovery.

Europe had suffered massively from the ruthless Mongol Invasions, desperate sieges, the start of a Little Ice Age, and a long, drawn-out terrible famine. The plague, which took the lives of perhaps half the population, was the coup de grace on a long line of catastrophes. It seems surprising that the scrappy and beleaguered European civilization survived at all, let alone that it arrived at a favorable outcome at the end of such tumult, and would rise to global pre-eminence shortly thereafter.

In many ways, this period in history can be viewed as a eucatastrophe, a terrible journey that somehow turned out favorably for the sufferers in the end. It seems especially strange given how this kind of devastating war+plague combination led to very different, devastating outcomes for other civilizations, such as the Inca and Aztec.

In our time, our global civilization faces mounting pressures: climate change, "forever" pollutants such as endocrine disruptors, tremendous systemic risks from long supply chains, rampant financialization, enormous public debt, along with the omnipresent threat of nuclear annihilation. The pandemic which has emerged in 2019 will not be the last unmanageable infection that stresses our civilization either.

Will these stressors finish us off for our hubris, or will we emerge anew? Can we find eustress in the midst of our difficulties? Will we fall under, or shall we snatch a eucatastrophe from the jaws of perdition?

Civilization depends upon people investing energy in it, whether in the form of attention, money, or belief. We lounge under trees on a sunny day at the park that were planted by people who knew they would never live to enjoy their shade. Civilization is a gift to the future.

Unfortunately, things seem to have turned in recent years. As our world has increased in pace thanks to technology, our time horizons have typically become much shorter, especially those in business, compensated with bonuses for short-term gains at the expense of long-term value creation.

Benefits are being enjoyed without being adequately paid for, whilst we borrow from the future to enjoy ourselves today. We see this in unsustainable debt, in the destruction of our environment and the species within it, and in escapism towards junk food and junk infotainment. These are symptoms of wider problems in society, perhaps the single greatest root cause of suffering in the world today: the poor accounting of shifted costs.

Shifted costs—negative externalities in economics terms—are what happens when someone does something which affects an unrelated third party in a negative way, who does not adequately make redress for the trespass.

Many economists tend to shrug somewhat at shifted costs; they are considered too difficult to account for, and so are largely ignored, written off as a sad inevitability of capitalism. Only the most gross and obvious of externalities get noticed and policed, the rest in a great long tail go unaccounted for.

Essentially, our entire civilization is constructed from mechanisms by which costs are shifted to be borne by others, whether as a cost to the environment and public health from pollution, or a cost to personal and social well-being by operating systems that are efficient yet not conducive to human fulfillment.

Exploitation happens at all layers of society. To some degree, we are all guilty of it, whether we are exploiting nature, or the agency of non-human animals, of enjoying cheap goods produced in places where labor is cheap due to lack of regulation of concern. Exploitation involves turning a blind eye to the shifted cost, whether as a producer or a consumer (though sometimes such costs are obfuscated).

Sometimes costs can be to society itself, for example through enjoying the efficiencies of globalization but without paying for the associated greater fragility that comes with it. Without down payments to a crisis management fund, when the inevitable disasters do occur, it's out of our control.

Another form of exploitation can stem from the misallocation of shifted benefits (positive externalities), whereby someone creates a benefit for others but does not profit from it. For example, unpaid personal care work generates tremendous value to society which would otherwise bear enormous social and economic costs in their vacuum.

A lack of accounting for shifted costs is the yoke by which modern equivalents of serfdom operate, and only by resolving this issue can we resolve the great failures of our age. It serves the interests of those with power to obfuscate shifted costs and benefits, as by doing so they can point the finger elsewhere. Thus, we have a dire lack of education in society about shifted costs. People aren't equipped to think of society in terms of externality tradeoffs, and thus easily get swayed by some ideology or other that has a correct observation on a small scale but misses the big picture. An ideological lens works well as a microscope, and poorly as a telescope.

However, this can be changed. By properly accounting for costs, we can account for damage to nature, damage to the sanctity of the family, damage to freedom, damage to purity of health-giving food, damage to societal trust and cohesion, damage to workers from unpaid costs of labor.

Accounting for shifted costs is the central issue that underpins the core values of every ideology and creed, for multipolar cross-partisan support, if framed in a way that can be understood. It can create a lingua franca between movements, to better communicate why a certain policy or approach is unjust, and to move past the bemused opacity to the views of others relative to reinforced polarization.

Accounting for shifted costs may be the answer to the failures of our society, socially and economically. We have an opportunity to bring this into being using a blend of emerging technologies and established law. We can understand and account for shifted costs through Artificial Intelligence, the Internet of Things, Distributed Public Ledgers, and Machine Ethics.

- Machine Intelligence. Helps us make sense of situations that appear to be too chaotic to control and enables us to automate the ineffable—that which cannot be adequately expressed in words or mathematics, but which we know when we experience. This is a fantastic resource for making predictions, generating improved solutions to difficult problems, and optimizing very complex variables. Recent research developments also hint at new formulae that could be applied to assist externality tracking systems.

- Machine Economics. Blockchain, distributed hash tables, and associated cryptographic technologies enable decentralized mechanisms to align incentives, create a permanent public record, and guarantee escrow in an affordable, trustworthy, and (mostly) scalable manner.
- Machine Ethics. We can instill prosocial behaviors and values into machine intelligence by collecting examples from multiple cultures, demographics, and geographies, informing the artificial intelligence of our general preferences on an individual and societal level.
- Internet of Things (IoT). Sensors are becoming more affordable and powerful all the time. Soon, they may even be commonly embedded within consumer electronics.

These elements combined enable us to detect, track, and tokenize cost-shifting, to account for its effects, and to understand which parties may benefit from an action, and which parties lose out. Once a general understanding of the true cost of a decision or transaction starts being known, one can then seek redress through standard litigation for damages, on an individual or class basis, with claims and depositions, which can be quickly administered through increasingly automated interfaces.

However, outside of civil tort, there are also fiduciary issues. Once the externalized costs are known with relative certainty, to not account for it creates mens rea, as it is essentially a form of fraud. Thus, a corporation (and in a just world its officers) are liable not only for true costs but also for errors of conduct for having ignored them.

Before long, with a few costly cases being won, externality costs or usufructs will start to be negotiated up front, instead of retroactively. Governments will use cost-shifting analyses to vet policies, to ensure that the effects of a policy are not unfairly born upon specific demographics, with the results of analyses made into publicly available information that they are accountable for.

If we are to find our eucatastrophe, I dearly hope that we not only discover how interdependent we truly are, but also take this opportunity to strike the root causes of our present societal failure to manage shifted costs, and their offspring—systemic risks. We must refuse to mutually divert the trolley onto each other's tracks for our assured collective doom. True and proper accounting of shifted costs is the best path towards lasting justice in a complex yet sustainable and enduring civilization.

I have begun to collect some ideas at www.pacha.org around these new opportunities to handle shifted costs in our economy, a concept I describe as Automated Externality Accounting.

The Internet once required one to connect to a single server at a time. It took the World Wide Web to enable us to surf between silos of information in a fast and user-friendly manner. Similarly, the elements to manage shifted costs already exist, they just need the right protocol and an interface to bring them all together. Repositories of pollution tracking, and the actions of bad actors exist today.

If we can wrap these in a protocol that facilitates the validation, integrity, and tokenization of this information, then we have an opportunity to transform our economy in the 2020s to the degree that we have transformed access to information in the 1990s. That might even change our world to an even greater degree.

NELL WATSON

Nell is a researcher in emerging technologies such as machine vision and AI ethics. She serves as Chair & Vice-Chair respectively of the IEEE's ECPAIS Transparency Experts Focus Group, and P7001 Transparency of Autonomous Systems committee on AI Ethics & Safety, engineering credit score-like mechanisms to safeguard algorithmic trust. She also chairs EthicsNet.org, a community teaching prosocial behaviors to machines, CulturalPeace.org, crafting Geneva Conventions style rules for cultural conflict, EDCsymbol.org, and Pacha.org, connecting a network of service providers to help enable the automated accounting of externalities (shifted costs) such as pollution. Nell serves as Senior Scientific Advisor to The Future Society, Senior Fellow to The Atlantic Council, and holds Fellowships from the British Computing Society, and Royal Statistical Society, among others.

WHEN PUBLIC GOES PRIVATE: ETHICS FOR WORKERS IN THE DIGITAL ECONOMY

SHEILA JASANOFF

Around the turn of the twentieth century, workers and labor unions won a series of victories that placed limits on capital's exploitative power. These gains were consolidated in large part through law.

Governments responded to worker demands by enacting fair labor standards, with restrictions on hours and conditions of work, as well as minimum wage rules, compensation for work-related injuries, and provisions for sick leaves and unemployment benefits. Later in the century workers won protection against discrimination on racial and gender grounds and, more recently, against sexual harassment and other forms of punitive conduct by bosses. Through these developments, governments acknowledged that assuring workers' well-being is one of the modern state's prime responsibilities. The massive relief efforts enacted in response to the novel coronavirus pandemic of 2020 attest to the continued vitality of this public mission. In modernity, a state that cannot take care of its workers is no longer politically viable.

What, though, are the private sector's responsibilities for workers? With the rise of the digital economy, large rents have appeared in the protections afforded to workers by the state. In the so-called gig economy, more and more people work freelance, at multiple jobs, from home, using personal resources such as apartments and cars—all conditions that lie outside the purview of the classic labor contract and hence outside of state-mandated protection. At the same time, a new white-collar working class has arisen, engaged in the work of the head rather than the labor of the hands. For these workers of the "creative class,"[3] jobs offer not merely income and security against life's accidents, such as catastrophic illness, but also the satisfaction of work that many see as innovative and socially beneficial. This is why Google's original motto, "Don't be evil," proved so seductive, attracting some of the nation's top software designers to the company.

Just as citizens want to believe that their country represents their values, so workers in the digital economy often want their employers to abide by principles and codes of conduct that converge with their own.

The ethical implications of these shifts in the way we work are profound. Most centrally, because so many worker needs and desires are either aspirational or outside the realm of traditional labor law, concerns previously addressed by public governmental action are increasingly being shifted to the private sector. In effect, we are living in a constitutional moment[4], in which corporate social responsibility has emerged as an essential complement to state regulatory powers. Are companies rising to the challenges of meeting workers' needs? Yes, to some extent, but scattered and ad hoc responses are by no means up to the magnitude of the task.

The entrepreneurs of the digital age benefited from a promissory environment in which it appeared, as in the 1960s, that a new wind of freedom would waft away the dilapidated cobwebs of ancient power and hierarchy, including its outmoded regulatory structures, and the Internet would emerge as a place of unchecked freedom. It may have been easy to believe this when authoritarian regimes were falling, and the digital medium offered a kind of instant access to the world that no one previously had even dreamed of. As a result, a domain of governance developed that was not subjected to the critical thinking that has accompanied other constellations of human political power, such as nation states and constitutional democracies.

Libertarianism, or a commitment to extreme personal autonomy and freedom from external constraints, is coded into tech companies' corporate DNA. It received prophetic articulation in John Perry Barlow's famed 1996 Declaration of the Independence of Cyberspace. There, Barlow, a former lyricist for the Grateful Dead, set out an explicit claim for ethical independence in the emerging digital world. Addressing the "tired" governments of the industrial world, he asserted: "You do not know our culture, our ethics, or the unwritten codes that already provide our society more order than could be obtained by any of your impositions." [5]

A quarter-century later, it has become clear that the unwritten codes Barlow celebrated are not as universally liberating as he took them to be, at least not for those falling outside of Silicon Valley's largely white, male, Western, and computationally gifted elites. Barlow mistakenly assumed that breaking out of the shackles of government regulation would free the denizens of cyberspace from all forms of repression and coercive power. This is akin to the flat earth fallacy; in that it wrongly presumes that social organizations can be free from barriers to complete egalitarianism. Firms, like governments, are embedded in preexisting forms of social order that constrain their capacity to discern ethical problems, let alone to rectify them. It is high time, therefore, for the companies of the Fourth Industrial Revolution to rethink their conceptions of social order in the light of their own internal topographies of power and to align their ethical thinking more closely with principles of good governance developed through millennia by theorists of democracy and collective self-rule.

Consider the evidence. In 2017, a controversial memo by Google engineer James Damore accusing the company of maintaining an "ideological echo chamber" and ascribing male/female disparities at work partly to biological differences, led to his firing. Damore's complaint to the National Labor Relations Board proved unsuccessful, reportedly because his comments were not deemed to fall within the category of protected speech. Ill-considered or no, his solo protest raised a legitimate question about the norms of workplace speech, but the episode created no precedent that future dissenters could usefully rely on. A 2019 group protest by Google employees had greater impact as the company announced it would not renew a Defense Department contract to develop artificial intelligence for improving the accuracy of drone strikes.

Engineers rebelled against a use of their talents that seemed to flatly contradict the "don't be evil" mandate, even though that is no longer the company's official motto. But the conditions under which such objections may be raised and are entitled to respect remain far from clear.

Turning to the bread-and-butter issue of pay, a drivers' strike in May 2019 involving 25 US cities and several international locations protested against rideshare company policies that caused driver incomes to fall below minimum wages when adjusted for expenses and wait time. In the health domain, Amazon workers across the United States, not unionized despite many efforts to organize them, staged walkouts to protest against unsafe working conditions during the 2020 coronavirus crisis. Meantime, in April of that year, French unions won a court order requiring Amazon to stop delivering all nonessential items until it could assure workers of adequate protection. With regard to equal treatment, in the summer of 2020, Françoise Brougher, former chief operations officer at Pinterest, drew a huge response with her complaint of gender-based workplace exclusion and discrimination at a company whose number two post she had held. [6]

These famous, or infamous episodes highlight the paradoxes of the Silicon Valley culture as it has diffused throughout the world. Somewhat like university employees, today's gig workers and digital creative classes sacrificed the safety of a heavily rulebound workplace for the promise of individual autonomy and collective improvisation. But they are discovering that no employment relation is free from power. Just as graduate students, faculty and staff in academic institutions have discovered the need for more formal norms and better institutions of self-governance, so digital workers too are awakening to a governance vacuum that has to be filled in order to protect fairness, equality and a reasonably pluralistic, lawfully held range of views in the virtual workplace. Ethics is a broad and vague term, but it encompasses the kind of infra-legal, yet binding norms that this moment of awareness calls for.

Rethinking corporate governance from an ethical standpoint is all the more essential because the largest tech companies have become statelike in their size and capacity to influence people's thought processes and social behavior. Facebook some years back advertised itself as the largest country in the world, and with user numbers pushing 1.7 billion in 2020, its potential influence has grown even larger. A 2020 US congressional hearing repeatedly took the CEOs of four tech giants—Amazon, Apple, Facebook, and Google—to task for their monopolistic practices. David Cicilline, Democratic chair of the antitrust subcommittee, noted that these "emperors of the online economy... enjoy the power to pick winners and losers, shake down small businesses and enrich themselves while choking off competitors." [7]

In democracies, any form of unchecked power is not merely suspect but also subject to being dethroned. Indeed, the doctrinal basis for doing so already exists in both antitrust law and constitutional law.

As far back as 1945, the US Supreme Court ruled, in Marsh v. Alabama,[8] that a company town, one wholly owned by a private enterprise, must respect the public's right to free expression, since in a balancing test constitutional rights should generally prevail over private property rights. Whistleblower laws provide further safeguards for employees who become aware of illegal conduct on their employer's part. Yet, as several of the cited examples show, these formal protections fall short of curbing the power of the Internet's emperors and its lesser aristocracy.

Concerned primarily with commercial imperialism, the American antitrust watchdogs did not sufficiently attend to another aspect of the unregulated behavior of digital media: their capacity to encourage or discourage forms of speech and thought that are crucial to socialization and the formation of political subjects. The spread of disinformation and conspiracy theories on social media has gained global attention, but as compared with traditional media, governed by well-established libel and slander laws, speech on the Internet remains a more murky terrain. Here, the ethical independence proudly affirmed by Barlow and others has condoned behavior—from Twitter shaming to election interference—that society rightly regards as contrary to democratic values. Employee unrest has prompted Facebook and other companies to revisit policies against hate speech and other forms of politically unacceptable communication, but a more systematic approach is long overdue.

What ethical values would rise to the top if corporations became more aware of power structures inside their organizations and did not take externally imposed mandates by state authorities as sufficient?

Transparency, first of all. Modern democracies have accepted that state institutions must open up their internal processes to some degree of public oversight under a variety of laws providing access. Board rooms, however, remain notoriously resistant to any critical outsider gaze. In one well-known example, the American documentary filmmaker Michael Moore, director of the 1989 classic Roger & Me, was shut down at an annual shareholder meeting of General Motors when he tried to air his grievances openly to the board.

Inside Job, Charles Ferguson's blistering account of financial industry misdeeds leading to the 2008 subprime mortgage crisis, offered another story of closed systems operating without adequate scrutiny under the convenient cover of a free market ideology. In economies where policy is often articulated through algorithms rather than laws (consider rideshare companies' surge pricing policies), decision-making has become even more opaque. Company ethical codes should make room for processes by which employees can access and criticize aspects of policy relating to their economic and social well-being, without fear of reprisals or other modes of silencing.

Transparency alone is powerless to change things if it is not coupled to mechanisms of accountability. The airport slogan "if you see something, say something" is instructive in this regard: it implies that, to have an effect, what one sees needs to be reported, presumably to someone with the authority to do something about it. Many organizations today employ ombudspersons to perform such a function. Their role is to hear complaints from workers and to resolve disputes, often through means short of formal legal proceedings.

Such in-house mechanisms, however, risk falling captive to internal power structures, unless they are granted a measure of independence that they do not always enjoy. And even independence, in the sense that those responsible for oversight cannot be overruled by the corporate board or CEO, may not ensure sufficient opportunities for worker self-expression and self-realization.

Facebook offers a telling example. In response to persistent criticism of its overly laissez-faire content moderation policies, Facebook in 2020 appointed a so-called Supreme Court empowered, according to CEO Mark Zuckerberg, to overrule even him with respect to decisions involving content removal. Newsworthy as this move was, the appointments were made without any outside supervision, and this "court" composed of international legal and human rights heavyweights offered little or no immediate benefit to workers within the company who had previously expressed unease with Facebook's content moderation policies. Internet governance still remains to a large extent unconstitutionalized, to the extent that one of its conceded "emperors" can appoint a judicial arm without advice or consent from self-constituted representatives of his "people." This concentration of power needs to be diluted, and revisiting corporate ethics is a potent avenue for reform.

Ethical obligations, moreover, do not apply only to corporate heads and their boards. The digital private sector, up and down the ladder, is ripe for a fuller examination of the ethical responsibilities that come with great personal and socioeconomic privilege. Employees at the upper reaches of software engineering have a special obligation to advocate for change. As highly skilled laborers, they command pay and prestige comparable to that of the nobility of a bygone era, and hence belong to both the ruling class and the ruled.

But the older pre-revolutionary monarchies functioned in part by dutifully adhering to the principle of noblesse oblige, which as yet has found few counterparts in the new information economy.

It may be difficult for the self-governing meritocracies of the digital age to accept that we do not live in a bifurcated world, with one ethical code for the best and another for the rest. Freedom in any civilized society has its necessary and proper correlation in responsibility. It is time for the capitalists of the digital revolution to shoulder the responsibilities that come with the creation of a new social order based on the control of data, personal information, and communication. Participants in this economy, at all levels, are citizens of a novel virtual polity whose norms remain largely unwritten. Both labor and management have a creative role to play in reimagining constitutional governance in this era of far-reaching transformation and change. In due course, we may even arrive at a newly written constitution that gives the force of law to some of their imaginations.

SHEILA JASANOFF

Sheila is Pforzheimer Professor of Science and Technology Studies at the Harvard Kennedy School. A pioneering social scientist, she has authored more than 130 articles and chapters and is author or editor of more than 15 books, including *The Ethics of Invention*. She has held distinguished visiting appointments at leading universities in Europe, Asia, Australia, and the US.

Her honors include the SSRC's Hirschman Prize, the Humboldt Foundation's Reimar-Lüst Award, a Guggenheim Fellowship, an *Ehrenkreuz* from the Government of Austria, and membership in the Royal Danish Academy. She holds AB, JD, and Ph.D. degrees from Harvard, and honorary doctorates from the Universities of Twente and Liège. Her work explores the role of science and technology in the law, politics, and policy of modern democracies.

THE ETHICAL PARADOX OF BUSINESS MODERNIZATION

VALTER ADÃO

> *"The greatest danger in times of turbulence is not the turbulence; it is to act with yesterday's logic."*
> PETER DRUCKER

THE PARADOX

We are wired to personify external events that threaten us, place our relevance at risk, and challenge personal and business paradigms. We give them names, and we spend vast amounts of resources to try to solve them. In the world of business, it becomes known as the common enemy and the reason for soft performance levels, business failures, and disruptions.

Until the first quarter of 2020, the personified enemy was the relentless progression of disruptive exponential technologies and the resultant wave of business digitalization. It has bred a movement of pop literature, both romanticizing and villainizing its impact on business and society, and predicts our ability to solve humanity's greatest challenges, in ways previously inconceivable. It has also framed an equal, but opposite dystopian outcome on a number of fronts, resulting in deep ethical concerns. The future relevance of the workforce has been brought into question and concerns over institutional and personal privacy have become central to the debate. Firms with a low acumen towards these and other ethical concerns, while benefiting handsomely from this global transformation, are facing increasing reputational and even financial risks.

Despite this, disruptive exponential technologies continue advancing and creating tremendous opportunities, new business models for services, products and delivery formats to compete with those currently on offer. Digitalization's progression, while enabled by technology, has progressed because of its overwhelmingly positive adoption—it provides the end user with diversity, affordability, and a friction-free and intuitive experience.

With the world currently reeling from the effects of the new coronavirus pandemic, the unthinkable has become inevitable. The personified risk and common business enemy has shifted to COVID-19.

Digitalization, the former threat, is now perhaps our best ally to solve the global pandemic. It presents us with the tools and solutions to enable the best possible economic and societal recovery and preparedness for a post-COVID-19 economy.

COVID-19's threat to jobs, before attributable to digitalization, can only be minimized by digitally enabled solutions, and attempts to halt the rapid spread of the virus, may only be addressed by the feared ubiquity of digital technologies. This is the paradox of our time.

Whilst the inclusion of ethical considerations remains critical for digital transformation initiatives; should the ethical debate not extend beyond the provision of guidance for the responsible deployment of digital solutions, towards positioning digitalization as an equally important ethical obligation for business and political leaders to embrace?

Digitalization in a digital or post-COVID-19 economy is irrefutable in its positive impact on societal, organizational, and economic competitiveness and resilience. Organizations and economies that transform in a deliberate and orchestrated manner, increase their endowment beyond their balance sheet, enabling them to navigate internal and external shocks quicker, and more agile than ever before. They are also better prepared to transition their workforce and ready them for the skillset required to thrive in an increasingly competitive and complex economy. Ethics change over time. They too, need to evolve to reflect changing needs of society.

THE DEBATE

At any given point, business leaders are exposed to phenomenal exponential technologies that have been shaped and directed, not only to solve some of the greatest challenges facing humanity, but also to enable an unprecedented wave of convenience and affordability, loved and embraced by the consumer.

The resultant effect is that business and government leaders are faced with technology choices not seen before, with positive business and societal dividends, but with both logical and emotive challenges. More than ever, organizations need to be seen as progressing, modernizing, and reimagining themselves, ensuring their relevance in an economic construct that is changing at an unprecedented rate.

Leadership, will, and confidence to make the necessary decisions to bring about this change are some of the key barriers to success within many organizations. It creates fear and stasis, both paralyzing and inhibiting strategies and policies to encourage and incentivize the digitalization of organizations and economies. Decision makers fear criticism, failure, unintended societal backlash, and the unknown implications of their choices.

Whilst digital transformation is, of course, enabled through technology, these observations should remind us that the human, and ethical dimension are as important as the technology being considered. Business leaders are faced with the challenge of deciding the extent and focus of their digital investments, as well as the consequences those investments will have on the organization, its workforce and society.

The digital value equation below, when considered holistically, offers a business only, directional guide for the deployment of investments.

$$\Leftrightarrow \underset{\text{(of the machine)}}{\boldsymbol{Capex}} < \underset{\text{(of the human)}}{\boldsymbol{Opex}} \rightarrow \underset{\text{Exponential Tech Dividends}}{(\boldsymbol{G})^n (\boldsymbol{P})^n (\boldsymbol{X})^n} = \boldsymbol{EV}$$

It's important to point out that the equation has no mathematical standing, but rather acts as a logic flow to precipitate key value principles that need consideration when guiding an organization through its digitalization choices, especially at the onset. When read from left to right,

1. The first half of the value equation, i.e., capex < opex, suggests that organizations need to look for evidence that capex investment into the machine (technology) needs to be less than the overall opex of the existing manual processes it is affecting—an overall consideration once the exponential technology dividends are incorporated (in the second half of the equation).

2. The second half of the equation unpacks the potential dividends that can be unlocked through digitalization. Irrespective of the complexity and features of the myriad of technology solutions positioned as the digitalization 'silver bullet,' only three broad digital dividends are of importance, namely: Exponential Growth (G^n); Exponential Productivity (P^n) and Exponential Experience (X^n).

c. G^n (Exponential Growth) indicates the potential for new sources of revenues, or new ways of solving for the organization's purpose. It may not be a financial construct, e.g., the saving of lives, reducing the spread of malaria, etc. This can be done by leveraging digital technologies to enable the innovation and creation of new products and services not conceivable before.

d. P^n (Exponential Productivity) indicates the potential for the use of digital technologies to reduce the cost of doing business (or fulfilling the organization's purpose). In all economic times, but especially the tumultuous ones, being the lowest cost producer (not to be confused with the provider of low-cost products) is an enviable position. All things being equal, the lowest cost producer will always have greater resilience over its more expensive-to-produce competitors. This is achieved by reducing the overall unit product costs, or by increasing production capability, without the proportional increase in capex or opex.

e. X^n (Exponential Experience) indicates the potential for the use of digital technologies to uplift the customer (and workforce) experience, by both creating friction-free and intuitive experiences, and developing a consensus-based understanding of the customer needs, preferences and past behaviors to best service them. The more frictionless, guiding and intuitive the experience is, the greater the chance of the consumer concluding a transaction successfully, staying connected longer, returning for further acquisitions, and telling others about their experience. In a highly competitive (and commoditized) world, where there is little differentiation between the features and benefits of products and services—think banking, mobile operators, insurance providers, etc.—a phenomenal customer experience is the last and decisive line of differentiation.

While the digital value equation simplifies the business input values and dividends organizations must seek to unlock, it raises an alarming question. One that has become the source of ethical debates regarding the digitalization of organizations and economies. When the first half of the value equation is considered—the Capex (of the machines) < the Opex (of the human)—it is inevitably contemplating the use of human replacing or human augmenting technologies. It triggers an emotive debate of the impact that these technologies and their adoption will have on jobs and the workforce, and the potential bifurcation of society along economic lines. The search for value from digitalization, cannot be separated from human and ethical considerations.

It must be acknowledged that digital technologies will eliminate jobs in the short term. Jobs with negative attributes such as poor safety records, low levels of efficiency and accuracy, etc., will be displaced, mostly in search of the dividends (see the digital value equation), enabled by exponential technologies that are becoming cheaper, more powerful, and no longer limited to the domain of wealthy organizations.

Paradoxically, for economies and organizations that are prepared and make the right proactive leadership decisions and orchestrated moves to digitally transform, the same technologies have the potential to create more jobs and prosperity than ever before. This is premised on the expansion of the economic base of organizations and economies, and the increased demand for the new skills.

Decades of economic data reaching back to the earlier industrial revolutions highlight that the rapid adoption of new technologies and innovations have catalyzed progressive and sustained economic growth and prosperity for the populations in the respective economies and industries. The converse applies where adoption has been resisted or slow—slower economic growth and generally lower prosperity of their populations.

A study by the World Economic Forum (WEF) leveraging the insights and opinions of business leaders representing organizations that employ 15 million people across a variety of sectors, skills levels and seniority levels, concluded that for every job lost to the adoption of cognitive technologies, approximately 1,74 jobs would be created. Similarly, a study undertaken into technology adoption in the United Kingdom by a leading global consultancy revealed that over a 10-year period, for every job displaced by technology, 4 new jobs were created.

Enrico Moretti, a Professor of Economics at the University of California, and the editor-in-chief of the Journal of Economic Perspectives, in his book, The New Geography of Jobs, concluded that for every job lost due to the advancement of technology, an additional 1.6 low "skill jobs" may be lost as a knock-on effect, but that the new technology-enabled jobs would potentially create 5 new service-related jobs.

These studies, while not exhaustive, suggest that through the structured and orchestrated adoption of digital technology, both economic dividends and the creation of jobs could be achieved. Organizations can be made more resilient, and with the appropriate plans in place, the workforce can be timeously prepared to remain relevant and in demand for the digital economy. Ironically, traditional attempts to protect jobs at the cost of technological progression reduces the competitiveness of organizations and economies. This in turn may be the biggest cause of job losses in the future. We need to embrace the paradox that while jobs might be destroyed by technology in the short term, only technology will be able to create and sustain the much-needed jobs in the digital economy.

PAUSE FOR PERSPECTIVE

In the 18th century, Frederick Engel described an economic observation, which Robert C Allen later coined as Engel's Pause. It may well provide the perspective required to understand and embrace the digital progression of economies and organizations, as an important and ethical imperative to ensure their competitive nature, whilst simultaneously ensuring broad and inclusive societal benefits.

Engel's Pause was first observed during the British Industrial revolution when new technology, specifically a labor replacing technology, was introduced. While the technology increased economic productivity, competitiveness, and further investments into industry, it also resulted in a drop in employment levels and wages of the workforce. The trend reversed approximately four decades later, only after a notable increase in the skills and knowledge proficiency of the workforce, resulting in the broad economic upliftment of society. Engel's Pause can be simply described as the time taken between the introduction of a new technology, and the eventual positive and broad socio-economic outcome made possible by the technology.

It is reasonable to accept that the process of digitizing economies and industries could lead to a similar current-day challenge; The Digital Pause. The time taken between the introduction of digital technologies and the readiness of the workforce to leverage the new technology with their newly developed skills to unlock similar economic and societal dividends.

Therefore, should the ethical responsibility not extend to ensuring the resilience and competitiveness of economies and organizations, by enabling and encouraging the adoption of digital technologies, while simultaneously ensuring that the existing and new entrants into the workforce are adequately developed and transitioned to be sufficiently skilled, knowledgeable, and prepared to create value in the new digital economy? Our focus should not be on halting the progression of technology, but rather on shortening the modern-day Digital Pause.

CONCLUSION

Leaders need to be equally true to both the responsible and ethical adoption of digital technologies, as to ensuring the completive nature and resilience of their organizations and economies. The increased productivity of organizations is a critical economic contributor, and essential to the sustainability of the workforce. Yet, moves to adopt technologies, and to modernize is faced with fearful and emotive responses by the workforce.

To navigate through this paradox, a change in perspective is needed:

1. The risk is the opportunity. Digitalization needs to be viewed as an opportunity that must be molded and directed to create new value, both to the business, the workforce and society.
2. Leaders must focus on the Digital Pause. The focus must be on shortening the Pause, not avoiding adopting technology, nor delaying the modernization of organizations. This perspective will provide the guidance required to navigate the paradox, ethically and responsibly.
3. The greatest threat is not the external event. Not making choices during this critical time, is the greatest threat facing leaders. It is as damaging as making the wrong choices. Steps to transition and prepare the workforce to minimize the effects of Digital Pause need to start early and simultaneously with the plans to modernize the organization. Plans to modernize must be elevated to one of the most important decisions leaders need to prioritize. A structured, timeous,

and orchestrated workforce transition plan will reduce the automation anxiety.

An error of knowledge is not an ethical failure, but it is, if it is a deliberate evasion of knowledge.

VALTER ADÃO

Valter is recognized as an expert in the fields of disruptive innovation, business re-imagination and emerging technologies in Europe, the Middle East and Africa, where he does most of his work. He is the Chief Executive for Cadena Growth Partners, a digital, innovation and venturing organization that operates at the intersect of strategic and innovation thinking with emerging digital technologies and design.

He is the former Chief Digital and Innovation Officer for Deloitte, managing and founding partner for Monitor Deloitte and managing partner for Deloitte Digital in Africa. Valter is also a TEDx Speaker, faculty member of Singularity University and recipient of the Constellation Transformation 150 award, which recognizes the top global executives leading digital business transformation efforts, and a Professor of Practice at the Johannesburg Business School. He was recently awarded as the Big 4 professional of the year, by The South African Professional Services Academy, who also recognized him as a top professional in South Africa's Digital Industry. Valter holds an MSc and an MBA, he has trained with Roger Martin, as a master strategist and is the recipient of numerous academic awards.

AUTONOMOUS SENTIENT TECHNOLOGIES AND THE FUTURE OF ETHICAL BUSINESS

BRIAN DAVID JOHNSON

In the coming decade, a constellation of technologies will come together to radically transform how we do business and live our lives. These autonomous sentient technologies will leave no organization or community untouched or altered. They will present both promise and peril for the future of ethical business. For organizations to prepare they need to understand what is coming and realize that they will need to fundamentally reimagine and go beyond long-held ideas and practices.

THE COMING AGE OF SENTIENT TOOLS[9]

These emerging technologies will include smart cities, the Internet of Things (IoT) and its industrial sister Industrial IoT. Robots will move from the factory floor and a warehouse into our homes, schools and care facilities. Computational power, connectivity (5G) and the ability to sense will only expand to the point wherever it is needed. Combined these technologies will bring about the age of sentient tools.

This coming age of sentient tools will give us technologies that are physically and culturally aware. They will have the ability to process large volumes of data and make probabilistic decisions. But most interestingly they will be social. They will know us as individuals. They will be aware of our families, coworkers and fellow citizens. There will be data and privacy concerns that will need to be overcome but the effect of this coming age of sentient tools will make computing and technology as a whole more human.

Autonomy will be an emergent driving force to fuel these changes. The past few years have witnessed the early implementation of autonomous vehicles on land, sea and air.[10] [11] These innovations will remap supply chains, infrastructure and push us to reimagine the movement of people and things. But autonomy will not stop there.

Autonomous digital technologies will push us to rethink artificial intelligence (AI), machine learning (ML) and the very nature of algorithms. The very term artificial intelligence coined in 1955 at a Dartmouth Conference[12] could become as outmoded as the information superhighway of the 1990s used to describe the Internet. AI and ML will operate across all emerging technologies. It will be the software that powers this coming age of sentient tools. All technology will use AI and ML. The use of the term could become meaningless because AI and ML will be subsumed by software in general.

BEYOND BIAS

The past 5 years highlighted the flaws and bias of industrial artificial intelligence[13]. It is widely believed that all data is biased. When all data is biased then all technologies that use that data become biased and the businesses and organizations that in turn employ those technologies take on that bias. But bias is nothing new. It is well known that all humans have biases and there are processes, procedures and areas of study that can help account for it.

In the next decade, when business develops these autonomous technologies organizations will need to move beyond bias. Bias is defined as "prejudice in favor of or against one thing, person, or group compared with another, usually in a way considered to be unfair."[14] The term itself is negative in its connotation. Bias is destructive and bad for business. It holds back technology developers and business organizations. If bias is a fact and all data has bias, then bias is the norm. This does not mean that we do not need to deal with it but in the development of autonomous technologies, it might help to deal with it in a different way.

A different way of discussing bias in the development of technologies and organizations is to ask: Why was the data being gathered? What was it going to be used for? Who gathered the data? It might be helpful to ask: What were you optimizing for?

In all technology development, an organization can't gather all the data. Systems can't solve all the problems. Developers have to optimize for something. A bias data set is a data set that is lacking (e.g., perspectives, participants, metrics, etc.). Being overt, transparent and defining what has been optimized for will reveal what could be lacking in the data. Understanding what you're optimizing for will help reveal bias in the data so that then it can be countered and accounted for.

BEYOND ETHICS

Autonomous sentient technologies represent considerable potential and peril for the future business. Organizations that adopt these technologies will need to thoroughly assess and understand their impact and risks.

Recent examples have shown how autonomous hiring software when fed with biased data begins to present discriminatory behavior.[15] This is not optimal for the organization and presents an incredible amount of liability and exposure for the organization.

This has promoted businesses, researchers and organizations to explore how to develop ethical AI.[16]

However, this is the wrong question. The correct question is: How do we make these autonomous technologies ethically compliant? How do we make these technologies so that they are compliant with the rules, culture, regulations, business practices and laws that govern the organization?

By moving beyond ethics and exploring how to make these technologies ethically compliant organizations can begin to functionally implement these industrial technologies and take best advantage of sentient tools in an industrial setting. To do this organizations will need to define their ethics, constructing an ethical framework under which the organization, leadership and employees can operate. For many organizations, this will already be in place. If it is not, then it would be wise to take the time and produce it.

Following this, the organization can move beyond ethics, pushing past the ethical conversations and focus more on how to make the autonomous sentient technologies ethically compliant to their ethical framework.

BEYOND THE TYRANNY OF ABSOLUTISM

Autonomous sentient technologies will push organizations to rigorously and continually reimagine who does business and how business is done. Thinking of AI as a single entity holds back developers and organizations from realizing the full potential of the technology. Why should there only be one AI? Why would an organization not have multiple? Imagine having multiple autonomous technologies each with a different pre-programmed algorithmic agenda. One could be optimized for profit. Another optimized for ethics and compliance. A third could be optimized for innovation and risk-taking. The fourth could be fine-tuned to help the previous three get along and communicate.

I wrote a science fiction prototype imagining the implementation of multiple AIs for IEEE Computer Magazine.[17] In the story, a CEO engages with her five top advisors to make an important decision. After arguing and discussing the situation, the CEO emerges from the board room with her direction set. The CEO is human. The five advisors are all AIs designed specifically to optimize the CEO's performance.

This tyranny of absolutism that there's a single AI or a single technology does not embrace the complexity of humans and business nor does it comprehend the coming abilities of sentient tools.

BEGIN WITH PEOPLE

But where to begin? For decades now organizations have developed ethics and had compliance officers and departments. Ethics and compliance and regulation are nothing new to business. In fact, one way to view employees is as autonomous beings that make decisions and take actions on behalf of the organization. These actions need to be ethically and legally compliant. There are existing training, checks and balances, and business processes to ensure as much as possible that employees are representing the organization in a fashion that is compliant.

The same processes and procedures can be applied to the development of algorithms and autonomous technologies. The drafting and development of the requirements documentation is a pragmatic place to begin. When drafting and conceiving of this documentation organizations should include a broad range of diverse inputs to understand the full complexity and pitfalls of technology. Involving compliance officers and ethicists is a good step in the right direction.

For organizations to navigate this future it will be important to always keep people at the center of all decisions and activities. Everything that a business does is about people. It begins and ends with people.

There might be a large volume of technologies, processes and procedures in between—but ultimately good business, ethical business is about people.

Never lose sight of the fact that technology is simply a tool. It is a reflection of the people that employ it. With this vision, organizations can not only conduct ethical business, but they can actually make the future better for everyone.

BRIAN DAVID JOHNSON

Brian is an applied futurist who has worked with governments, trade organizations, start-ups, and multinational corporations to not only help envision their future but also specify the steps needed to get there. He is the futurist in residence at Arizona State University's Center for Science and the Imagination, a professor in the School for the Future of Innovation in Society, the Director of the ASU Threatcasting Lab, and worked for a decade at Intel as their first appointed futurist. He has contributed articles to publications like the *Wall Street Journal*, *Slate*, and Wired *Magazine*, holds over 40 patents and is the best-selling author of both science fiction and factbooks (*WaR: Wizards and Robots*, *21st Century Robot* and *Science Fiction Prototyping*). He has directed two feature films and is an illustrator and commissioned painter. In 2016 Samuel Goldwyn released *Vintage Tomorrows* a documentary based upon Johnson's book of the same name.

Photo Credit: Sarah Jenkins

(2)

ORGANIZATION - IN THE MACHINE ROOM

INFUSING ETHICS INTO YOUR BUSINESS: INSIGHTS FROM BIOMEDICAL ETHICS

DR. TIFFANY VORA

No doubt you've been told that yesterday's science fiction is today's business opportunity—and with this radical acceleration comes an increasingly complex and constantly evolving ethical landscape. While ethics underpins an organization's culture and, I would argue, the success of its product portfolio, "ethics" is a job too big for just one person—even someone with an ethics degree. To close this gap, I believe that both top-down (from leadership) and bottom-up (from every employee) approaches are crucial.

To extract insights that you can apply to ethics in your company and your industry, let's explore the general ethical principles that underlie medicine and biomedical research. Why medicine and biology? Because today's biomedical ethics rests on a rich history of deep thought into what "moral behavior" means, both from the top down (in health and research organizations) and from the bottom up (how doctors and scientists behave).

For at least a thousand years, physicians have sworn an oath at the end of their formal training. While this oath can come in many flavors [18], common cornerstones are trust (both with patients and with colleagues) and doing good. Today's biomedical ethics is similar to traditional medical oaths, with foundations of justice, doing good, and respect. It is based on the 1979 Belmont Report, which was first formulated in response to the Tuskegee Syphilis Study. During this decades-long experiment, hundreds of black men suffering from syphilis were frequently misled about the study or received no treatment at all. As a result, the Belmont Report sought to ensure that future research would be justified and ethical.

Things have gotten a bit more complicated since 1979. As Sarah Franklin of the Reproductive Sociology Research Group at the University of Cambridge recently wrote in Nature [19] "The stereotype of bureaucratic, box-ticking ethical compliance is no longer fit for purpose in a world of CRISPR twins, synthetic neurons and self-driving cars."

Just as box-ticking ethics tacked on at a study's end doesn't cut it for science anymore, it no longer suffices for your business—no matter your product or your industry. As a leader, you're empowered to embed ethics into the DNA and culture of your business, as well as into every project and product from the very beginning.

Let's explore the three foundations of biomedical ethics—justice, doing good, and respect—as principles upon which you can infuse ethics into your business and your industry.

JUSTICE

In biology research and medicine, the concept of "justice" encompasses legality, respect for a patient's rights, protection of vulnerable people and communities, and fair and/or equal resource distribution. The latter aspect is especially thorny, because "fair" and "equal" are not necessarily the same. For example, if every patient in an emergency room were treated equally, then a person suffering a heart attack would have to wait while another person had a splinter removed.

From a business point of view, must a product or service be offered fairly, let alone equally, to everyone? From a purely market-driven, capitalist perspective, the answer is no: it is "just" to expect payment for a product. Does it follow, then, that a potentially life-saving intervention should be withheld from our patient in the hospital waiting room if he cannot afford to pay? While assuming a neutral position about medical urgency would support a hospital in refusing to treat a non-paying patient (a top-down view), few would argue that such a decision is just—and a physician's oath would directly reinforce her commitment to just treatment (from the bottom up).

How can a business chart a compass toward justice, particularly for scenarios that are less extreme than an emergency room? In a review of Naomi Oreskes' *Why Trust Science?* for The Scholarly Kitchen[20] Lettie Conrad reminds us that being neutral is not necessarily the road to a just and ethical business—just as we see in our emergency room example. Rather, "by honestly examining and declaring our personal and organizational perspectives, privileges, and proclivities, we can contribute to a more open, transparent... ecosystem." In medicine and research, ethics review boards and explicit transparency requirements for publication contribute to both the strategy and the tactics underlying just practices.

For the concept of justice to be foundational to your business's mission, culture, and operations, it is crucial to explore what "just" means, from the bottom up (your employees) and from the top down (your leadership). This goal is ambitious, but achievable, particularly if you begin with small conversations in a safe space within your company that are focused on raising questions, rather than immediately seeking answers.

For example, you could start within your company, probing what "just business" even means for your industry, then expand the conversation to include trusted external advisors. Broadening the conversation to your customer base and your industry will ultimately position you to craft your strategy and your tactics for achieving justice.

By being willing to grapple with the concept of justice, an ethical business leader can do more than simply exploit a new market—you have a chance to truly influence the world. Children, the elderly, the differently abled, minority groups, and others have needs for products and services, but there may be important historical, social, and other reasons why they have not accessed them to date. Will having your product or service actually improve the lives of your customers—according to their values? Even though our hospital example is requiring our patient to wait longer for treatment for his non-urgent situation, could the hospital be delivering value to him during that time? How would the patient like to benefit while waiting?

Building a dedicated space for stakeholder voices, from the very outset of a product, shows respect to your potential customers, earns their trust, and enables a business that is just. These voices can offer crucial insights into biases in your product or how you intend to market and sell it. Unfortunately, it's impossible to avoid bias completely, which is why medical and scientific training focuses on ferreting out bias, especially our own. We can be hobbled by all sorts of cognitive biases, like confirmation bias ("this is proof that my idea is right"), status-quo bias ("things are great the way they are"), and self-serving bias ("my career is at stake here"). And when we add artificial intelligence to the mix, we have to consider algorithmic biases, too.

The key question is, "What would it take to change my mind?" If you discover that nothing will change your mind, then critical thinking, ethics, and leadership deserve more of your attention. As Tom Nichols urged in *The Death of Expertise*,[21] strive to cage your ego long enough to learn something.

Constantly asking, What am I missing? What do I have wrong? What am I assuming? helps keep you and your endeavors honest, ethical—and just.

DOING GOOD

Until mid-2018, Google famously included a clause in their code of conduct reminding employees, "don't be evil." Some physician oaths include a clause to "do no harm." Is "do no harm" the same as "do good?" And is just not being evil enough anymore?

Several bioethicists believe that the answer to both questions is "no." In her 2019 Nature essay that we referenced earlier, Sarah Franklin pointed to Warren T. Reich's 1978 statement that medicine had moved away from a simple commitment to preserving life. Our example patient could die during a heart transplant, after all. As Franklin writes, "In the world's most advanced medical facilities, a higher quality of life could now be worth dying for." Has a surgeon "done good" if her patient dies on the table? The answer depends on the surgeon's worldview and values—as well as on her patient's worldview and values. Our patient likely believes that his surgeon will not actively harm him, since doctors are known to swear an oath, and he has provided informed consent before beginning a procedure that could hurt or even kill him.

How do we uncover a company's worldview and values? The best mission statements clearly lay them out and reflect a company's day-to-day, from the top down and the bottom up. The mission statement is a rallying cry, an operating manual, and a social contract rolled into one text—an oath, to extend our analogy to medicine. In the best scenario, every employee, from the executive suite down, can not only tell you their company's mission: they can tell you what they've done, today, to live that mission.

Importantly, your company's mission statement can reveal whether your business understands the difference between "do no harm" and "do good." From a legal perspective, a written commitment to doing good may feel like a dangerous promise. And that promise is dangerous—if you break it. If you want to make it a habit to "do good," seek out small ways for individuals and for your organization to "do good" on a daily basis. By relentlessly doing good, you show respect to your customers and your employees by validating their trust in your leadership and your company. Remember this point about respect, which we will explore next.

Imagine our surgeon telling our patient, "I'm committed to keeping you alive" versus "I'm committed to you leading your best life." In my mind, the former statement fails to respect the patient's autonomy and agency; it disregards his values. But for the latter statement, the patient must define his best life, in his own terms. The surgeon has accorded respect to her patient as a step on her path to doing good.

From the rise of Benefit Corporations to the surge in Environmental, Social, and Governance investing, we are seeing a shift toward defining "doing good" as not just a company's overall goal, but as each and every step that the company takes toward meeting those goals. Along the same lines, Pope Francis drew eyes in 2019 as he challenged business leaders to merge economics with ethics.

Together, these trends tell me that in the very near future, "doing good" will not be a bonus. Doing good will be business as usual. Are your company and your industry ready for that future?

RESPECT

In medical terms, "respect" encompasses respect for dignity, for autonomy, and for privacy. For animal research, ethical behavior accords the animals with dignity, with acknowledgment that they feel pain, and with awareness that their lives have intrinsic value. Several guidelines for ethical research on animals stress the need to balance benefit and suffering; for an experiment to be approved, the researcher must demonstrate that the overall benefit (to people, to animals, to the environment) outweighs the suffering inflicted on the study animals. The suffering of human subjects also must be carefully considered. And it's not enough to say these things in words. Doctors and researchers must, through their daily actions, manifest their commitment to respectful, ethical behavior, from the initial design of a study or treatment all the way to the end of their relationship with their subjects.

Some of the most valuable commodities today are data, attention, and trust. By treating your customers and stakeholders with respect, your company can earn their data, their attention, and ultimately their trust. I believe that trust will soon be the single most valuable asset that a business can hold. The foundations of your business's trust reserves are transparency, inclusiveness, commitment to a mission, and relentless respect—both within the business and in all aspects that face customers and partners.

Notice the analogy here: respect, like a foundation, should be engineered from the beginning, not tacked onto a project just before launch. In addition to ensuring informed consent, our respectful surgeon includes her patient in discussions of his treatment plan—before decisions are made—and ensures that her patient's voice is heard without compromising his care. Similarly, the early stages of biomedical clinical trials have increasingly involved patients and their advocates in trial design and approval, often with the benefits of increased transparency, respect, and partnership—in all directions.

Your employees also deserve your respect as their leader, and that respect constitutes a foundation of trust within your company. The most effective scientific and medical research teams masterfully combine hard-nosed analytical mindsets with psychologically safe spaces. Respect should anchor the meetings of our patient's care team—with respect accorded not just among physicians, but for our patient as well. Crucially, our surgeon will give the other members of the care team her full attention and share her most honest feedback, because her patient's life depends on their plan.

As a leader, you can foster bias-busting, respectful collaborations both explicitly (through verbal tags) and implicitly (through modeling, body language, and consistency), both within your company and for conversations outside it. What will you gain from liberally showing respect? A group of partners that you can trust to call out your biases, whether personal or business. To follow up when you call them out on their blind spots. To question whether a product will land the way management wants it to. To raise the right question, instead of the question everyone else is asking (or thinks they're asking). And to find answers that may not be the ones your company wants but are closer to the ones that your company needs.

Think of those trusted, respected partners as your business's care team.

YOUR ETHICAL BUSINESS FUTURE

By digging into the formal ethics framework that underlies medicine and research science, we've identified principles—and experiments—that could empower your business to be an ethical business, from the top down and the bottom up.

Ultimately, your company's ethical position may or may not be aligned with the climate in your industry or even in your culture. Perhaps you've made your best guess at the ethical landscape that will exist when your product comes to market, after encouraging your stakeholders to share their concerns and visions with you. Or perhaps you're building the product, the market, and the zeitgeist all at the same time. Today our surgeon and transplant patient enter into a known ethical landscape—but what if 10 years from now our surgeon is transplanting a 3D-printed organ, or a human organ grown in a pig? This is the main reason why "box-ticking" ethics are no longer sufficient: when the time comes to tick those boxes, no one may have drawn them yet!

No matter the scope of your company's ambitions, you and your business must have an ethical position from which to operate—both strategically and tactically. Should this position be flexible? Yes! Be willing to change your mind once it becomes clear that your goals or your ethics strategies are untenable, whether from cultural, technical, or market forces. Overall, navigating toward justice, respect, and doing good will help you lay the foundation for making the future instead of just chasing it.

DR. TIFFANY VORA

Tiffany is an educator, writer, research scientist, and entrepreneur who lives in Silicon Valley. Her Ph.D. research in the Department of Molecular Biology at Princeton University brought her into the emerging fields of genomics, systems biology, computational biology, and astrobiology. She previously served as a Visiting Professor at the American University in Cairo and an Instructor for the Department of Bioengineering at Stanford University. Among other activities, she is currently Faculty and Vice-Chair of Medicine and Digital Biology at Singularity University, a member of the Homeward Bound project for women leaders in STEM, and a Nonresident Fellow at the GeoTech Center within the Atlantic Council. Overall, Tiffany is passionate about translating the leading edge of science and medicine into insights enabling humanity, prosperity, and peace.

Photo Credit: Nick Otto

MAKING EFFECTIVE AND ETHICAL BUSINESS DECISIONS

BENJAMIN ROSMAN

When deciding on a course of action in business, there is typically a tension between what is good for the business (and particularly the bottom line), good for the employees, and as more of a recent concern, good for society and the environment. This presents a dilemma in thinking about making business decisions.

We can look to the science of decision making to guide us through this challenge, by focusing on the desired outcomes, or utility, of what happens following a decision. It is important to note that what anyone actually cares about is typically the downstream effects of a decision, rather than the immediate consequences.

In fact, thinking only of the immediate consequences is what is referred to as acting greedily.

For example, consider the case of automating some existing role in a company, leading to redundancies. There are obviously many effects to take into account here, which can be treated as lying along two primary dimensions: who is directly affected by the decision (the business, the employees, and society), and then the timeframe of these effects (short-term vs. long-term). For instance, automation may result in immediate cost-saving, yet may have longer-term negative impacts on the perception of the company. There would also be implications on the wider economy because of increased unemployment, which would be offset against the greater demand for automation and what that would mean to different sectors of the economy. Every alternative to that decision would come with its own desiderata; whether that would involve keeping those people employed but with shorter work hours, looking at innovative approaches to human-machine collaboration that plays to the strengths of both, or maintaining more of a human workforce.

Thinking long-term presents a far greater challenge than just the short-term: if I care about more than just immediate consequences, I need to be able to predict what will happen, how other entities in my ecosystem may respond, how I, in turn, would respond to that, etc. This is further exacerbated by the fact that all of these quantities possess different degrees of uncertainty. To make truly effective decisions, one needs to factor all of these considerations into the process.

The problem is that, while the long-term effects may have tremendous ramifications for the business, these are typically not explicitly codified, making them challenging to factor into the reasoning process. If one could foresee all eventualities, this would be a tremendous boon, but unfortunately, this is seldom possible.

Instead, we can work with larger teams of stakeholders to consider different downstream and broader outcomes, and coarsely categorize these based on the expected probabilities of them occurring.

One is then faced with the problem of how to think of value in the future. The challenge is not just in enumerating all that might occur, but also quantifying these effects. How does some immediate effect trade off against the exact same effect happening a year down the line? We know from research into behavioral economics that the human brain discounts future rewards: these outcomes are worth less the further into the future we look, precisely because they are less guaranteed to come to pass. It can thus be useful to consider the notion of discounting, or explicitly reasoning about the relative value of the same outcome at different points in time. One useful approach to this is to think in terms of the expected utilities: being the utility one may derive from some consequence multiplied by the estimated probability of it happening. In this way, the value of some significant future event is somewhat offset by the estimated probability of its occurrence. Making decisions by weighing up these values ensures that we are to some extent taking the future into consideration.

As an example, consider choosing between two options: X and Y. Option X is guaranteed to lead to an outcome with a profit of $30. On the other hand, option Y may result in some event A that yields a profit of $100 but is expected to happen with a probability of 20%, or to an alternate outcome B which has a probability of 80% and produces a profit of $10. This gives the expected utility of option Y as the weighted average of their outcomes, which is $100*0.2 + $10*0.8 = $28. In this example, option X is the better choice when the probabilities are factored in, even though option Y has the chance of a larger payoff.

This is where it is important to weigh up all the ethical ramifications of a decision. Explicitly considering how this could affect employees or the broader society may warn against something that seems positive in the short-term but could ultimately affect the sustainability of the business. The converse is true for many disruptive decisions as well: what may harm short-term growth could place the company in a far stronger position down the line. It is important to take into account that businesses succeed through interaction with a greater ecosystem, and the health of that environment and external perceptions thereof can have significant effects on the long-term stability of an individual organization.

This problem of thinking ahead does not only occur at the level of decision making for an entire business, but at every level within it. It can often be the case that while the general direction for the business has taken potential long-term effects into consideration, this has not been done at the various tiers throughout the business. For example, Key Performance Indicators (KPIs) are typically set by line managers to guide the performance of employees, but these are often done without an overview of the entire business.

This challenge is known as the goal alignment problem and can easily result in a situation where employees at each level of an organization are pulling in slightly different directions and optimizing for goals that have been set at a local level, with the effect of diffusing the direction of the entire organization.

The solution to these joint problems lies in thinking deeply about incentives and utilities. Here we can take inspiration from the wide range of literature on behavior learning in artificial intelligence (AI), and note that at its core, this problem resembles that of an intelligent agent learning to play a game such as chess with a long sequence of moves in an adversarial setting, or having a robot learn a task such as cooking, where every action has dependencies and effects that may only be realized at a later point.

When facing these challenges in AI, one typically considers various approaches to subdividing one monolithic goal, such as long-term financial success, into multiple smaller pieces that are aligned in their aims. One such method is to define subgoals to be reached on the path to the final goal and strive for these.

This is still fraught with challenges, much as how giving a beginner chess player the subgoal to capturing the opponent's queen may help her learn to play the game but will result in behavior that gives a circuitous route to victory. Other approaches involve a top-down decomposition of the task, as would happen when different divisions within the business are assigned their own goals. In this case, it is again critical that each goal is clearly aligned to the overall goal, and not merely left as the result of a box-ticking exercise.

Any time one is required to set goals, there is a great risk that the resulting behavior could deviate from the intention. This happens naturally, as we humans are often unaware of not just the consequences of our actions, but additionally many of our own biases and assumptions. It is usually not even clear what our goals are in their entirety, and failing to specify some aspect, such as environmental impact, opens it up to exploitation in that direction. The best mitigation procedure is then to monitor closely and continuously the behavior that arises from having set certain goals and adapt these regularly to ensure desirable outcomes.

In short, making good decisions within an organization involves considering impacts on all stakeholders, focusing specifically on the long-term, and making sure subgoals within the organization are well aligned. To this end:

- Engage widely with experts to forecast all potential downstream effects of decisions on all stakeholders and estimate the probability of these occurring. This should include not just financial aspects, but also implications for staff and the broader ecosystem, to avoid missing something that may have significant long-term effects.
- Ensure that anyone setting subgoals at any level within the organization has a larger view of what they should be aiming to accomplish and understands not only the full context of what their team is expected to accomplish, but why.
- Refine goals repeatedly at all levels, with constant feedback up and down the organization to understand where behavior has deviated from what is desired.

BENJAMIN ROSMAN

Benjamin is an Associate Professor in the School of Computer Science and Applied Mathematics at University of the Witwatersrand, South Africa. He received his Ph.D. in Informatics from the University of Edinburgh (UK). His research interests focus on decision theory, machine learning, artificial intelligence, and robotics, and he has published over 65 academic publications in these areas. He is a Co-Founder and organizer of the Deep Learning Indaba, a machine learning summer school with a focus on strengthening African machine learning. He is a recipient of a Google Faculty Research Award, the first in machine learning in Africa. He is a SingularityU Faculty Member, and a Senior Member of the IEEE.

MANAGING THE ETHICS OF DATA DRIVEN SOLUTIONS

ELAINE WEIDMAN-GRUNEWALD
AND ANNA FELLÄNDER

In our data-driven world, we're used to having massive amounts of information instantly available to navigate nearly every aspect of our lives. Data-driven technologies and AI bring exponential benefits to companies, individuals and society in terms of both efficiency gains and convenience. It may even help solve complex problems like cures for cancer, species extinction, and climate change. But at the same time, it is vital that organizations consider the societal and ethical implications of their use of technology to avoid unintended pitfalls and risks, such as discrimination, privacy intrusion, unethical nudging and social exclusion.

Two converging trends exacerbate this situation. First, data gathering by companies for product development and marketing, digital security and more are picking up speed, while the question of who controls the data remains controversial. Second, Artificial Intelligence (AI) is applied without the ability to trace and explain the use of private data and how the algorithm arrived at a specific conclusion. Exploitation of private data should be based on transparency and accountability. Most people are unaware of how their data is used and the insights created when data sets are combined—and when these insights become highly privacy-intrusive. The promise of AI and tech solutions is exciting and can be lucrative, but it is also risky because the nature of the risks is difficult to predict and once you get it wrong, the impact of that decision can scale exponentially.

Few companies are prepared to manage these dilemmas. While many larger, established companies may have an ethics and compliance function or ethics board, relatively few have included ethical and societal risks as part of the business agenda when it comes to the company bottom line. Addressing new emerging risks that result from data-driven technologies requires a new lens, a broadening of typical risk and compliance functions. Three areas, in particular, are pertinent to managing the ethics of data-driven solutions in the workplace:

- Use of data-driven technologies and AI in recruitment
- Companies deploying data-driven solutions to deliver products and services
- Organizations using data-driven solutions to optimize processes and create uniquely tailored client relationships

No matter how companies use data-driven solutions, they need to act early and decisively to curtail or avoid privacy and ethical risks. Responsibly managing data in the workplace is going to be a fundamental aspect of ethics at work going forward. The journey won't be the same for every company because they are at different levels of digital maturity, but every business would benefit by starting now to take appropriate actions to protect against ethical risks. In this chapter, we offer guidance and practical tools for businesses to move ethically into an ever more digital future.

THE ETHICAL PITFALLS

The AI Sustainability Center AB® describes four main pitfalls of digital risks:

- Misuse or overuse of data: The AI application/solution is intrusive (using overly broad or deep open data), or data could be used for unintended purposes by others.
- Bias of the creator: Values and bias are intentionally or unintentionally programmed by the creator who may lack the knowledge/skills to appreciate how the solution could scale more broadly.
- Immature data or AI: The algorithm is based on insufficient data or the AI model is not trained or tested enough for market-readiness. Insufficient training of algorithms on data sets and lack of representative data could lead to incorrect and unethical recommendations.
- Data bias: The data available is not an accurate reflection of reality or the preferred reality and may lead to incorrect and unethical recommendations.

If these pitfalls are not managed well, they pose a broad range of risks. These include privacy intrusion, amplified discrimination and inequality, social exclusion and segregation, as well as faulty conclusions, recommendations and predictions, and misinterpretations.

Policy frameworks are starting to recognize the problems. The European Union, for example, has developed a set of ethical principles for "Trustworthy AI."[22] The EU white paper published in February 2020 includes seven specific requirements that should apply to "high-risk" AI applications. These are: human agency and oversight; technical robustness and safety; privacy and data governance; transparency; diversity, non-discrimination, and fairness; societal and environmental well-being, and accountability.

However, despite some guidance at the government level, traditional tools used for detecting risks are either insufficient or not updated to accommodate new kinds of ethical risks. By taking advantage of new tools, such as the risk scanning tool described in the next section, and anchoring business models within a strong ethical foundation, companies will be favorably positioned for future regulations. There is most often a trade-off between the accuracy of the AI model and the ability for explainability. Yet this is the only way to go as we expect future regulations will make explainability a prerequisite to ensure the transparency and accountability of any AI application.

OPERATIONALIZING YOUR ETHICAL PRINCIPLES

Companies are increasingly using data-driven solutions to deliver products and services and to optimize their own products and processes. Managing that data responsibly requires the right governance framework and risk management measures to handle new types of risks as well as measures to mitigate the risk. This includes integrating ethical risks into normal risk handling, a strong focus on accountability, staff training and competence development, explainability of data models, and transparency. Companies can also benefit and build trust by benchmarking their risks and continuously monitoring and reporting on performance over time.

To be trustworthy in the use of data-driven solutions, the minimum requirements are to ensure the following fundamentals are in place: governance, accountability, transparency, and explainability. Since AI is self-learning and self-propagating, the effects of even a small decision can scale in unexpected ways. Setting minimum requirements and being aware of possible ethical and societal outcomes, should be at the top of the agenda in boardrooms and C-suites.

Companies need practical tools to evaluate the societal and

ethical risks of digital solutions before they are deployed as well as practical ways to operationalize ethical principles and practices in their use of data-driven solutions. One example of an early tool is the AI Sustainability Center and MetricStream Inc.'s risk scanning tool which is designed to provide a cross-functional perspective. The self-assessment risk scanning tool reveals possible gaps and vulnerabilities in governance and technical frameworks. It is designed to help companies to identify and ultimately mitigate potential risks, avoid common pitfalls, and meet emerging regulatory frameworks.

The box below provides a snapshot of this assessment tool, the kinds of questions an organization might consider to see where it sits from the perspective of data-driven risks:

EXAMPLES OF HOW TO ASSESS YOUR AI AND DATA-DRIVEN ETHICAL RISKS

- Does your organization have any ethical guidelines, principles or codes specifically related to AI and/or data-driven technology?
- Is information about how you use AI and data-driven technology easily available for those affected and/or using it?
- Do you have a process for detecting unwanted bias in your data?
- Can you trace the decisions made by the algorithm(s) in the solution given a specific outcome/result?
- Do you have employee training around ethics in relation to data, data-driven technologies, and/or AI?
- Do you take any specific measures to reduce possible unwanted biases in the coding/programming?
- Do you have quantitative (or other) criteria for determining when the model used is mature enough/sufficiently trained?
- Can you explain in simple terms how the algorithm(s) in the solution came to a certain conclusion?

- Can you explain in understandable terms to the relevant stakeholders how the data used in the solution is selected?
- Do you have a process for checking whether the solution is used for its intended purpose?
- Are you confident in your organization's ability to detect, then shut down a malfunctioning AI system in a timely manner i.e., before any serious problems are caused?
- Is there a "human in the loop" during the life cycle of the solution?

The answers to these questions yield insights that are akin to a quick health check to determine possible risks or trouble spots. To get a more complete picture of actual risks, an organization needs to go deeper by following up on potential risks with a risk assessment and then prioritizing which actions would make sense to mitigate those risks.

COMPANY CASES: PUTTING DIGITAL RISKS INTO PRACTICE

We present two cases of companies applying an ethical lens to their use of data-driven solutions. The first is JobAgent®, a Swedish startup in the HR-tech space, which specializes in reversed recruiting, matching talents to hiring companies. JobAgent uses AI as an important tool in its process but is well aware that AI-based recruitment can present serious sustainability risks. Many companies in the recruitment industry using AI have a so-called black-box approach, which means they cannot explain the recommendations given by the AI. This can result in a number of risks:

- Productivity loss: The recruitment may be based on irrelevant variables which increase the risk of the wrong person being matched to the wrong place.
- Discriminatory risks: This occurs when you can't backtrack

and explain the AI that you are using. Ethnicity, gender, age or other irrelevant variables might come into effect.

- Bad societal catch 22: This means that the algorithm is overly based on what the talent has done before with regards to work experience and especially work titles, such as women being screened out for executive and board roles because they haven't had the opportunity before.

To address these challenges, JobAgent applied the AI Sustainability Center and MetricStream's risk scanning tool. A crucial finding was the need to build its AI from a glass-box rather than a black-box perspective, with transparency on how the algorithm works, and why it gives the recommendations it does. In addition, JobAgent created governance features to constantly monitor its AI and ensure that human biases don't contribute to making the AI faulty. The risk scanning tool highlighted the fact that a risk that might appear small in developing a specific functionality or feature could have huge effects in the future when that functionality scales. It also underscored the importance of explainability for transparency and retaining the trust of users.

The second case is Telia Company, a major telecoms and media company operating across the Nordics and Baltics and a founding member of the AI Sustainability Center. For Telia Company, privacy preservation is a brand and trust differentiator. It has introduced nine Guiding Principles on Trusted AI Ethics[23] which apply to operations and employees as well as product design, implementation, testing, use and follow up of AI. These are: responsible and value centric; human centric; rights respecting; control, accountable, safe and secure, transparent and explainable, fair and equal, and continuous review and dialogue.

Sustainability and ethics are also part of Telia Company's Group Enterprise Risk Management Framework.[24]

One of its solutions, Crowd Insights, helps cities improve traffic congestion, planning, safety and security while preserving consumer privacy. Telia applies the AI Sustainability Center framework to assess and mitigate data-driven risks in use of the solution. To ensure privacy, the data is aggregated and irreversibly anonymized before it can be used in the Crowd Insights service. This limits the level of location granularity and demographic profiling that can be used.

Both cases illustrate that the real challenge for companies is not setting a principle, policy or commitment to managing digital ethical risks, but to actually implement the right approach. As mentioned above, this rests on proper training and risk handling. Importantly, the complexity of the technology requires cross-functional approaches to ensure that legal, societal and technical risk assessments are all captured.

Cross-functional teams and training are critical in coding the values of a company, and a society—not just the most effective or powerful algorithm. This is one way that companies can manage the ethical trade-offs between maximizing profit and sustaining ethical principles. You might not benefit from the maximum profitable algorithm—but this must be weighed against a potential loss of trust.

As sustainable AI is an emerging field, and many risks difficult to predict with traditional compliance and audit measures, we offer the following recommendations and early steps for companies to consider.

RECOMMENDATIONS

1. If you don't have them already, consider establishing ethical AI principles, and integrate them cross-functionally.
2. When assessing the level of risk in your organization, be sure to include multiple perspectives and the right subject matter expertise in your risk assessment.

3. Make the societal and ethical risks of data-driven solutions part of your company's overall risk framework.

4. In addition to seeking to reduce or avoid risks, like privacy intrusion, companies should also consider proactive measures that can protect and preserve privacy.

5. To build stakeholder trust, companies should be transparent and publicly state how they are—and aren't—using the data they collect. Some 89% of consumers wish companies would take additional steps to protect their data.[25]

6. Explore methods and tools that can be integrated into risk frameworks to help to identify and characterize data-driven risks.

CONCLUSION

In an ever more digital future, every company needs to be conscious of ethical and societal risks, adjust their business model accordingly, and put measures in place to assess and mitigate these risks across the organization. Awareness of the ethical risks is the first step in managing them. Democracy and the right to privacy hang in the balance. In some instances, as responsible governments and businesses, we must simply say no, recognizing that while we have the ability to use the data, we will not do so. And, as long as we do not have the right explainability models in place, AI is best used as a complement to human decisions, not as a black-box substitution.

Data will remain one of the most valuable assets on the balance sheet. Chances are we will look back on this period when data increasingly defined our world and reflect on that how we gave away our privacy was naïve. Sustainable companies will recognize that management of that data as well as algorithms on large, combined data sets, cannot be relegated to technical teams alone or that its use should only be driven by profit. In the future, organizations will need to earn our trust in order to use our data. The winners in the new data-driven world will be the organizations that can most skillfully balance that ethical tightrope, maintain their values, and prioritize transparency and sustainability in line with the seductive profits.

ELAINE WEIDMAN-GRUNEWALD

Elaine is a founder of the AI Sustainability Center. She is an expert in the technology sector and effects of digitalization, as well as the global sustainability and development arena, where she has had leading positions and roles, including Chief Sustainability & Public Affairs Officer at Ericsson. She is a Board member of SWECO AB, The European Sustainable Growth Acquisition Corp, the International Women's Forum Sweden, and the Whitaker Peace and Development Initiative, and is actively engaged in the ethics of technologies. She recently published her first book on why and how business leaders can take action on sustainability: *Sustainability Leadership: A Swedish Approach to Transforming Your Company, Your Industry and the World*, co-authored with Henrik Henriksson, former CEO of Scania.

ANNA FELLÄNDER

Anna is the founder of the AI Sustainability Center, which helps organizations identify, measure, and govern the ethical and societal risks in AI. She is one of Sweden's leading experts on the effect of digitalization on organizations, society, and the economy. Most recently, Anna was Chief Digital Economist at Swedbank and has spent 10 years working for the Swedish government, including as Senior Advisor to the Minister of Digitalization. She has also held advisory positions at Stockholm's Royal Institute of Technology and as a Board member for AI start-ups.

UNDERSTANDING HUMAN VALUES TO DEVELOP VALUES-LED TECHNOLOGIES

GUENDALINA DONDÉ

"*The best way to catch the technology train is not to chase it, but to be at the next station,*" suggests Professor Luciano Floridi, who is one of the most authoritative voices in the field of digital ethics.[26] Against this backdrop of uncertainty about future developments of digital technologies, businesses have the opportunity—and the responsibility—to be pioneers of the ethical framework that will be applied to technological innovation. This is certainly recognized by companies in many ways. IBE research shows that the use of data and privacy risks, which are closely interrelated with the adoption and use of artificial intelligence technologies, for example, are frequently mentioned by companies as issues of concern. In a recent survey the IBE conducted among large listed companies in Europe, issues around data management are the most frequently mentioned as need addressing by Ethics & Compliance practitioners, overtaking bribery and corruption for the first time since the survey started in 1995. But what does it mean in practice? How can companies make sure that they are waiting at the next station rather than chasing the train?

THE ROLE OF THE LAW: HINDRANCE OR OPPORTUNITY?

First of all, it is important to acknowledge that they are not facing this challenge on their own. Governments and international institutions have been working on a clearer definition of the "rules of the game" through *ad hoc* laws and regulations (at the EU level, the General Data Protection Regulation—or GDPR—is a good example of this).

Legislative interventions are important to establish a basic normative framework, especially in contexts where the risk of ethical lapses might be higher or where human rights might be disregarded. By imposing some minimum standards that organizations have to comply with, they start to address the concerns expressed by some that companies—in the tech sector or otherwise—are using the limited regulation of digital technologies, especially in developing countries, to their advantage (as the Financial Times rhetorically asked its readership in a 2019 article about the so-called "African Silicon Valley, are tech companies Africa's new colonialists?)".[27]

However, this is not sufficient. Relevant legislations indicate, metaphorically speaking, the moves that are not allowed in the game. They say nothing about the best moves to win the game (which means, in this case, using and developing digital technologies in a way that truly benefits society). To define that, businesses need to develop their own ethical standards, going above and beyond legal requirements in order to rebuild and support the trust of their customers, employees and the public as a whole. This can be done both through a set of core principles that apply to digital technologies and through governance systems that ensure a good management of technology. The role of board members is also important.

One might immediately think about tech companies and their responsibilities in this field, and it is important that they are ahead of the game. However, it is important to bear in mind that they are not the only ones that are called upon to set ethical standards for the use of digital technologies. All businesses across all sectors need to be involved in this conversation, given how pervasive these issues are across industries and sectors.

A VALUES-LED APPROACH

Over the past few years, an abundance of ethical principles for digital technologies have been developed by a variety of organizations and institutions, both at national and international level, and the overlaps between them send a positive signal that we are moving in the right direction. At the IBE, we have developed an interactive framework of fundamental values and principles for the use of Artificial Intelligence (AI), as follows:[28]

A	Accuracy	Accuracy means that companies need to ensure that the AI systems they use produce correct, precise and reliable results. They need to be free from biases and systematic errors deriving, for example, from an unfair sampling of a population, or from an estimation process that does not give accurate results.
R	Respect of privacy	The rise of AI has been described by some as the death of privacy, while others have compared to an Orwellian Big Brother ready to scoop on everyone's private life. Certainly, machine learning technologies have brought about new ethical issues related to the respect of privacy. Recognizing this, the European Commission reinforced the principle that everyone has the right to the protection of personal data by a comprehensive reform of data protection rules that culminated with the implementation of GDPR.
T	Transparency	Traditionally, many organizations that have developed and now use AI algorithms do not allow public scrutiny as the underlying programming (the source code) is proprietary, kept from public view. Being transparent and opening source material in computer science is an important step. It helps the public to understand better how AI works, and therefore it improves trust and prevents unjustified fears.

I	Interpret-ability	Interpretable and explainable AI will be essential for business and the public to understand, trust and effectively manage "intelligent" machines. Organizations that design and use algorithms need to take care in producing models that are as simple as possible, to explain how complex machines work.
F	Fairness	Fairness and justice remain paramount for ethical businesses when dealing with AI. As AI systems are able to perform tasks, previously undertaken by humans, in a more efficient and reliable way, the workplace is going to change, and it is therefore important that companies pay attention to how this will affect its employees and customers.
I	Integrity	As the saying has it, integrity is doing the right thing even when nobody's watching. In the context of AI, we should ensure that it is used only for its intended purpose, even when there is no means to enforce this. When designing or selling an AI system, it is important to ensure that the end user will respect the agreed uses of the technology.
C	Control	Much of the scepticism around the future of AI is fuelled by the fear that humans might lose control over machines, which would then prevail and possibly wipe out humanity altogether. To have full control over AI systems, it is important that both companies and algorithm designers only work with technologies that they fully understand. Being able to explain the functionalities of a technology of which they appear to be in control of is essential to build trust with employees, customers and all stakeholders.
I	Impact	Sometimes companies might be tempted to adopt new AI systems because they want to be ahead of the game and on top of the latest technological advancement, rather than because they really need them or because they benefit their business. Just because a company can use a certain AI technology, it doesn't mean that it should. Measuring the impact of AI is important to help companies avoid unnecessary costs and potential risks deriving from the use of inadequate or inappropriate technologies.

A	Account-ability	Accountability is central to the definition of good practice in corporate governance. It implies that there should always be a line of responsibility for business actions to establish who has to answer for the consequences. AI systems introduce an additional strand of complexity: who is responsible for the outcome of the decision-making process of an artificial agent? It is difficult to provide a univocal answer and a rich debate has flourished on this topic. Although the question of responsibility remains largely unanswered, a valuable approach would be for each of the parties involved to act as if they were ultimately responsible.
L	Learning	To maximize the potential of AI, people need to learn how it works and what are the most efficient and effective ways to use it. Employees and other stakeholders need to be empowered to take personal responsibility for the consequences of their use of AI and they need to be provided with the skills to do so.

FROM VALUES TO PRACTICE

The ARTIFICIAL framework presented above is an important starting point for organizations to reflect on the challenges that technology can pose to the business and how to overcome them. However, one of the most important challenges is how to move from this sort of high overarching statement of principles to more granular procedures and practices that can be applied at the coalface. According to our research, most experts agree that codes of ethics can be an important tool to do so. There are two levels at which these types of codes could work. First, outside bodies could develop overarching industry codes. Second, these principles could be written into the ethical conduct codes of individual companies.

In the UK, the House of Lords Select Committee on AI report (2018) raised the possibility of an AI Code.[29] It noted that companies have started to develop their own principles and it stated that companies using boards, committees and processes within a self-regulatory framework will generate confidence and trust among their clients.

The challenge is to make them of practical help to employees. This must be done without creating silos in which technology staff are treated differently from other employees.

Some practical suggestions for companies to consider might be:

- Design new and more detailed decision-making tools for meta-decisions, to help those that design algorithms and construct AI systems to ensure that they 'do the right thing' and act in line with the company's ethical values. This can come in the form of dedicated company policies that ensure proper testing and appropriate signoff from relevant stakeholders, both internally and externally.

- Engage with third parties for the design of AI algorithms only if they commit to similar ethical standards: the design of these systems might be outsourced, and it is important to conduct ethical due diligence on business partners. A similar principle applies to clients and customers to whom AI technologies are sold. Testing a third-party algorithm in a specific situation is also important to ensure accuracy.

- Introduce 'ethics tests' for AI machines, where they are presented with an ethical dilemma. It is important to measure how they respond in such situations in order to predict likely outcomes in a real-life application, and therefore assume responsibility for what the machines will do.

- Empower people through specific training courses and communication campaigns in order to enable them to use AI systems efficiently, effectively and ethically. These training courses should be directed not only at the technical personnel building the tool, but also at senior business managers who should understand the assumptions, limitations and—at a certain level—inner workings of AI technology.

- Conduct impact assessment of the digital technologies adopted. Given the rapid adoption of digital technologies in business, there is a risk that the governance systems required to mitigate the potential risks of its deployment are overlooked. Data science teams should have structured controls and testing around their development process, which are overseen centrally by the business. Because AI tools are often self-learning, control and testing procedures should be dynamic and constant. This includes a risk assessment and impact analysis of each AI tool, and approval by management. It is important to ensure that the ethics team is involved in this process, to ensure that it is in line with the organization's ethical values.

- Engage with stakeholders, internally and externally. This can provide useful evidence in terms of what works and what doesn't, giving companies an indication of the best direction forward. This is relevant because introducing standards that are removed from business practice can block the potential of technology. If the potential and the impact of AI are not fully understood, there is the risk of going to the other end of the spectrum and being unnecessarily "conservative," missing out on potential opportunities.

- Include a decision-making model focused on the use of digital technologies. Many organizations include in their code of ethics guidance to support individual decision-making through a decision-making model or guide which often takes the form of 'questions to ask yourself.' This could be applied in a similar manner before adopting or using digital technologies. Some questions to consider might be: what is the purpose of our job and what technology do we need to achieve it? Do we understand how these systems work? Are we in control of this technology? Who benefits and who carries the risks related to the adoption of the new technology? Who bears the costs for it? Would it be considered fair if it became widely known? What are the ethical dimensions and what values are at stake? What might be the unexpected consequences? Do we have other options that are less risky? What is the governance process for introducing this technology? Who is responsible for it? How is its impact to be monitored? Have the risks of its usage been considered? Is the potential gain proportional to the ethical risk?

In conclusion, digital technologies offer great potential, and their scope of application is growing exponentially, but it is important to be aware of the ethical risks that they bring too. The definition of a legal and ethical framework that can be applied to digital technologies is far from being defined. This is why businesses, together with governments and society as a whole, have an important role to play in defining how we, as a society, can make the most of the opportunities offered by digital technologies, minimizing the risks and ethical challenges. Ethics and compliance practitioners, in particular, have a wonderful opportunity to shape tomorrow's business approach to ensure that the ethical values that are often engrained in an organization's DNA will be enhanced and not compromised by the new challenges that technology is posing.

GUENDALINA DONDÉ

Guendalina is Head of Research at the Institute of Business Ethics. She advises organizations on how to make their ethics program, code of ethics and policies more effective and conducts benchmarking exercises on specific issues. Before joining the IBE, she collaborated with the inter-university center for business ethics and corporate social responsibility EconomEtica in developing the code of ethics for the Italian Association of Management Consultants and worked for CSR Europe, a European CSR Business Network based in Brussels. She holds a master's degree in Business Ethics and CSR from the University of Trento in Italy.

THE ETHICS OF ARTIFICIAL INTELLIGENCE

RAY EITEL-PORTER

What is ethical leadership? The concept will mean different things to different individuals, and it will vary according to context. Ethical leadership in the charity sector, for example, will involve different priorities and concerns to ethical leadership in the petrochemicals or retail sectors. However, there are commonalities.

One such commonality is apparent in the ethics of Artificial Intelligence (AI). It is a concept that all ethical leaders will need to understand and embrace in the years ahead. This is because AI deployments are accelerating: according to one estimate, the global market size for AI systems is expected to reach $733.7 billion by 2027.[30] Soon, AI will be used extensively by every organization and will therefore have a significant effect on society and individuals.

The impact of AI has the potential to be overwhelmingly positive. The technology has already been used in healthcare to identify new drugs, help select candidates for clinical trials and monitor patients, for example.[31] AI can also contribute positively to sustainability by, for example, helping the agriculture industry better monitor and manage environmental conditions and crop yields, while reducing the use of chemicals.[32] And there are countless other use cases across industries that promise to drive efficiency and help find insights to improve organizational decision-making.[33]

However, with the huge potential of AI also comes a responsibility to ensure the technology is used ethically.

SEVEN PRINCIPLES FOR THE ETHICAL USE OF AI IN BUSINESS

The ethical use of AI involves ensuring that seven principles are rigorously respected. These principles mitigate unintended negative consequences of AI on society and individuals and by extension, help protect the reputation of businesses using AI. The principles are as follows:

1. **Soundness.** AI model development should question not only "can we do this?" but also "*should* we do this?" There may be situations where the technology could enable potentially useful activities but an organization's ethical principles consider it to be inappropriate.

2. **Fairness.** Are there factors influencing AI outcomes that should not be? Is there an expectation of similar outcomes for different subgroups, and is this delivered? Have we eliminated all bias against minority groups? One of the arguments against the use of AI-based facial recognition software in the US, for example, is that such technology misidentifies people of color more often than white people.[34]

3. **Accountability.** What is the chain of command for dealing with potentially biased/erroneous outcomes? AI itself cannot be held accountable for its actions: for that, we need a human "owner."

4. **Transparency.** Do we understand how the model works? If not, how can we be sure it is behaving ethically? Many AI models are currently so-called "black boxes," although research is underway to develop greater transparency.

5. **Explainability.** Linked to transparency is the concept of

"explainability": can we explain, in nontechnical language, how an output was arrived at? Explainability is required to build public trust in AI and to meet regulatory requirements. Where explainability is lacking, the backlash can be pronounced, as Apple discovered with the seemingly biased loan decisions made against female applicants by the algorithm that supported Apple Card. The inability of customer service representatives to quickly explain how its algorithms came to its conclusions added to the discontent.[35]

6. **Privacy.** Are we using personal data in accordance with the permissions granted? Does the model ensure against inferences that breach privacy?

7. **Sustainability.** Cloud computing has made access to massive amounts of compute power both easy and relatively cheap, yet the environmental impact of running these servers is often overlooked. Data scientists should be trained to code as efficiently as possible and to consider the carbon footprint of running another large compute job to achieve what might just be a minimal improvement in accuracy.

These principles can help businesses harness the power of AI responsibly. But how does an ethical leader ensure their organization follows these principles? Here are some practical steps.[36]

1. Put in place AI principles, oversight and governance

The first step is to create a core ethical framework. Here, businesses can draw on generic frameworks for inspiration, such as The Alan Turing Institute's "Understanding Artificial Intelligence Ethics and Safety."[37] However, each ethical framework should be unique to each company as it will factor in its circumstances (industry, sector, market, etc.) and its brand proposition. For instance, an e-commerce brand differentiating through customer experience excellence should look to enshrine that priority in its principles, whereas an aviation company will put safety above all else.

The ethical framework, along with any strategies resulting from said framework, should be informed and supported by an AI ethics board. The board will combine AI, industry and ethical expertise for a comprehensive oversight function. The board should be viewed as a high-level source of advice and approval for both broad AI ethics strategies and specific use cases.

A final foundational step is to put in place a robust governance process to detail how decisions relating to AI ethics are arrived at and recorded across the enterprise. For businesses in highly regulated sectors such as pharma or finance, it makes sense to adapt existing governance systems and processes. Employees will be more likely to successfully use governance structures they already understand, and the approach avoids duplicating effort.

In the governance structure, it's important to track responsibility for the difficult trade-off decisions that come with AI implementations. For example, the more data that an insurance company can collect on an individual the more accurate their policies will be, but what level of intrusion on that individual's privacy is acceptable? Processes must be put in place to record who made such decisions, when and why. If the reasoning behind such decisions is later questioned by regulators, customers or other interested parties, a clearly documented explanation must be forthcoming.

2. Embed ethical AI through training and metrics

Leaders can set the ethical direction of AI in their company, but they must also ensure that principles and governance structures are understood and acted upon by all employees. This in turn requires a comprehensive training program tailored to seniority and job role.

The senior business leadership will require training on why responsible AI matters and the ways in which they can embody this message. Managers will need to be trained in more granular issues, such as how AI ethics impact projects, and what practical steps they need to take with regard to governance. Meanwhile, data scientists need a grounding in the specialist skills required to control fairness, bias and explainability in AI. It will also be critical to make sure the organization at large has an understanding of what AI is, why it matters and how to use it responsibly.

Alongside training, leaders should establish metrics so they can measure compliance with AI principles and the business benefit of these principles. The aim is to ensure that AI ethics is not forgotten about as employees go about their daily duties. Until such a time as AI ethics are hardwired into business practices, they must be kept under constant review, so long as the measurement does not unduly slow AI development or innovation.

3. Foster dissent and diversity

Another way in which leaders can help ensure the ethical use of AI is to enable any employee with concerns about an AI model to express these concerns freely. Dissent around AI should be welcomed as a way to "stress test" models from an ethical perspective.

Leaders should also build AI teams with an eye to diversity, as a diverse team with a broad range of perspectives will help mitigate against unconscious bias. This should be addressed as soon as possible: studies already suggest that because the AI profession is currently overwhelmingly white and male it is at risk of perpetuating historic biases.[38]

PROFESSIONALIZING AI: THREE RECOMMENDATIONS

To further ensure that AI is used ethically, business leaders should help drive the professionalization of data science within their organization, while also ensuring that responsibility for preventing unintended negative consequence from AI is borne by all employees equally.

Here are three recommendations to help leaders professionalize the field of AI within their organizations:[39]

1. Define accountability against job roles

Accountability needs to be built into every stage of the AI development lifecycle. That means precisely mapping the ethical responsibilities of each role, as well as ensuring that these responsibilities are complied with and enforced. For instance, the people building an AI model need to understand that part of their role is to ensure that training data is unbiased, and that the model's function does not break the company's ethical framework.

It is also important that each technical and business role linked to AI development is supported by clear pathways for escalating concerns around AI models should such concerns arise.

Finally, leaders should ensure there is a process in place to oversee each model in production to ensure it continues to behave as expected and that the use case context is still appropriate.

2. Ensure training remains relevant and democratize learning

As discussed above, it's essential that everyone in the organization is trained to an appropriate level in the ethics of AI use and model development as it pertains to their roles. This must include regular updates for the latest guidelines and regulations from government and industry bodies.

There's also a broader requirement to ensure that *all* employees understand AI technology and ethics at a base level. Leaders should be looking at how best to democratize data and AI literacy to prepare the workforce for this rapidly advancing technology. This work involves defining the minimum level of AI knowledge required from employees, regardless of their roles, and building a training program around that requirement.

3. Build AI standards with ethics in mind

Currently, there are no regulated professional standards or kite-marks for AI ethics. Consequently, leaders should encourage the creation of internal standards that are consistent with their core ethical principles. Such standards could include mandates around governance controls such as independent reviews and audit trails, for example. While these standards may be developed internally, it is important to ensure that any external partners in AI deployments also comply and that the standards are in force throughout the AI development process—including after the AI is operational. Here, the ethics board discussed above would prove useful, as it can help ensure policies remain relevant and can help resolve escalations. It is worth considering including an independent, outside voice to join the board to ensure controls are as robust as possible.

RESPONSIBLE LEADERSHIP IN AI

Much is demanded of today's business leaders and what it takes to succeed has changed significantly over the past few decades. Embracing data-driven decision-making and transforming an organization to leverage the power of data science can provide significant competitive advantage. It's little wonder that 93% of high-growth businesses are already investing in AI.[40]

But with the power of AI comes risk: the risk of unintended consequences. An ethical leader will ensure that their organization goes beyond the regulatory minimum requirement and takes the moral high ground by implementing governance, controls and training to minimize the risks of AI. Wherever AI is deployed, both business and technical colleagues must consider the principles of soundness, fairness, accountability, transparency, explainability, privacy and sustainability. Those that do will be able to reap the rewards of the technology with a clear conscience and help lead their industry towards widely adopted ethical principles.

RAY EITEL-PORTER

Ray is a Managing Director at Accenture and Global Lead for Responsible AI. He led the formation of the Accenture/Alan Turing Institute Strategic Partnership to create a channel for cutting-edge research in data science and AI into real-world applications and has 20+ years of experience in technology start-ups and corporate leadership positions. Ray is also an editorial board member of the academic journal AI and Ethics. He cares deeply about encouraging greater innovation with data and analytics in business, schools, and further education and has chaired the English government's Data Skills Taskforce since 2015 and worked with TeenTech to create the first National Data Science Prize for schools.

DON'T DESTROY SECURITY AND PRIVACY TO SAVE IT

JAYA BALOO

Likely you've seen in TV shows and movies a scene where police or intelligence agents are hot on the trail of a villain and are trying to get information, usually crucial to saving lives. But the information is "encrypted," putting the investigation and lives at risk. No problem, some stereotypical "hacker" character (in a hoodie) says, we've got a "backdoor" and can "break" the encryption. Voila, a few (unnaturally fast) keystrokes later they have the information they need, they catch the villain, save lives, happy ending, and story over.

But we know life isn't like TV shows or movies. "Backdoors" like that don't exist in encryption today.

And while an element like that might make for a good story, the reality is that if it were true, we would all be living in a much less, and not more, safe world.

In the United States, there's an absurd saying: "Sometimes to save a village you have to burn it." The saying supposedly comes from the Vietnam War and points out the absurdity of using a noble end to justify horrific means to that end when those horrific means destroy the very intended noble end itself.

We're looking at this same absurd situation when it comes to encryption. People with noble ends, stopping crime, terrorism, child pornography and trafficking, are proposing means to those ends, weakening encryption with backdoors, that would in fact destroy the very end goal of security and privacy for everyone.

The situation is made even more complicated when we look at the very likely coming impact on current cryptography from quantum computing. That is looming as a force of its own that threatens past, current and potentially future encryption and by extension security and privacy for everyone.

This creates a real-world ethical challenge for us in cybersecurity. How do we protect people's security and privacy while also trying to solve the valid problems of stopping crime, terrorism, child pornography and trafficking while also being mindful of the threats posed by the coming sea change quantum computing will likely bring?

Ethics is never easy: it's a discipline that requires grappling with hard questions and this is no exception. Part of the process of ethical grappling is understanding the full scale of the problem stated and that's what I'm going to do in this essay, as well as highlight possible solutions that I feel best balance the best (or least bad) answers to these problems.

I believe these issues can be addressed in a balanced way. But like all good solutions, it requires several nuanced elements to come together. We should not weaken encryption—now or in the future. We should continue to work with legitimate agents that need legitimate access to information that may be encrypted to find effective, targeted ways to get that information without weakening encryption for everyone.

And by continuing to support the strongest encryption possible, we can mitigate the risks that all encrypted information, past present and future, face from quantum computing.

WHY WEAKENING ENCRYPTION IS ACTUALLY INEFFECTIVE AND DANGEROUS

We are today witnessing a revival of the "Crypto Wars" of the 1990s/2000s.

As a refresher, in that era, governments like the United States treated encryption products like munitions with strict export controls around them. For example, you could use 128-bit encryption on your Windows NT 4.0 webserver in the United States, but if you wanted to stand up that same server in France, you'd have to use the weaker 40-bit encryption version. At the same time, law enforcement agencies pushed hard for a special backdoor for encryption that (in theory) only they could use. This all culminated in the failed "Clipper Chip" initiative.

Those Crypto Wars ended with the Clipper Chip dying and export controls being lifted. In the years since, we've seen global adoption of strong encryption in conjunction with the exponential growth of life on the Internet. Arguably, the stellar growth we've seen in the past 15 years or so is a positive result of how the Crypto Wars of that era played out.

Today, however, the basic ideas behind the Crypto Wars are back on the table. After a series of high-profile events where law enforcement claimed that strong encryption was impeding their work, we saw law enforcement and governments once again calling for backdoors in encryption, ostensibly only for their use. The most notable example of this is in the wake of the San Bernardino attack of 2015 where law enforcement encountered problems accessing encrypted data on the attacker's iPhone and said that this is where a backdoor would be critical for them to have.

The arguments for backdoors being made today mirror those from the Crypto Wars. The objections to those arguments remain fundamentally the same. Implanting backdoors or weakening encryption in any way jeopardizes security, privacy and data integrity for everyone at all times.

Benjamin Franklin famously said in Poor Richard's Almanack in 1735: Three may keep a secret so long as two are dead. That saying holds true with encryption. The idea that special backdoor decryption keys will always, ever only be used by trusted entities presumes perfect technical implementation and flawless process execution—neither of which are realistic. Aside from the risks of loss or misuse of the legitimate keys by legitimate entities, the reality is that the chances that any built-in backdoor will be independently discoverable by other untrusted entities are very high.

Put simply, building any kind of backdoor into encryption means it's already broken on day one. It's only a question of when, not if, untrusted entities learn that it's broken and how to exploit that for their own gain. And once encryption is broken, it's broken for good. We've seen this already with encryption schemes that have had to be retired because they were broken due to computational weakness. For example, the 40-bit encryption you had to use in the 1990s outside of the United States isn't used today because it's essentially useless.

Often discussions around the benefit to law enforcement for backdoors for encryption rely on the analogy of a wiretap on a physical telephone line. Wiretapping with a court order is a legal activity with a long-accepted history. However, this analogy is specious and inaccurate when we talk about encryption backdoors. Wiretapping is a practice that legally breaks the confidentiality of specific individuals at a specific time by targeting the relevant endpoints: it doesn't disrupt the confidentiality and integrity of all calls of everyone using the phone system at all times—which is precisely what encryption backdoors do.

It's also worth continuing the wiretapping analogy in a different direction to show that there are viable alternatives more in line with traditional wiretapping methodologies. Law enforcement and intelligence agencies have a number of alternative tools at their disposal that can gather information that is encrypted in transit without relying on backdoors and is targeted to specific individuals the way wiretaps are. With appropriate warrants, these agencies can target individuals' computers and devices in a way that accesses data that has been encrypted in transit in an unencrypted form on the device. There are also ways to break encryption on specific devices without breaking encryption for everyone at all times.

Also, there is a practical point around effectiveness. If a specific encryption algorithm is known to be backdoored, the very people that this backdoor is meant to target will simply use other, non-backdoored encryption for their purposes.

All of this is to say that while there are reasonable arguments of the ends that advocates of backdoors want to achieve, the means to those ends are actually ineffectual and dangerous putting everyone's security and privacy at risk in a fruitless quest to try and understandably and legitimately target a small, admittedly dangerous subset of people.

HOW QUANTUM COMPUTING WILL CHALLENGE CURRENT (AND PAST) ENCRYPTION

We are in the middle of a developing revolution in computing that could be bigger than the computing revolution itself and possibly as big as the industrial revolution: quantum computing.

While we're not there yet, even some of the most conservative forecasters estimate we're only ten years away from quantum computing being a major disruptive force. And when we look at quantum computing, one of the major ways that it will be highly disruptive is what it will mean for past, present and future encryption.

To understand the impact, it helps to cite an example from television. In the HBO Series Silicon Valley, the main characters realize that they've created an artificial intelligence (AI) that is on the verge of being so powerful that it will be able to break all known encryption, easily, in a matter of days. They recognize that this literally puts the entire Internet at immediate risk because there will be no way for there to be secure payments, secure communications, basically there will be no security or privacy. I won't spoil the story and tell you how that ends, but the important thing to understand is that with quantum computing we really are facing that scenario in real life and facing it in just a few years.

Fortunately, there is work being done in encryption by both physicists and cryptographers on two separate solution tracks that can potentially meet this challenge. But there's a question of whether it's coming fast enough to prevent this kind of apocalyptic reckoning. A key point in the work of both these groups is that we need to be strengthening current encryption today as much as possible as soon as possible to mitigate the potential negative future impact of quantum computing on encryption.

However, we don't have encryption in place today that we can confidently say will withstand the power of quantum computing. And we've already seen what happens when encryption algorithms that were once thought to be "secure" are broken by increased computing power.

The Data Encryption Standard (DES) was a 56-bit encryption algorithm that was developed in the 1970s. In 1999, nearly 30 years after it was developed, a DES key was broken by distributed.net[41] and the Electronic Frontier Foundation[42] in 22 hours and 15 minutes, effectively killing DES. It's worth noting DES was 16 bits stronger than what people were limited to for export during the Crypto Wars, meaning that encryption was even weaker.

After DES was broken, people who built and used server

software, browsers, websites, and mobile devices all had to go through a protracted painful process of changing encryption algorithms to ensure they were all using more secure encryption. It was a process that took years. And any resting data that was encrypted using DEC that is still accessible is now functionally not encrypted. Like the Silicon Valley episode alluded to, information encrypted with DES effectively became plaintext overnight.

As quantum computers come into their own in the coming years, this is what we have to look forward to as more encryption algorithms that once took the lifetime of computing power to break are cracked in hours or even seconds.

HOW MOVES TO WEAKEN ENCRYPTION AND QUANTUM COMPUTING COLLIDE

We stand at a point in time right now where people are lobbying to weaken encryption with backdoors while at the same time we can see a near future where existing encryption algorithms without backdoors are likely to fall to the power of quantum computing.

These two trends run the risk of colliding and making the current situation around encryption and by extension, security and privacy for everyone worse. And they portend to make the future even worse.

Current encryption is facing a clear and present danger already from quantum computing. Moves to weaken existing encryption with backdoors will only make the risks we're facing significantly worse. When something is already weak in the face of a coming onslaught, further weakening it, no matter how good the ends are, is the wrong and dangerous thing to do.

Further weakening existing encryption with backdoors will only hasten and make more likely the cryptographic apocalypse that Silicon Valley fictionally outlined and we've seen hints of in the demise of past encryption algorithms.

Our focus around encryption now should be on strengthening, not weakening encryption to better prepare for the impact of quantum computing.

And as I've outlined, the approach of introducing backdoors into encryption is understandable but misguided: it sacrifices security and privacy for everyone in a quest to understandably target a small but dangerous subset of individuals.

CONCLUSION

So what should we do to address these two colliding streams today?

We should be doing all we can to strengthen encryption to mitigate the likely impact of quantum computing. As I said, there are promising trends in this space and they should be pursued with all due speed.

We should recognize the valid ends those arguing to weaken encryption with backdoors have but stand firm in saying that's the wrong, and dangerous direction. We can work to find other means to those same ends, ones that protect security and privacy for everyone while giving governments and other legitimate entities the tools they need to meet those ends in an appropriately limited and targeted fashion—just like with traditional wiretaps.

It's not a simple answer: it's a nuanced answer. But that gets to the heart of ethical conundrums: there's almost never a simple answer, nor should there be.

These issues reflect the fundamental tension between individual freedom, security and privacy and the collective need for safety and security. Those two are almost always in tension but it's a healthy tension that reflects some of the best and most important characteristics of our open and free society. We want to preserve freedom, security and privacy. And we don't want to destroy those very things in our efforts to preserve them.

JAYA BALOO

Jaya is Chief Information Security Officer at Avast and has previously worked as CISO at KPN, the largest telecommunications carrier in the Netherlands, Practice Lead Lawful Interception at Verizon, and Technical Security Specialist at France Telecom. She has been named the top 100 CISOs globally and ranks among the top 100 security influencers worldwide. Also, Jaya was selected as one of the fifty most inspiring women in the Netherlands by Inspiring Fifty. She sits on the advisory boards of the Netherland's National Cyber Security Centre, PQCrypto, and Flagship Strategic. She serves on the audit committee of TIIN capital, a cybersecurity fund, and is also a member of the IT Committee of Sociale Verzekeringsbank. She is currently a member of EU Quantum and formerly of the EU High-Level Steering Committee for the FET Quantum Flagship.

SEEKING WISDOM IN BUSINESS

ARASH AAZAMI

"We have come this far because we are the smartest creatures that have ever lived, but to continue we require more than intelligence. We require wisdom."

With these words David Attenborough concludes his latest documentary "A Life on Our Planet."

THE UNSUSTAINABILITY OF BUSINESS AS USUAL

In 2009 I was leading a subsidiary of a large energy company in the Netherlands. It operated a pretty conventional business model, buying electricity and gas in bulk, and adding a margin before selling it to individual customers. This company, like many energy companies, wanted to play their role in the energy transition, and dedicated a part of its resources to be "green," advising customers to use less electricity for example. But something did not feel right. How can a company want their customers to use less energy if their business model is based upon the volume that they sell? Because like every other energy company at that time, the more energy they sold, the more they earned. The bottom line of this business model: we could only be incentivized to sell as much as we could.

We were, like almost every company, in the business of being intelligent. We bought products, did something smart to them and added a margin to them, and then we would sell them to the customer. In most cases this is not a problem. Practically every business in the world works like this. But still it didn't feel "right." What if your product—energy from predominantly fossil resources—harms the environment? What if the nature of our product and the system we were playing in were designed to keep the customer locked in, dependent, and paying whatever we would ask them to pay? We were, after all, providers of a basic need.

Everybody needs energy every day, regardless of cost and availability. Nobody and no business will ever function without energy. The business of energy, as long as it is based upon scarce resources owned by a few and needed by many, products that harm the environment in irreversible ways when we burn them, is fundamentally unfair. But because it is a basic need, and we have only just begun to shift towards renewable resources that can be harvested by everyone, people will still buy large quantities of fossil fuel, and energy companies possess an unbelievable amount of power. This power requires something beyond intelligence: wisdom.

I learned that practically every business decision we make is not based upon wisdom, but intelligence. Wisdom has yet to find a place in the workspace.

THERE IS NO PLACE FOR WISDOM... YET

And that is when I realized we needed an entirely different type of energy company, all the way to the fundamentals of our business model.

Instead of "sell more to earn more" I wanted a company that would earn more as it sold less energy.

This is how customers could get actual help decreasing their energy footprints, reducing their environmental impact, whilst benefiting the company that fulfils their need. But how would that ever work?

How can you design an inverted business model?

In a world where we define practically every success by "more," I was faced with the challenge to find a way to define success by a decrease. How would a customer pay for something they did not get? How would our solution ever be valued by our customers, and by investors?

Oftentime wisdom even seems to be in the way of success. I assume that many of you have experienced more than once that when you question the framework upon which your business is built—its ethics, fundamental strategies, its "why"—you get either rolling eyes or a reply sounding like "We have discussed this topic already and it is not something we can change today, so let's just go ahead and not lose more time."

But if intelligence so clearly prevails over wisdom in our business rationale, what does this say about our organizations, our economy and society? Is it enough when we base ethical decisions upon our intelligence? Or does ethical business require something else, something deeper, less individually oriented? I believe that in order to conduct business in an ethical way, we need to incorporate, embed and nourish wisdom within our organizations. Even when this wisdom would make us ask the big questions: "Is our organization doing the right thing?" "Should we keep making money the way we used to?" "Would it be wise to change the business fundamentally, or maybe even choose to cease to exist?"

I believe that deep within we all want to be well-doers. We all believe in something. We all want to contribute to a better world. We all have a heart, desiring for the happiness of others and ourselves. Every individual has a purpose to fulfil.

But often it seems like there is something in between our purpose and ourselves minding our daily business: our intelligence. Most of the time when we are about to decide to take a leap into our purpose-driven lives our head takes over. The heart wants it, but the mind speaks louder. "Now is not the perfect time," "Who am I to change the way things are?" "What if I am wrong?" "What will my parents, friends or colleagues think?" We usually end up telling ourselves that this is not the right moment, not the right environment, or maybe even not our purpose, and spend our lives "doing this one thing that I do not fully support to create space to do the things that I really believe in." We seem to live in constant cognitive dissonance from our intuition. However much we want to be well-doers with lasting positive impacts on our environment and society, we still let smart prevail over wise for our own benefit. Every day.

FIND INSPIRATION IN ENTIRELY DIFFERENT FIELDS

With me this is no different. I wish to really contribute to the betterment of the world and society, but fail miserably most of the times, trying to survive and reaping this world's benefits at the same time. But I also got lucky. Years ago, I became a member of an international forum on the subject of ethics in the workplace: EBBF—Ethical Business Building the Future. Their members span all continents, and practically every line of business, NGO and governmental organizations. Since 30 years EBBF members from an enormous variety of backgrounds and professions gather once or twice every year to explore the subject, share ideas and experiences, and contribute to common knowledge and understanding of the subject of ethics. This community helped me to not feel alone in my desire to incorporate ethics in my daily business activities, and more than once provided breakthroughs in my thinking.

It was at an EBBF conference that I met Graham. At that time a director for Procter & Gamble in China. I told him about my dilemma: "how can I build a sustainable, lasting and profitable energy company that earns more when it sells less?" He looked at me and replied, "Ah, you are looking for Chinese medicine!"

He explained to me that we are used to pay the doctor when we are sick. But this incentivizes the doctor to make sure we are always a little bit unhealthy. If we would be completely healthy the doctor would not earn any money. He then explained to me that in China the doctor gets paid as long as the patient is healthy. That way the doctor is always incentivized to keep their patients as healthy as possible.

This example inspired me so much that I set my heart to design a similar model for energy companies. Why do customers not pay us for the energy that we save, and not for the energy that we deliver to them? I designed a business model where energy was delivered at zero margin. The customer would pay us exactly the price we paid to the producer or wholesaler. Of course, in itself this is a horrible business model, but it incentivized us to sell our customers as little energy as possible, and it lowered the customers' energy bill. Now what if that little money our customer saved this way were invested into something else? Into reducing the energy need of our customers, in the form of energy savings solutions and renewable energy production for and by our customers? I found out that these solutions often allowed for far better sales margins than energy as a trade commodity, bought and sold in bulk. So, what if we could invoice our customer a fixed amount of money every month, and gradually turn that into their own energy transition fund? At first—although our cash flow is stable—the amounts of money we would make are very small, but when invested properly their impact is high. We went on and designed an algorithm that calculates the best energy savings investment opportunity for every customer, using their building data, energy consumption data and a wide array of possible partial energy savings and renewable energy generation solutions.

BUILD A NEW MODEL THAT MAKES THE OLD OBSOLETE

From here onward it was simple: put all these small energy investments in order of return. The best performing solution, costing the least amount of money had to come first. For example, this would be adjusting the client's thermostat, or refitting energy saving light bulbs. Then the second-best solution would follow, then the third best, and so on. The money saved from implementing the first solution would finance the second. The money saved from implementing the first and the second together would then finance the third solution. And so, we created an "energy transition machine" that would help our customer through every step to get to energy independence, carbon neutrality and seriously lower energy cost. And so on. Soon the amount we could invest into their energy independence increased to very serious levels, allowing for more and more costly, but important investments like solar panels, insulation and shares in neighboring wind farms, whilst never requiring a higher energy bill for our customer. This was a Chinese medicine approach to energy. I named the business model the "Path to Zero."

With this business model, I founded the world's first "energy independence company" in 2010, and although it required quite some explanation to our prospective customers, "this is too good to be true, how can you make money when you sell less?" we grew exponentially during the following years. On average our customers paid the exact same amount as they were used to paying their previous energy supplier, but through our Path to Zero business model their energy use and dependencies were reduced by 30%

during the first three years, only to increase in the years to follow.

Every customer had a dashboard where they could monitor when they would reach 100% energy independence if they would follow the steps on their Path to Zero. Many customers even increased their monthly payments because they wanted to reach zero earlier.

YOUR OWN CHANGE DOES NOT MEAN THE WORLD HAS CHANGED

This all sounds like a success story, and for a few years it was indeed. But even so the company does no longer exist. The business model was and is sound, but the company itself was not, and neither was the energy sector of which it was part. Where did it go wrong? Well, for one, although putting no margins on supplied energy, the company relied upon buying energy from companies who demanded margins, often also supplying customers of their own. This created a split incentive where our suppliers would not want to see us supplying energy at a price lower than what they billed their own customers. We would have needed to be completely vertically integrated, becoming the owner of energy production facilities and independent of our suppliers, to overcome this. Also, the market for energy supply is heavily regulated, unlike the market for energy savings or renewable small-scale energy generation. At one point the Dutch authorities to which we reported at that time compared our energy prices to other suppliers and decided we were too cheap and disturbing the competitive field within which we operated—not taking into consideration that we actually sold energy as a full-service package, including energy savings and renewables generation solutions. This meant we had to increase our prices and make some profit on energy supply if we were to continue, even though we did not want this.

Meanwhile, the Path to Zero began to yield serious amounts of money. As customers would start to spend less and less of their monthly payments for energy supply and save up more and more for their next step on the Path to Zero, our operations started to look like those of a bank. We managed money on behalf of our customers and invested that into energy solutions. But we were far too small to operate as a licensed bank and fulfil all our duties according to the laws for financial institutions. Another dilemma arose: should we grow into a bank at enormous cost or ask a regular bank to do all this for us at equally enormous cost?

So, both the market and the authorities could appreciate us, believe that our model was good and in service of the needs of our customers, and a catalyzing force for the energy transition, but could not provide us with an environment within which we could thrive on the long term. This meant we had to change the entire energy sector, change the law under which we operated, or change our business into a conventional "old fashioned" energy company.

I personally was adamant upon continuing with developing the Path to Zero as it was intended to. "If this requires me to change both the sector and the law, I guess I will have to do that too then" was my initial thought. I was ready to take up this challenge but knew that would put the company's future at risk too.

However, I was not the sole proprietor of the company's shares and voting rights. The Path to Zero had become the intellectual property of a mid-sized company with a good number of co-workers, fellow shareholders and some co-founders, not to mention suppliers, licenses to operate on national markets, and thousands of clients.

Meanwhile our main supplier of energy went bankrupt themselves, and that put our entire operation at risk. We lost a huge amount of money, stress levels within our organization rose to extremes, and we very quickly had to give up half of our business to a conventional supplier in order to be able to survive and serve the other half with our Path to Zero model. I personally was ready to give up the energy supply side completely and leave that to more conventional players on the market, as long as we could keep offering our Path to Zero plan for our customers. Other shareholders—understandably—argued that we could still earn a lot of money by becoming a more conventional energy supplier.

We did not find a way to bring our visions together. And in the end the company itself was not doing well anymore. Externally it looked like it was doing okay, but internally it was severely held back by conflict and lack of aligned visions of the people supposed to lead it. We were dwindling.

DESIGN, DESIGN, DESIGN

This showed one big design flaw: I architected a business model that was intended to be good for all, but let only a few people, including myself, be the owner of it and amass the wealth it would generate. In retrospect I would have put the Path to Zero into a foundation or open-source structure and built the company around the operationalization of this intellectual property. Making a profit because we would make an impact, rather than making a profit because we own something that the rest of the world doesn't.

Around that time, I visited the country where I grew up, Niger, for the first time since I had left 26 years earlier. When I was there, I saw how something I took for granted made a huge impact on the lives of people. Niger is one of the most challenged countries in the world in terms of access to modern forms of energy. 84% of its people live in energy poverty, meaning that they rely upon collecting biomass so that they can cook, and regard electricity as a form of energy that is out of their reach. The impacts of energy poverty are tremendous: up to half of people's waking hours are spent on fulfilling their very basic energy needs. With so much time lost this makes it practically impossible for many Nigerians to develop themselves out of poverty. I realized this was what I wanted to contribute to all along. This was my big "why."

Whatever company or organization I would serve had to contribute to the simple but enormous goal of universal access to abundant renewable energy. If my current company could no longer serve that goal because it became more conventional, I had to leave and start something new.

It was time to make a very difficult decision. Take up the fight and take over control of the company again, at the expense of my fellow shareholders and a part of the company or leave. I left. I found this an utterly difficult decision to make, and I put my own career and future at risk by doing so, but this was the only way left to give the company a chance to thrive, albeit not providing the services and products that I had envisioned. I thought to myself that it would be easier to build another company based upon the same principles later on, than to try and redirect this company from where it was at that point. A flawed product or service can always be repaired, but a flawed company design is almost impossible to mend.

LET GO OF WHAT YOU CANNOT CHANGE, AND CHERISH WHAT YOU CAN

If I could have sold my shares at that point I would have, but no one wanted to buy them from me. I was too much "the face of the company" and leaving would imply a perceived devaluation of the share price.

This revealed another flaw that I made: the company was perceived to be "mine," instead of "the community's." It relied too much upon me, and that made it impossible to grow beyond my own limitations as an entrepreneur and leader.

I decided to still take distance from my shares and put them in control of a middleman, a lawyer whom I had worked with for years and trusted. I said goodbye to my colleagues, my voting rights and my control over the company, and spent a year thinking about what I could best do to serve the grand goal of universal access to renewable energy.

A year and a half later, this once very promising scale-up lost its fight for survival in the fiercely competitive market for conventional energy trade. It went bust. My share value was reduced to zero, but that was a risk I knew I took and could do nothing about when I decided to leave the company. I was sad for the team that worked so hard to build this up, but realized we had a lot to celebrate also. For one we showed that it was possible to build up a disruptive energy company out of nothing. We proved that we could systematically reduce energy footprints and dependencies for thousands of users. And we were able to set a precedent upon which the laws governing the energy sector could eventually change.

We did many smart things that yielded results, not for us, but perhaps for the world, one day. We at least tried. Intending to build an ethical business—not making profit on energy sales but on increasing energy independence—even where it seemed to make more sense both commercially and legally to follow the conventional, and perhaps unethical path. And although the design of the company was flawed and the entire business was lost in the end we learned immensely valuable lessons to guide us through our next steps.

ABC: ALWAYS BE CHANGERS

After six years of traveling the world, working with experts, governments, entrepreneurs, scientists, and a vast scale of people putting ethics on the forefront of the decisions they make in their work and life, a next initiative is under preparation. We want to make energy from abundant renewable resources peer-to-peer. We develop intellectual property but will not be the owner of it. We will not even be the owners of shares in the company, but the stewards of these shares that will be held by a foundation. We never intend to sell the company, because it is not ours. We work together with lawmakers, producers, distributors, tech companies and many others. Our aim is not about individual success, but about the well-being of the entire collective. We intend to bring abundant renewable energy to the commons. And we have our hearts set to further contribute to our goal: universal access and participation to a globally unifying energy system.

I realize that a company is a tool. It is not a goal in itself. I regard a business entity as a vessel to help make one's dream come true. A company is always an experiment. If it works it deserves to be nurtured, celebrated and thanked. If it happens to not work, and maybe even be in the way of realizing the dream that got you going, then do not be afraid to let go of it. Make space for a new vessel, improved and enriched with your experience and increased knowledge and network.

For me the litmus test is simple and two-fold: does it bring a smile upon the face of your stakeholders? Think of yourself as a shareholder, your clients, your suppliers, your co-workers and their families, and then think of the effect of your business on society, and on the environment. Is there a reason to smile for all of them? Then they will want you to succeed, and an entire ecosystem is bringing its forces together to make that dream come true.

David Attenborough was right, we have come this far thanks to our individual intelligence, but for our further progress as a species now is the time to nourish our collective conscience, firmly rooted in ethics, and aspire to wisdom in our decision making.

ARASH AAZAMI

Arash is a purpose-driven entrepreneur and innovator, half Persian, half Dutch, and raised in Niger, West Africa. His initiatives merge energy, digital tech, and finance. In 2010 he founded the world's first energy company that earns more as it sells less energy. Arash recently launched Unify.energy, building self-balancing 100% renewables-based peer-to-peer energy networks. His vision leads to an "Internet of Energy," enabling users worldwide to exchange energy from abundant renewable resources. He is also a faculty member at Singularity University and develops strategies for governments on optimizing social, economic and institutional impacts of the energy transition.

ETHICAL DESIGN: THE COMPETITIVE EDGE OF THE 21ST CENTURY?

CHRISTIAN VILLUM AND CHRISTIAN BASON

Living in today's technology-driven world, we are all subject to the consequences of design decisions in our everyday lives. Choices that affect not only the shape and function of digital technologies, but their ethics and thus the lives and welfare of consumers. The consequences of design choices and our ethics—that is, the concepts and principles that guide us in determining whether our actions ultimately help or harm society—sit in the very fabric of the products and services that we make, for better and for worse. But with the rapid scaling of digital technology, these consequences are propelled to unprecedented heights.

Companies' ability to design ethically is proving more important than ever.

To illustrate this point, let's consider a flashy new credit card that captured headlines around the world. Developed in partnership between Apple, a technology firm, and Goldman Sachs, a bank, the card promised customers a range of cutting-edge features. According to the marketing pitch, this included no fees, daily cash back and seamless integration into Apple's mobile devices, as well as a "new level" of privacy, security and transparency. Finally, the card allowed consumers to analyze their spending patterns and calculate how much they could save in interest charges by paying off different portions of their balances. All of this is powered by some rather savvy artificial intelligence algorithms.

Now let's meet three people who all played different roles vis-à-vis the Apple Card.

First, meet Steve. Steve is a customer who was excited by all its smart features and thus signed himself up for it.

Second, meet Tim. He's the CEO of Apple. Tim has a lot of employees; let's pick one of them—we'll call her Lucy. She is one of the programmers who took part in crafting the Apple Card algorithm.

Steve, being really happy with his card at first, convinced his wife to get one, too. But soon he made a startling discovery: despite the couple having a shared economy, Steve's credit limit on this card was ten times higher than his spouse's. No one could explain why: the Apple Card's algorithm simply made this highly sexist assessment. Dozens of other customers stepped forward and soon social media overflowed with scathing critique of the new product.

Tim naturally didn't decide for his new prestige product to be misogynist. But he faced massive pushback from this story, as did his company and its banking partner. We can imagine him being even more frustrated by this incident than Steve.

Lastly, our imaginary Lucy (the only made-up character of the three in this true story) surely didn't put that specific gender bias attribute into the software code either. In fact, we could imagine she was ashamed of having helped put it into the world and probably considered changing her job as a way to make amends.

NAVIGATING UNETHICAL DESIGN

All three people in the Apple Card story felt the undesirable consequences of unethical design, regardless of where they were placed in the value chain.

Before we move on, let's up the ante a bit: what's Steve's last name? Wozniak. Legendary computer scientist and former co-founder of Apple alongside Steve Jobs. Wozniak left Apple many years ago, but you would imagine that a guy of his position would somehow fly above algorithmic discrimination. But no. No one is above that. And here is the real stinger: This is not just any algorithm cooked up by two guys in a basement for quick cash. This is the best artificial intelligence that the world's leading technology provider, in partnership with the world's most profitable bank, could build. It sets the highest possible bar for the future we're heading towards. And still it fails to tackle the ethical dilemma on which it stands: How to give people credit in a fair, balanced and transparent way.

The Apple Card debacle is emblematic of one of the big ethical challenges of the 21st century: technological solutionism. This balances extreme digital convenience against minimizing complex systemic challenges to a mathematical normative logic. This logic goes as follows: technology has an answer (actually, an app) for all our problems. In fact, solving Apple Card's problem with misogyny is seemingly manageable: plenty of solutions can address algorithmic bias like the one Apple Card is having by using well-known complex statistical methods to correct it, but that only fixes the symptoms of the problem and doesn't address the root cause. Our society is still defined by biases that are largely invisible at face value, but all too present in the data that it generates. Including the very data that was used to train the Apple Card algorithm. Our current solutions don't fix the problem. They just gloss it over.

The wider point is that algorithms, by definition, are biased to some degree since they weigh certain parameters more than others. The challenge is to choose which biases we can live with.

Since biases of the past may not be the biases we want in the future, the algorithms that control people's lives are inherently political: They are always up for negotiation.

OPPOSING THE TREND

Unsurprisingly, the opposition towards unethical black box artificial intelligence algorithms is growing. With global currents such as the Silicon Valley "tech-lash," we have seen Google employees doing walkouts to protest their AI development work being used for military purposes. We also see a growing Chinese state surveillance overreach which has reached a disturbing pinnacle by introducing a social credit score system to limit social services, access to train tickets and flights to misbehaving citizens. It is becoming ever clearer to citizens (and CEOs, programmers, etc.) around the world that ethics are not automatically baked into the digital products and services they either make or use on a daily basis.

This begs the question: will a more ethical approach among companies to shape our digital future be not only a utopian fantasy, but an actual demand from an increasing part of the global population in general, and global workforce in particular? Could it be that Steve, Tim and Lucy—or at least Steve and Lucy—want a different digital future? Or, more accurately, could it be that they demand a different digital future?

If so, it appears that finding a way to systematically act ethically is any company's best bet of remaining relevant in the future we are heading towards. Perhaps not only to stay relevant, but to stay competitive. Is ethical design the key competitive edge in the 21st century?

DESIGNING FOR ETHICS

Within industrial design, a rule of thumb says that 85 percent of a new product's environmental impact is defined in the design phase. This means that if firms wish to reduce their products' footprint when it comes to sustainability, they must carefully consider how they approach the earliest phases of product development. A similar point can arguably be made when it comes to the design of digital products and services, including artificial intelligence algorithms. It is the early, front-end considerations concerning the ethical properties of a product or service that often times define how it ultimately will perform.

However, while much is still to be learned in firms and among designers about products with low, zero or even positive environmental impact, the field of "ethical design" in the digital space is even less mature. The example we opened this chapter with is a case in point: if some of the most powerful and smart firms in the world can make such grave mistakes when it comes to ethics in their consumer-facing products, what hope is there that more down-to-earth organizations can fare better?

There is a pressing need to see ethics as a design challenge, and to start working in more reflected, nuanced ways to ensure ethical design becomes part of corporate and organizational practice.

In addition, just like companies are now realizing there can be a competitive advantage in sustainability, there may well also be one when it comes to ethics.

As famed designer Charles Eames once suggested, design is the process of arranging elements in a way so as to achieve a particular purpose. As a systematic, creative process for innovating in a human-centered way, design embodies a range of working practices that provide opportunities for making more ethical, responsible products and services.

Today, questions of ethics are not necessarily—perhaps even rarely—embedded into digital design work. However as the pace of technological development increases and more and more "intelligence" becomes available to engineers, coders and developers as well as leaders and CEOs as they build future products, we need to find ways to bring ethics and design much closer together.

The question then becomes: how might one embed ethical practices into the way in which products and services are designed? And might we start with one country—Denmark—to find out what the answer might look like?

TOWARDS DANISH ETHICAL DESIGN?

Danish design has always been rooted in a strong societal awareness. During the formative years, starting in the 1930s, the highly functional, clean, well-crafted and unadorned aesthetic became characteristic of "scandi" coolness. At the same time, another aspect of Danish design emerged from the so-called cultural radical movement: the idea that design should make life better for all.

Back then, it was mostly a question of uncluttering the home with simple, affordable yet modern furniture. This was achieved in part by using new technology in treating and shaping wood, in part through designing for industrial mass production. Later, during the rapid economic growth throughout the 1960s, 70s and 80s it led to progressive design for such areas as play (think LEGO), air quality in homes (think VELUX) and water quality (think Grundfos). Today, the ambition of making life better through design is as strong as ever; it is still inherent to the Danish design DNA. Characteristics of this DNA include a human-centered approach, a holistic view of product environmental impact, and an ambition to create truly transformative products and services.

In this age of accelerating technological change, this means that design originating in Denmark should also consider the hidden, but potentially life-changing (or threatening) functions of technology in a deeply ethical way. We imagine that Danish designers (as well as CEOs, coders, etc.) could be among the first to embrace industry-wide codes of conduct or guidelines as they endeavor to shape the products that will shape our future.

Indeed, we (Danish Design Center) are currently working with a number of experts, design agencies, the Industry Foundation, and the Confederation of Danish Industry to create an "ethical compass" tool for designers engaging with clients that wish to leverage the power of artificial intelligence, data and data ethics, and behavioral design in new product offerings. The vision is to turn ethical design into a competitive parameter for Danish companies by making ethics an integrated design material in the development of new digital products, services and business models.

The compass will be co-designed together with larger corporations that are already in the process of applying ethical thinking to their digitalization strategies. Subsequently, the compass and associated tools will be tested with a range of small and medium-sized enterprises within fintech, healthtech and mobilitytech.

The tools will be made available as open source, and thus free for all to use, and at the same time they will be part of an educational offering targeted at designers and design agencies who wish to make ethics part of their offerings, and to SMEs who see the opportunity to strengthen their global competitiveness by building and selling ethical products.

This is one bet on finding a way to integrate ethics in design decisions at the earliest stages of the innovation process. Just as Danish design paved the way for what became the welfare state, and one of the world's wealthiest societies, it must now pave the way for a more ethical society well into the 21st century.

CHRISTIAN BASON

Christian holds a Ph.D. and is CEO of the Danish Design Centre, Denmark's lab for sustainable growth by design. Before that, he was Director of MindLab, the Danish government's innovation team. He has authored seven books, most recently *Leading Public Design*; his writing has appeared in, amongst others, Harvard Business Review and Stanford Social Innovation Review; he is a lecturer at Oxford Saïd Business School, the European School of Administration, the Henley MBA, and Copenhagen Business School; and he is a member of the board for the Royal Academy of Architecture, Design and Conservation, The Rockwool Foundation's Intervention Committee, the Centre for Leadership, and a member of the World Economic Forum's Global Future Council on Agile Governance.

Photo Credit: Agnethe Schlichtkrull

CHRISTIAN VILLUM

Christian is Director of Digital & Future Thinking at the Danish Design Centre where he examines new ideas in the span between technology and design thinking. He has a background in maker technology, new business models, sharing cultures, open data, and open design, internet culture, and hacktivism. His previous work includes cofounding and heading the experimental Platform 4 Art & Technology hub, being a frontrunner in the use of Creative Commons content licenses and building global communities for the UK-based non-profit Open Knowledge Foundation. He is also editor and co-writer of the book *Open Source City.*

Photo Credit: Agnethe Schlichtkrull

THE EXPONENTIAL PROFESSIONAL - ETHICS IN AN AGE OF HUMAN-MACHINE CONVERGENCE

MIC MANN

The origins of the word "professional" have their roots in Middle English between the 11th and 15th centuries, as an individual "professed" their duty to the church when they were ordained as a member of the clergy.

By the end of the Medieval era, the word gained secular meaning and was no longer merely confined to religion. Within this new context, an individual professed to be duly qualified and knowledgeable within their specialized trade, to serve the greater public good.

Divinity, law and medicine became the three traditional learned professions of the time. As professionals became gatekeepers of specialized knowledge, so professions were passed down from one generation to the next within a family structure.

Professionals became defined by a few key similarities. Their admission to the profession was reliant on their credentials as experts due to their extensive education and practical training through formalized knowledge and qualified teachers. Professions were built on principles of ethics and values aimed at serving the greater public well and benefiting humanity. Their activities were regulated by relevant codes of conduct or overseen by laws that were stipulated by specific governing bodies.

With the industrial revolution, significant disruption came to the traditional professional. There became an increasing need for new professions because of the advent of novel technologies such as miners, factory workers, spinners and weavers—as outlined in Carr-Saunders and Wilson's classic 1933 study *The Professions*. With the invention of electricity and the light bulb, you could light up your home with the help of an electrician. The same happened with the mainstream introduction of the internet, and so the same will happen again in the future with the rise of artificial intelligence, quantum computing, robotics, virtual reality, augmented reality, blockchains and distributed ledgers, 3D printing, IoT and the like.

With the rise of the digital economy, access to professional industry skills and knowledge are rapidly shifting from a limited model that was once only available to the elite minority who could afford to study, (still in 2017 it is reported that around 59 million children in developing countries do not have access to basic education) to a future model of abundance with democratized access to education through the internet and with the help of exponential technologies.

Exponential technologies are going to continue to disrupt occupations as well as our ways of working and engaging with each other, in many ways. Professionals are going to need to reskill themselves to remain relevant in ever-changing times. In the past, it was reasonable to have a career that lasted a lifetime, between 30 and 50 years. The recent *IBM Study: The Skills Gap is Not a Myth, But Can Be Addressed with Real Solutions* published in 2019, found that we need constant upskilling and reskilling throughout our careers in order to remain adequately qualified. It stated that professionals require up to 36 days annually of learning and training to close current skills gaps, which are continuously expanding due to the rise of new technological disruptions. Professionals need to learn new skills and find innovative applications of their knowledge and experience.

The future will be shaped by scalable learning through alternative teaching outlets, such as online platforms and free, 24/7 online digital entities programmed with unlimited knowledge transference capabilities and personalized to each student. Not only will this decrease the amount of time and money that it takes to qualify as a professional, but it will also make it more accessible and holds the potential of enabling new professionals to go off into the workplace without substantial student debts.

At the same time, many occupations will be aided by exponential technologies in tasks that humans could never perform with such dexterity, computational power and physical speed. This human-machine convergence will result in an increase in productivity and a decrease in the amount of time, energy and effort required to complete intricate work. As a professional's tasks and workflows change, so new metrics for successful practice will need to be developed such as collaboration, culture and wellness.

In the next few years, humankind will augment itself with machines in the form of AI-designed, 3D-printed prosthetics and exoskeletons. These mechanical orthopedic devices will ultimately in the further future be wirelessly connected to our brains and perform actions with a mere thought. Not only will they give us extra-human strength, endurance and durability, but they will also level the playing field in terms of physical strength and remove a gender and age bias within the workplace. In this way, the human-machine conversion will democratize physicality.

PROFESSIONAL ETHICS IN AN AGE OF HUMAN-MACHINE CONVERGENCE

According to the MacArthur Foundation, 65% of school children will get jobs that haven't been invented yet. Part of the problem is the fact that most new professions are not created with a code of conduct or ethics in mind. As we evolve into the future, we need to consider how to educate the youth and how to incorporate ethics into new professions enabled by technology. Human-machine convergence will be able to relinquish some of the ethical responsibilities traditionally associated with human professionals over to artificial intelligence, big data and other exponential technologies that have far greater computational abilities to make logical decisions that are not fraught with emotions and biases—if we manage to eliminate algorithmic bias, which is currently a huge issue. We will witness a joint partnership between human and machine, as AI algorithms improve with each iteration. The five codes of ethics of behavior that come from the accounting industry—integrity, objectivity, professional competence, confidentiality and professional behavior—or something similar—must be required to rely on these technologies before making critical decisions.

In Human Resources, hiring processes in the next 5–10 years will be transformed as they become centered around psychometric testing that is equipped with cameras, speakers and various quantifiers that will be responsible for measuring e.g., an applicant's micro facial expressions and body language, dilating pupils, heartbeat, breathing and underlying mood—to determine the integrity of their statements and other stress indicators. Advanced Artificial Intelligence algorithms will compute massive amounts of data to do this. These data sets need to be based on replicable research in the workplace over time in order to be totally accurate. AI will eventually help determine an applicant's personality, character traits, work attitude, leadership qualities, emotional landscape, and mental health to better match them with a suitable role. Formal structures and transparency on criteria, when hiring, will need to be put in place to avoid any types of discrimination, bias or avoidable stress levels in applicants. These in-depth, AI-assisted assessments could hold the possibility of increasing the applicant's—who get through the eye of the needle—long-term job satisfaction based on an accurate understanding of who they are, their work aspirations and fit within the organizational culture.

We're already witnessing the possibilities of such capabilities. Beyond Verbal, an Israeli AI start-up created the Moodies smart-phone application that maps out emotional analysis through vocal intonations or so-called biomarkers, in real time and on an ongoing basis. It uses AI algorithms to determine the physical health, wellness and emotional state of the speaker.

We'll see journalists submit articles via plagiarism platforms that will run live fact-checking while undertaking a grammatical autocorrect function with humanlike vocabulary capabilities. In this way, copywriters' campaigns will also be screened for originality.

Similarly, leaders, influential individuals and those featured in the media will be broadcast with a simultaneous fact-checking livestream that will vet or discredit their statements to hold them accountable to the public. I imagine that these simulcasts will also reference and pull up their previous media appearances as a means of live cross-checking.

Again with replicable research and large data sets, we will be able to confirm more accuracy using AI when evaluating insurance claims. The claims will be processed with the aid of high-tech screening platforms through a smart device that will be able to determine the veracity of claims via numerous emotional and polygraph screenings that can also be undertaken remotely.

The legal sector, which is built on a strong code of ethics, will see human lawyers, juries and judges replaced by AI-driven robo legal aides that take facts into consideration, without being clouded by emotional biases, and also have a historical overview of the entire ambit of the legal case at hand. To get to this point there will need to be a number of barriers overcome in AI advances. Furthermore, the crowdsourcing of juries that is enabled by new platforms will help to balance the bell curve of judgments in a more objective manner.

An AI assistant might become an ethical requirement for various professionals across many industries. Medical professionals might be bound by the advice of AI assistants that analyze large data sets and the risk outcomes before undertaking an operation or treatment method. Similarly, there will be fewer cases of medical malpractice as robots will minimize the possibility of human error e.g., during surgery.

While human contact and emotional responses will remain vitally important in psychology and psychiatry, they, too, will be enabled with AI assistants that will record and download client sessions, with their permission, to advise on verbal biomarkers, subtle mood changes and behavioral irregularities.

These large data sets will assist human practitioners with ongoing diagnosis and treatment while providing a new range of insights into deep-seated issues that might have been suppressed. This data could become integral to speed up and fine-tune the healing process in a personalized manner.

As an example, Socos Labs' Co-Founder Vivienne Ming is doing AI research to assist diabetic patients and those with mental health issues, while exploring social influence and conformity, attitudes and persuasion, how stereotypes impact discrimination, group behavior, as well as aggression.

In the same way, board members might have to rely on AI assistants to crunch the large data sets, analyze historical information and suggest investment or divestment decisions that are devoid of emotions and biases. Companies will rely on distributed ledger systems to encourage complete transparency across their entire supply chain and financial spending, without the possibility of human interference and fraudulent transactions.

When it comes to complete transparency in the workplace,

Bridgewater Associates, a hedge fund founded by Ray Dalio that employs over 1,600 people, supports a radical truth and transparency approach that Dalio outlines in his book *Principles*.

Most meetings are recorded and made available to all employees via the company archive. If an employee mentions an absent colleague, they're required to send the recorded session to the said co-worker.

Just as this kind of radical transparency from Ray Dalio attempts to instill ethics within a company through accountability, so there's potential for socialized ethics within the workplace through surveillance cameras that represent a modern-day Panopticon approach. Though always on, cameras would begin recording once activated by specified AI-determined visual and audio markers—such as raised voices, strong language, unusual and sudden movements—which would be pre-specified and fine-tuned over time with the help of machine learning.

These markers would also alert human security guards to investigate the situation. If with the help of real-time AI predictive analysis or human intervention, it turns out that there is no threat or it has been neutralized, the cameras will stop recording. Though an infringement on personal privacy, which has become a controversial issue in recent years, a heavily monitored environment could encourage compliance with codes of conduct through the knowledge that one could be caught red-handed and charged with evidence in court. There is a lot of work to be done in terms of technology development to enable an ethical type of surveillance system, and laws differ from country to country and state to state varying the distribution and usage of this technology. Ultimately, I believe there should be a consensus between the state and the people on their privacy laws.

Another possible model of how ethics will unfold within the

workplace in the future is through a gamification or points-based approach that is supported by a customized smartphone application. An example of this is Yellow Solar Power in South Africa. Yellow is already using a points model and gamification to drive sales and good behavior. Employees' base salaries are aligned with their KPIs to complete tasks within their role and compliance with the company's code of conduct when dealing with customers or internal colleagues. Still, employees are incentivized to earn additional points when they undertake other responsibilities or extended work hours. These points can be exchanged for money, end-of-year bonuses or chosen incentives.

However, on the back of the global COVID-19 pandemic, we've seen a massive shift towards remote working environments, especially within location-independent industries, whereby corporate office space has been replaced with home offices or membership-based co-working spaces and coffee shops.

As digital migration accelerates with the enabling power of exponential technologies, so we'll witness a shift in how business leaders operate to ensure their employees remain productive and ethically undertake their work, when there might be fewer organizational checks and balances in place.

Business leaders of the future have to be more empathetic, transparent and rely on consistent and clear communication, especially as remote working does not inspire as great a sense of community as physical space and in-person relationships. Leaders need to lead by example, consistently upskilling themselves by actively taking time to learn and creating a framework of trust, freedom and responsibility between all colleagues. New working relationships need to be formed, with the aim of eliminating friction from work processes and tasks. Online communication platforms have become the new medium for the message, from Slack channels to personalized messenger platforms and branded company apps, as well as more interactive virtual reality environments. Leaders need to embrace these technologies as they will enable a more connected and collaborative workforce.

WHERE TO FROM HERE?

I predict that the not-so-distant future will see workplace ethics largely outsourced to exponential technologies, in the form of compulsory AI assistants, constant surveillance, AI-assisted checks and balances; all of which will become ethical requirements for all professionals. In turn, though, professionals will have to surrender much of their data and privacy to enable these new moral systems, which will create a problem in terms of how this personal information will be stored, used, who will have access to it and for what purpose. We can anticipate the establishment of various AI-driven ethics committees within companies to governments that ensures that technologies are developed and used for our best interests and in the name of good. There will be varying degrees of this dependent on the country, and organizational dynamics. As an example, this would most likely happen first in China and take longer or not be implemented at all in Europe.

Blockchain technologies will also enable a new type of workforce that is decentralized and can be based on skill level and not judged by gender or race. In the future, I believe we will be able to have multiple online identities. As an initial construct, each person can have one public identity, a pseudonymous identity or an anonymous identity. When using your pseudonymous identity, on a blockchain application, your attributes related to skill level can be presented to customers and the work can be completed without the customer knowing the real identity of the person doing the work, making the transaction totally unbiased and based on skill.

The coming together of technologies like AI and Blockchain, robotics, augmented and virtual reality and the convergence with humans will have profound implications on how we evolve the workplace as professionals. Increasingly we will see new gamification strategies in the workplace that make the employee feel a sense of progress and improvement. Designed to increase motivation, work satisfaction, loyalty, and incentives, there will be new types of rewards systems enabling more prosperity, fulfillment and happiness. We need to consider each step in the process and ask ourselves, how do we build this world we all want to live in?

Reference and reading list

Carr-Saunders, A. M, Wilson, P. A, 1933. *The Professions*, Clarendon Press, Pennsylvania State University.

Dalio, R, 2017. *Principles: Life & Work*, Simon and Schuster, United States.

Susskind, D, Susskind R, 2017. *The Future of the Professions: How Technology Will Transform the Work of Human Experts*. National Council of State Boards of Nursing. Published by Elsevier Inc.

MIC MANN

Mic is Co-Ceo of SingularityU South Africa and Mann Made. He is a storyteller, futurist, entrepreneur, investor and speaker on how exponential technologies can help to #futureproofAfrica. After completing his honours degree in scriptwriting, directing and producing film at AFDA, Mic joined as co-owner of the family business, Mann Made. Over the last 5 years Mic and his partners have been educating, inspiring and empowering South Africans through programmes, events and online. They have built a community of change-makers that want to make a positive impact. Mic is also the host of online show Exponential Africa which focusses on bringing the best thought leadership and innovation to African and global audiences. He is regarded as one of the leading experts in Virtual and Augmented Reality globally, developing some of the most exciting new digital spaces and environments with his studio and regularly speaks about VR, AR, the future of work, the new online global economy, gaming, education and the changing role of professionals. Mic is a strong advocate not only for local communities in South Africa but for all of Africa on a global scale.

THE ETHICS OF BLOWING UP YOUR JOB DESCRIPTION

CARIN ISM

The discipline of foresight has a serious design flaw: a built-in misaligned incentive, rigged against the very purpose of the practice. It reads like this: if a leader gets informed of what's coming, if a leader has a (virtual) paper trail, in which it can be confirmed that an imminent threat was indeed known to them, this, in and of itself, produces the possibility that the leader will be held accountable. There is duty, there is responsibility, there is guilt that can be assigned to whoever knew what was on the horizon. The solution to this might sound simple: for any given leader to not just keep themselves informed, but act on the information they receive.

However, as anyone who's ever attempted to lead an organization forward will know all too well, what needs to be done—especially in relation to long-term consequences—are often actions that are less than popular and comfortable for everyone involved. Hence, keeping reactive, rather than proactive, comes with its perks. To keep yourself in the proverbial dark, pushing problems ahead, and leave them to the leaders, or generations that will succeed oneself, can be a more immediately comfortable choice.

Deep, bold leadership, on the other hand, is, of course, defying personal risk, making sure you have as much overview as possible, and finding ways to take those potentially unpopular actions, focusing, not on personal discomfort, but on the bigger picture and values at play.

I start this text about the ethics of the future of work by highlighting this: the uncomfortable nature of being, or striving to be, a leader with fortitude and vision. And I start it here because, on the horizon, for what we now call work, is the prospect of its absence. And this prospect currently tends to make people extremely uncomfortable. So threatened in fact that hardly any leaders—be it of organizations or states—have dared to take command on the impending situation—with the famous Oxford Martin School study e.g., suggesting 47% of all jobs being automated by the early 2030s.

Leaders are still tackling the fact that algorithms' capacities are measuring up and surpassing those of humans with unhalted and more than exponential speed. Automation researchers have exclaimed it is both technically possible and—in terms of market forces—inevitable. However, this inevitability is handled reactively. As if each cashier replaced by a self-checkout machine, or each delivery by drone was some kind of singular event, and not part of the making of a full-fledged paradigm shift. If you look around, if you hear the speeches or read the annual reports, the narratives are still soiled with and built on claims that there will be jobs to go around, and that jobs are a good thing in and of itself. Which, of course, is anything but certain.

Finding a leader who has taken the necessary step back to achieve an overview of what their organization or state could look like 'post labor' is rare, if not unheard of—at least publicly.

Now if you are reading this, and think about your position within a certain context and organization, finding that it's both beyond your paygrade and mandate to enact or even start to envision changes of this scale, let's spend a moment directing the light on the concept of a bureaucracy, and how that model is what makes so many of us so used to thinking about what is and what isn't on our plate and in our job description.

The bureaucracy originated in China and became a global staple as industrialization and the concept of the state were widely established. In the bureaucracy, large projects like building a railroad or de-risking the lives of a population through social services, get defined and broken down into small, manageable tasks, clustered into work descriptions and paired with a chain of command. The bureaucracy states what needs to be done and makes people as replaceable as cogs in the wheel for execution. This model means that from the board member to the CEO to the manual laborer, everyone can say that they lacked the full picture of what was going on, and as such, everyone can always play the defense card of "I was only doing my job." This has, of course, been studied and described as the banality of evil in the context of genocide and war. But here, in the context of a paradigm shift for business and work that no one has been explicitly tasked with handling in a proactive manner, we might speak of the banality of missing out on opportunities, and, ultimately, the banality of becoming obsolete.

Bureaucracies have served us well to organize vast amounts of people for extremely ambitious pursuits but staying loyal to the chains of command fails us in the face of a new and emerging economic system. One that provides an update to what sits at the core of any society—be it tribal, slave-based, agricultural, modern or beyond: every society needs to reconcile and find a way to solve the fact that not everyone can create what they need to survive. Some are too old, some are too young, some are otherwise unable. And so those who can create, those who can work, need to create a little extra. Who is tasked to produce that extra, and how that extra is distributed, is the material foundation defining the inner workings and ideology of any system.

Now, as we are shifting from a model where humans were the

only viable option as to who was equipped to produce that extra, and entering an era where we can task machines with the task of production instead, we need to either build bureaucracies explicitly aimed at figuring out what the transition will look like, or at least disregard our loyalty to what is currently in place.

Acting like an ethical person, rather than just a conscientious employee, now must encompass asking questions and taking actions outside of one's job description. Essentially, if no one is at the wheel, everyone, arguably, has a moral obligation to take it. Meaning, wherever you are, right now, in a certain context, and/or the hierarchy of a certain bureaucracy, this is a moment in history that presents you with an opening: to think about what kind of value your organization is creating, and how that value could be created without people being necessary in the process. Furthermore, you, I, and everyone is equally tasked with thinking about how work being automated will lead not to peril, or the poverty many associate with unemployment, but rather to a new system for distributing that "extra." Some version of universal basic income (UBI) or universal basic services, are on the table of suggestions, but the jury—meaning we the people—is still out, still undecided as to what a suitable new system would be.

Imagine for example that, today, during the stress and opportunities presented by the coronavirus, a Fortune 500 company announced that they want to automate their entire process by 2030. And that they will invite all their employees to figure out how to make this happen. Regardless of where in the value chain a certain person might be working, everyone will be invited to suggest how either your individual job, or the entirety of the operation could turn from something requiring human efforts to something that does not—all with a maintained or increased production of value.

Now add to the equation that this imagined company would pledge to keep paying, not a wage that's given out in exchange for labor, but an UBI to everyone who has been employed within the organization, once the workers are made obsolete. Would that company not attract more talent and be a more exciting place not only of work, but of community, than almost any other? This idea, in all its radical disruptive power, is up for grabs. Something that, along with so many other concepts previously unimaginable, is now becoming ripe for prototyping. In the midst of the transformative changes happening within industry after industry, either directly linked to the challenges and opportunities of the dematerialized situation COVID-19 fast-tracks, or the fallout from an economic system strained from previous crises that's now put to yet another test. It's a time for creativity, as every strategy, including sticking with whatever was seen as the status quo some months ago qualifies as an experiment right now.

Acting ethically, be it as an organization, state or human, in times characterized by uncertainty, means the opposite of putting your head down and complying with an obsolete protocol. Acting ethically is activating the fullness of your intellect and capacity to learn and act on that knowledge. Acting ethically is acting on the agency each human is born with, that no reductive job description or vision statement can take away. What is a company other than a vehicle for organization, and for action amplified by the strength in numbers? And what is a leader other than someone who has the courage to act on an idea, on conviction, on a value they hold dear?

CARIN ISM

Carin is Co-Founder of the Future of Governance Agency (FOGA); faculty in distributed ledger technology and governance at the Nordic branch of SingularityU and, together with Julien Leyre, the author of *How to Rule A World*. FOGA created the first governance study in a Mars simulation, where Ism was the principal investigator. She is the previous Director of Research at Bitnation and was the Executive Director of the Global

Challenges Foundation, which ran the largest global governance innovation competition to date, focused on UN reform and the mitigation of global catastrophic risks. Carin identifies as an Effective Altruist and is the Co-Founder and former Chair of its Swedish branch. She is devoted to upgrading the tools available to distribute power and improve how decisions are made and enforced. Carin is the recipient of the 2019 Joseph Jaworski Next Generation Foresight Practitioners Award in International Policy.

INVESTING WITH DEMOCRATIC VALUES IN MIND

ALEX GLADSTEIN

A huge part of business and work is the strategy for the formation and accumulation of capital and the choices that firms and their leaders make with regard to their financial investments. These choices, while not always obvious to or even knowable to the average employee of a company, help steer not only an organization's performance but also its morale and culture.

So, if we're going to talk about how businesses can move ethically into the future, we must discuss investment. In a sense, the kind of investments we make today will determine the society of the future. And, unfortunately, that future is headed in the wrong direction unless we make a drastic change.

In the past two decades, there has been an increasing social and global pressure to "do good" with your investments. In other words, to try and improve the world, beyond just focusing on pure profit-seeking.

Recently, many private individuals, corporations, and funds have decided to partake in "impact investing," where they portion some of their investment strategy into companies and industries that can meaningfully improve society or the planet. Primarily, these impact investments are driven by the United Nations Sustainable Development Goals.

The "SDGs," as they are popularly known, are 17 ambitious and admirable goals ranging from zero hunger to clean water to quality education. They were unveiled by the UN in 2015 and have since steered trillions of dollars of investment. According to the Global Impact Investing Network, as of April 2019 the world's annual impact investing market is $502 billion.

Beyond the money, there are dozens of global conferences, investment arms, media outlets, strategic advising firms, family offices, and governmental task forces that evangelize impact investing with the SDGs as the GuideStar.

The problem is, while the SDGs look beautiful and sound wonderful, they are missing some very important topics. And this is not by mistake. Today, the UN working group that controls the SDGs and their future direction includes dictatorships like Belarus, Iran, Turkey, China, Zimbabwe, Egypt, Saudi Arabia, Vietnam, Nicaragua, Thailand, and Kazakhstan. The "2030 Agenda" that these governments are following is bringing us closer to a future without human rights.

If you review the SDGs today, and take a close look at the 10,000+ words that make up the descriptions of the 17 goals, you'll notice a few glaring omissions. Take, for example, the words "democracy," "journalism," "elections," "freedom," or "privacy." They are simply not listed. So, regardless of how friendly the SDGs appear, we need to consider that anyone following them as a compass for their investments and for how the world should look is pushing us towards a world without democracy, without independent journalism, without privacy, and ultimately, without freedom and human rights.

Now, when we consider that the SDGs are driving the overwhelming majority of impact investing, and when we consider that impact investing is this growing global movement which allocates more than a half-trillion dollars per year, we know that there is an opportunity for change.

Today, the most popular areas to do impact investing range

from agritech to healthtech to edtech to cleantech. These are, no doubt, fabulous areas to invest. Companies and technologies that make our society more educated and healthier and that make our planet more bountiful and greener are very attractive targets.

However, what about democracy? If businesses moving into the future are steered in a way where "doing good" must fall into the SDG paradigm, then, if we don't make a change now, anything not included in that paradigm will wither and lose interest to the world's investors.

I propose a new area of impact investing that can complement what is currently being driven by the SDGs: "demtech." This area would include, for example, citizen journalism; open access to the Internet; private communications; self-sovereign data; censorship-resistant money; and decentralized communications.

The good news is, there are massive opportunities for investment in these areas. To give a few examples, had you sat down in 2005 with "demtech" as a guide for your corporate, public, or private portfolio, here are some investments you could have made within these guidelines.

Perhaps you may have been an early investor in Twitter, a platform that has given human rights activists a voice around the world and continues to grow in prominence since its IPO. Or perhaps you were an early adopter of Bitcoin, a currency that can't be controlled by governments or corporations that has increased in value from less than $1 to more than $30,000. Maybe you chose to invest in a particular privacy company, like the virtual private network provider TunnelBear, which was sold to McAfee for $400 million, or the encrypted communications platform Keybase, which was recently acquired by Zoom. Or you worked on the Signal project, an open-source encrypted messenger app that now boasts of more than 100 million daily active users, and whose tech was adopted by WhatsApp and Facebook Messenger.

These are just a few examples to give you some ideas of what's possible. All of these technologies can strengthen democracy in the face of increasing authoritarianism, surveillance, and state control. All have performed fabulously well for their early investors. And none of them would be recommended by anyone following impact investing guidelines set by the SDGs.

So, as we look forward to the future of business and work, there are undoubtedly opportunities for this sort of investing and prioritization to take on a bigger role. Whether it's entrepreneurs who might be driven to create companies in this area, or venture capitalists who might consider investing in startups in this area, or even public funds that may wish to allocate a small percentage of their investments into companies and technologies like these—there are enormous areas of potential impact.

You may think that business and human rights can't coexist. How can we achieve both at the same time? I'm telling you we can, and we must.

ALEX GLADSTEIN

Alex is Chief Strategy Officer at the Human Rights Foundation. He has also served as Vice President of Strategy for the Oslo Freedom Forum since its inception in 2009. In his work, Alex has connected hundreds of dissidents and civil society groups with business leaders, technologists, journalists, philanthropists, policymakers, and artists to promote free and open societies. Alex's writing and views on human rights and technology have appeared in media outlets across the world including The *Atlantic, BBC, CNN, Fast Company, The Guardian, The New York Times, NPR, TIME, WIRED,* and *The Wall Street Journal.* He has spoken at universities ranging from MIT to Stanford, briefed the European Parliament and US State Department, and serves as faculty at Singularity University and as an advisor to Blockchain Capital, a leading venture firm in the fintech industry. He is also co-author of *The Little Bitcoin Book.*

CORPORATE ACTIVISM: CORPORATIONS READY TO FIGHT – AND DIE – FOR THEIR BELIEFS

NILLE SKALTS

"As many punches as I've taken about all kinds of stands, publicly, I would do it again in a minute. At the end of the day, you want to live your life having done what you believe is the right thing to do, and not having taken some generic stance or safe route..."
ROSE MARCARIO, FORMER CEO OF PATAGONIA.

SILENCE IS NOT AN OPTION

On June 2nd 2020, Blackout Tuesday, a day of collective action to protest racism and police brutality in response to the killings of George Floyd[43], Ahmaud Arbery[44], and Breonna Taylor[45], as mega-brands posted black tiles, shared carefully drafted and somewhat flavorless statements, or twisted iconic slogans telling us 'For Once. Don't Do It,' one particular company, Ben & Jerry's, stood out. With a corporate voice they called out the toxic institutional racism that continues to permeate business, government and wider society, extending the call to action: 'We Must Dismantle White Supremacy: Silence Is NOT an Option.' They went on to issue four policy-oriented pathways and followed up with 12 Ways You Can Help Eradicate White Supremacy.

Not your average invitation from a global corporation. But very real and frequent for the Benefit Corporation Ben & Jerry's, owned by global mastodon Unilever, and designed around a pertinent ethos and the "peace and love" worldview of its creators. While some corporations, like Nike, courageously use their megaphone to amplify a cause, they neglect taking a good long look inwards to truly practice what they preach in every business decision they make. To them it is a campaign supporting a cause, rather than the essence of why they're in business and the backbone of all decision making. For Ben & Jerry's it isn't woke-washing or dipping your toes in the world of corporate social consciousness, it is the continuation of decades of fighting for social justice internally and externally. It is the foundational essence of the company that provides the main impetus for their action. It is a deep dive into expressing the identity and intent of the company, the commitment to progressive values and the desire to mobilize fans, not as employees and consumers but as citizens, in that same fight. To partner with grassroots organizations to do something about it. Using the business model as a lever to change what is deemed wrong with the world. It is living ethics to the extreme. It is corporate activism.

Corporate activists are unusual business icons. Corporations who firmly believe that business has the right to exist only if it helps society flourish. Who live by the mantra of aligning their values with the way business is run. Like Ben Cohen, co-founder of Ben & Jerry's says: "If you don't like the way the business world operates, change the way you run your own business."

As many brands scramble to get on the social justice bandwagon, Ben & Jerry's keep doing what they have always done.

Despite warnings and massive reactions to 30 years of an overt stance on progressive issues, Ben & Jerry's is doing fine, mixing activism with a thriving and profitable business. For companies trying to understand how not to be lambasted for raising their voice and not following up, and who are looking for how far they could go, Ben & Jerry's is a good place to start.

WHAT IS CORPORATE ACTIVISM?

Corporate activism is using business as a lever for progressive social change. Corporate activists have strong values and opinions on injustice, crisis and political agendas, a strong desire to make right what is wrong. With all their being they put themselves at the forefront of that, which runs against their value systems, and share worldviews with activist leaders, borrowing their methods, tools and approach to alter the social order of society.

As I here define corporate activism it is radically different from what Harvard declared "mainstream" in 2018, in reaction to the "Kaepernick moment," where Nike borrowed the voice of Black Lives Matter-activist Colin Kaepernick, as a carefully selected, strong image to a campaign with the message of "Believe in Something. Even if It Means Sacrificing Everything" attached to their iconic "Just Do It" statement.

Why is it different? The activism in support of Black Lives Matter by Nike compared to Ben & Jerry's is grounded in radically different ambitions. One is expressing support for a cause, the other is dedicated to driving systemic change. The difference lies in the intention. Where Ben & Jerry's explicitly start with their progressive values and the change they seek, Nike responds to the signals of a young, affluent primary target audience, who longs for a different world, and who is drawn by an icon ready to sacrifice it all.

It differs in the extent to which it transcends the entire business. While Ben & Jerry's relentlessly strives for linked prosperity, Nike is criticized for not extending social justice to the entire value chain. It shows in narrative and in invitation to contribution. While Nike borrows the voice of activist Kaepernick and amplifies the reach to millions, Ben & Jerry's mobilize all of us, the average citizen, for action and co-creates solutions through grassroots movements. It shows in the degree of commitment regardless of costs. Where Ben & Jerry's is an "activist who just happens to sell ice cream" as corporate activism manager Chris Miller defines the company, Nike is a corporation momentarily lending its voice to an activist cause. It is not yet in the DNA of the company, merely a great starting point and an amazing campaign, which leaves us hopeful, yet hungry for more.

THE VITAL BEHAVIORS OF SUCCESSFUL ACTIVISTS

If we look closer at the characteristics of the corporate activism of Ben & Jerry's, we see four vital behaviors that serve as a compass for successful activists.

1. They have ethos with a fundamental stand on why they exist and their role in society

Corporate activism stems from the very core of the corporation. Ben & Jerry's is founded on and dedicated to a corporate concept of linked prosperity. The mission that guides decision making consists of three interrelated parts: the Economic Mission that asks them to manage the company for a sustainable financial growth; the Social Mission that compels everyone to use the company in innovative ways to make the world a better place; and the Product Mission, that drives them to make fantastic ice cream. Central to the mission is the belief that all three parts must thrive equally in a manner that commands deep respect for individuals in and outside the company, and that supports the communities of which they are a part.

It is the essence expressed in a genuine desire to push progressive social change. For Ben & Jerry's activism "is squarely rooted in the things we believe and the change we seek to make in the world, we're not thinking about what issues our fans care about..." as Chris Miller explains. With social justice at its core, Ben & Jerry's engage in shaping, renegotiating or changing the norms of society and use its platform to raise awareness of issues ranging from inequalities to racism or climate change, never hesitating to link products directly with ideals, such as ice-creams named Justice ReMix'd, Empower Mint, or Pecan Resist.

2. Their DNA *is radically different, and they design their whole business to benefit all stakeholders*

A corporate activist must lead with progressive values fully reflected internally. Ben & Jerry's has built the company on design criteria where values filter through everything, from innovative legal forms, impact business models, and to profiles uncommon to most other corporations.

Ben & Jerry's operate with an impact business model, based on interdependence and linked prosperity, creating systems value for the entire value chain. It treats its product as a way to create progressive change, and regards customers not only as such, but as citizens as well.

They measure success differently, looking primarily to scale the impact they seek, rather than growth in traditional terms and with the commitment to compete, not to be best in the world, but best for the world.

They organize differently and they hire for it. Most of the

current directors are activists themselves or have extensive experience in grassroots organizations, and allegedly more members of the board have been arrested while protesting than not. Employees are hired for passion, ability to build movements and desire to change the world. "Activism" is not your typical corporate department, but Ben & Jerry's has one, headed by the world's only corporate activism manager. They meet every week to identify pressing social justice issues and work closely with grassroots organizations and civil society to mobilize and create change.

They have updated governance, and are incorporated as a Benefit Corporation, an innovative corporate legal form that explicitly recognizes companies' commitment and accountability to all stakeholders, not just shareholders. This, coupled with the mission lock, allows the corporation to stay true to the values.

Despite being bought by Unilever, Ben & Jerry's is still able to drive advocacy work thanks to an independent mission board with the power of veto, that oversees the company, empowered to protect and defend brand equity.

3. They take an unapologetically bold stance on polarizing issues, build movements with grassroots and mobilize fans for action

Activism calls for followers. Ben & Jerry's is renowned for repeatedly taking an unwavering position on social injustice, but their activism is not merely a point of view, but a compelling point of action. Core to the work is turning customers into activists. With an inviting approach they reach beyond an audience already mobilized, tapping the potential of the dormant activist. They give the employees and customers a platform for action, as when they helped mobilize hundreds of thousands of Americans to sign the Paris Agreement, or followed up their call to dismantle white supremacy with concrete ways each one of us can help eradicate it, making personal action possible.

Specific to Ben & Jerry's activism is also that they never do it alone. They always partner closely with grassroots movements and facilitate collective action groups rather than creating campaigns internally. Rather than merely donating massive amounts of dollars, Ben & Jerry's develop long-term partnerships. After they decide to align with a cause, the team seeks out leading advocacy groups, spends substantial time working on persuasive language together, then using the corporate muscle to give leverage to the co-created campaigns.

4. And... they're ready to live and die for what they truly believe in
The inherent condition of activism is, that some will be pro and others against. It demands a strong ethical grounding and courage to always act according to values, also when opinions are violently divided and at the detriment of profits.

Ben & Jerry's practice consistency standing up for values whenever they're threatened. The engagement has evolved from relatively uncontroversial issues related to climate change to the most controversial issues of white privilege and racism. And they are prepared for pushback. When they overtly proclaimed solidarity with Black Lives Matters in 2016, a shitstorm hit them, the call center was overwhelmed with calls from angry Americans who didn't share the same beliefs and called for an ice-cream boycott. But all employees were ready to fight, standing strong shoulder by shoulder. And the shareholders were ready to accept the potential damage to the business.

THE TIDE IS WITH CORPORATE ACTIVISM

Bold, brave and with conviction, B Corps like Ben & Jerry's are shaping a new playing field for business. They deliberately address issues of racism, inequality or climate change, going beyond what is previously seen. They redefine the role of business in society in the process. It is the contours of a paradigm evolution, where the business of business is finally, 50 years after the epic definition of Milton Friedman, not only to deliver value to shareholders, but to truly help society flourish.

The tide of history is with the proactive. With a seemingly endless round of social and environmental problems that urgently needs addressing, this type of activism is much needed. Never has the world to such an extent needed business to help solve the most pressing challenges. Never has there been so many declarations from corporate leaders calling for a reset of capitalism. Never have we, the people, expressed such desire to change the world for the better.

Activism is likely to be a constant for corporations in the future. Consistency between ethics and actions and standing up for your values when they're threatened is what defines the future of business. Going forward we will see companies acting to affect the wider system within which they operate, assuming moral obligation, and prioritizing ethics over everything else. This will give us, not only as responsible employees, consumers and investors but as engaged citizens, the opportunity to amplify our voice and act. It will be the onboarding ramp for a new breed of activists, and a way to reach the future generations, who have diminishing faith in the ability of the political systems to drive change and are looking for new ways to become part of making change. They will cheer the rise of the activist corporation.

NILLE SKALTS

Nille is a corporate activist, movement builder, and regenerative change agent in business facilitating the transition to a regenerative economy. She is the Co-Founder of Danish change agency Märk, a certified B Corp, and Founder of the Nordic B Corp Movement. She is a lecturer in Corporate Activism at Copenhagen Business School and The Royal Danish Academy for Architecture, Design & Conservation, a master facilitator, and the Co-Founder of the Danish Facilitator Association. Nille has been an advisor to the Confederation of Danish Industries on the SDGs and was appointed to the Danish Government's Task Force dedicated to building a Civil Society Strategy.

Photo Credit: Stine Heilmann

THE ART OF UNLEARNING: WHY ORGANIZATIONS NEED TO RETHINK BUSINESS AS USUAL

EVELYN DOYLE

It's a cool Monday morning in October 2019 and I am not sitting at my desk at Patagonia's Amsterdam headquarters. As the HR Director for Europe, I am often travelling for work—to visit the brand's global headquarters in Ventura, California, to meet our partners across Europe, or to lead and take part in events around the world. But today is different.

Today, I am standing on the edge of Amsterdam's historic museum district with a phone in my hand.

In front of me is a very serious-looking police barrier and on the phone is a criminal lawyer. I am here because, just past that barrier, a group of my Patagonia colleagues (and my boss, our general manager) are lying across what is normally a busy traffic interchange, arm in arm with hundreds of others, taking part in an Extinction Rebellion human blockade. The council has ruled that this act of civil disobedience is illegal, and the police have been given the go ahead to use force to remove protesters, one by one. I have worked in HR for many years but can confidently say: this is a first.

When I think back to that day, I'm hit with a rush of divergent emotions. There's fear for my colleagues: what will happen to them? Will they be hurt? Will they be arrested? If so, what happens next?

And is this going to have a long-lasting impact on their freedoms to live and work in the Netherlands?

Then there's deep frustration. I am exasperated that they have had to take this action in order to help those in power see what is clear to us: that we are in the middle of an impending climate crisis—of our own making—and need to take definitive, systemic action, right now, to change course.

But, overwhelmingly, there is a huge sense of pride. In that blockade is a cross-section of my colleagues, both in terms of professional roles, background, nationality and age. I work with them every day; we often share stories from our lives over coffee and lunch; I employed many of them myself. The general manager Ryan—a sharp-witted American who was then the most senior person in the European organization and is now our global CEO—is lying in the street, near to our receptionist Christelle—a nurturing French woman—who intended only to come and bring food to the protesters this morning, but then felt compelled to join them.

There are many Patagonians involved. I'm so proud of my colleagues, that they have taken this step, and proud to work for a company that encourages and supports them to do so—a company that recognizes the importance of people and organization coming together, to form one interconnected ecosystem. And it's my responsibility as HR director and as a colleague and friend, to make sure that they stay safe, whatever today throws at them.

Before joining Patagonia six years ago, I worked in Russia, Africa and Switzerland, holding leadership roles in the fields of human resource management, talent management and culture and organizational development initiatives for global companies, in with-profit, non-profit and social entrepreneurship sectors. I have always been passionate about playing a role in positively transforming work environments and business models and help-ing employees find their voice. But, looking back, I can see that, before Patagonia, I was invariably operating within set parame-ters—around company or shareholder profit.

The concept of bringing my "true, human self" to work—and encouraging those I employed, and developed, to do the same—would have been as foreign to me as suddenly deciding to entreat colleagues to bring their pet goat to work.

And, at Patagonia, that is exactly what I do. We are all actively encouraged to be ourselves, and not forced to make a distinction or tradeoff between what we believe as concerned citizens, as parents, as children, partners and friends, and the things we do when we go into "work." What's more, we are trusted, and trust others, to make our own smart decisions and to use our unique voices to serve our reason for being: we're in business to save our home planet.

This employee autonomy, that runs like a red thread through the global business, was what led a junior graphic designer to come up with the idea to give away 100 per cent of Black Friday 2016 profits to grassroots environmental groups (we expected this would cost us $2m; it ended up being $10m). It was what galvanized two members of the design team when they hid a secret message under the size labels of our Regenerative Organic Cotton Stand Up Shorts this election season: Vote the Assholes Out. And it was on the mind of Patagonia's founder Yvon Chouinard, in 2018, when he announced—without consulting the wider business—that he was changing our decades-old reason for being to this new one: "We're in business to save our home planet," and then told the whole organization: "You're smart people, you work it out."

Chances are, you are a business leader or manager reading this, and thinking: but how do I do all of that? What is the secret sauce that guarantees you a workforce of committed visionaries, from the people who run payroll to those who answer customer calls—and everyone in between? At the risk of disappointing you, the answer is: there is not one magic ingredient. You have to do the tough work, through every part of employee engagement, and you have to live and breathe your values, your core, your DNA every day, in every way—not just as some employee engagement statement.

The work begins with yourself, as an organization, as a leadership team and as individuals. It takes an extraordinary approach to prioritize intellectual curiosity and storytelling, and to truly support your employees to grow, navigate, work as a team and find their independent voices. But all of this is vital in order to nurture a company culture of activism and responsibility. In the words of the author of Designing Regenerative Cultures Daniel Christian Wahl: "What might we do, not simply to wreak less havoc or do less harm, but to leverage the natural connections we have with living systems, to contribute to the integrity, resilience and long-term viability of people, places, and ecosystems?"

At Patagonia, our reason for being is central to everything we do, from the paid environmental internships we offer all employees to the lunch talks from NGO partners across Europe, our generous maternity and paternity policies and the family room we have at our headquarters to enable our teammates to bring their kids to work or to nurse them. It's there in Earth University, our refreshingly different, innovative employee learning and development program, that takes inter-departmental groups out into nature to learn through, and with nature. During this experience, they practice what it means to take care of our environment and share experiences, to immerse in systems and regenerative thinking models and learn about themselves, develop skills and come home better equipped for the challenges ahead. It's there in the fact that we aren't afraid of hiring mavericks—and actively seek to nourish their radical ideas and non-conformist viewpoints.

And it's there in our bail policy, that says we will pay bail for all employees, all over the world, arrested for taking part in environmental action.

Our singular focus —we're in business to save our home planet—provides a constant reminder that acting with purpose should not be without consequence. Sometimes it can hurt the bottom line. And sometimes it should. If you aren't prepared to take bold decisions when everything is at stake—to "bet the ranch" on your purpose —then you are not walking the talk. At Patagonia, we weigh these decisions every day as an organization, asking questions about degrowth and measuring profit and loss on planetary impact, rather than money. This has been there in Patagonia's DNA since the very beginning when Yvon Chouinard realized he was harming the place he played in and loved, and immediately stopped making hard steel pitons, replacing them with more delicate aluminum chocks.

Today, this takes place in every department and at every level—for example, our #StopHateForProfit boycott of Facebook advertising, which has had clear negative impacts on our ability to communicate with our audiences and to reach new communities for our environmental NGO partners, but has also brought us one step closer to living and breathing that reason for being. Through this work, purpose becomes something not solely dictated by the leadership team but constantly redefined by each individual employee.

So, if you are the owner, founder, or in a position of power at a business or organization, ask yourself: what is your company purpose? And what is your own purpose for being there? If the answers to these questions go beyond being purely financial, the most important thing is to act and to ensure your vision and purpose are clearly articulated and demonstrated in how you lead and how you nurture employee voice and activism. Employees are increasingly keen to work with leaders who demonstrate humility, empathy and authenticity, and for organizations that understand the need, not only to take, but also to give back to the planet. On the back of a strikingly different year in so many ways, people are reevaluating every aspect of their lives and work and are waking up to the interconnectedness of people and planet.

Empowering a community of passionate employees starts before they even join your organization. At Patagonia, we challenge ourselves to hire people, not CVs. Someone could have the best skills for a role, but they must also bring a connection to our values—through such things as a love of the outdoors and a dedication to social and environmental justice issues. Hiring mavericks who will add to your culture takes time; it requires rigorous work and demands an organization of leaders who understand and accept that hiring is not just another KPI. I commit to meeting so many different people speculatively, sharing a coffee and a far-reaching conversation to understand what drives them. And, as with every step of the process, putting in the work reaps rewards—your employees are your most valuable asset as a business, after all. I implore you: find those exceptional people, nourish them and support them on their own journeys, help them find their voice and how they can connect their role to your purpose and share the good times and the bad, as an organization, along the road. Your employee community—just like your customer community— expects more and more of you today. Understanding we are part of the ecosystem, rather than standing outside of it, needs to be the constant message and demonstration via concrete actions; such as allowing everyone to bring their whole "self" to work.

Get started right now. Take one step and keep walking. Surround yourself with those who share your purpose. And give them the tools to live and breathe it every day and to bring it to life in ways you couldn't even imagine.

Don't be fearful when they take your business in directions you didn't anticipate. Remember: every business is a living ecosystem that needs to regenerate. And sometimes, what you unlearn is more important than all of the things you think you know.

It's important to acknowledge that as a company, Patagonia has not always been at its best. While each business has its unique strengths, it inevitably has weaknesses too. We know that to become a just, equitable and antiracist company, it means taking a tough look at ourselves, hearing directly from our BPOC and BIPOC colleagues, and taking decisive action focused on creating a more diverse and inclusive environment – not just within Patagonia but in the outdoor industry and arguably, in the communities and places where we live, work, and play. And that's exactly what we're doing.

That Monday in October ended well, comparatively speaking. All the Patagonians taking part were rounded up onto a bus and deposited far outside the city to walk home, in the hopes they would have no energy left to return to the blockade. But within the organization, their actions lit a fire. Every employee had friends who had been in the group and had heard their stories of the day, had felt empowered by their actions. As a collective, we were all clear on our reason for being and were working it out for ourselves. We still are.

EVELYN DOYLE

Evelyn is HR Director, EMEA, for Patagonia, based at the brand's European HQ in Amsterdam. Originally from Ireland, Evelyn has lived and worked in Russia, Africa and Switzerland, holding leadership roles in the fields of human resource management, talent management and culture and organization development initiatives for global organizations in with-profit, non-profit and social entrepreneurship sectors. Evelyn is passionate about positively transforming work environments and business models, nurturing employees to develop their individual voices, and architecting culture through regenerative approaches.

At Patagonia, she is responsible for building an internal community that embodies the brand's reason for being: we're in business to save our home planet. Outside of her work at Patagonia, Evelyn is a member of the advisory board of Net Impact Amsterdam, sits on the board of directors of NGO Design-athon Works, and is actively involved in supporting grassroots groups working to find solutions to the environmental crisis. Her loves include music, keeping up to date with news and cultural developments from around the world, all things food and spending time with her son.

HUMAN – AT THE CORE

I THINK, THEREFORE I AM – NEURAL SOVEREIGNTY AND NEURAL RIGHTS IN THE 21ST CENTURY

DIVYA CHANDER

Cogito, ergo sum

RENÉ DESCARTES, DISCOURSE ON THE METHOD (1637)

Descartes posited that the thinking mind was axiomatic proof of our existence. Drawing on the logical extension of this axiom, if your mind is what defines you, then do you have the right to your own mind? Do you have the right to "neural sovereignty," potentially the last bastion of Selfhood? Is it more important than even your genome, that other code of life?

Recent advances in neurotechnology have made the science fiction of *Black Mirror* and *The Matrix* science fact. The technologies are glorious, beautiful, and exquisite, and have the potential for creating real human advancement. But the Collingridge dilemma (named for David Collingridge's 1980 book, *The Social Control of Technology*) applies to this technology as much as it does for any of our most forward biotechnological advances, such as gene editing and synthetic biology. Collingridge stated that "when change is easy, the need for it cannot be foreseen; when the need for change is apparent, change has become expensive, difficult and time-consuming."[46] The challenge lies in being able to predict the potential impact of a new technology to enact policy to stay ahead of it, so that we as an international community and as an evolving ethical species, can anticipate the need for regulation and what limits to apply to it, so that it does not violate basic human rights' norms. Make no mistake—given the enormous power to collect humans' data, the obligations for businesses in today's society are as deep and profound as the obligations of the governments of nation states and international regulatory institutions.

This essay is about exactly this effort—to understand neuro-technology and its cutting edge, and to stay ahead of the effort to self-regulate its misuse, precisely by understanding the myriad ways in which it can be exploited. Companies and businesses that adhere to such principles in advance, should be both recognized and rewarded to encourage the voluntary participation in such initiatives.[47] IBM did exactly this in working towards a crowdsourced, iterative framework for ethical artificial intelligence, which they committed to upholding in their own company and day-to-day practices.[48] Facebook Reality Labs claims to have integrated a series of responsible development principles for their neuro-capable devices,[49] which you will see are not comprehensive given the risks outlined in what is to follow; but paying lip service to this means there is pressure in this domain. Therefore, early adoption of ethical neurobusiness practices can potentially form the basis for helping to craft and accelerate the adoption of ethical neurotechnology principles, as well as trust in your company, its brand, and its uptake.

THE NEW EDGE – HOW TECHNOLOGY HAS ENABLED US TO READ AND WRITE TO THE BRAIN

Everything we talk about next will hinge upon a singular

understanding—that of the neural code, the fundamental code of life that endows us with the ability to exist and navigate the world. In other words, in order to translate stimuli, objects and phenomena, from the outside world, or generated within the organism, what is the alphabet? How do you translate one form to the other? How do you get from the activity of nerve cells to complex percepts? Is the definition of consciousness embedded somewhere in this code, or is it something different altogether?

CAN YOU READ MY MIND?

In 2011, Jack Gallant and his postdoc, Shinji Nishimoto, published a seminal paper in mind-reading.[50] Placing student volunteers into a magnet (an fMRI machine), the scientists presented YouTube movie trailers to the subjects, and measured the brain activity in response to those movies from one of the early visual processing areas in the brain, called the visual cortex. From these neural recordings, they created the equivalent of a data dictionary—linking patterns of brain activity to the statistics and properties of the visual imagery—a fancy way of saying that lines, orientations, edges, movement, luminance, contrast, and color were mapped to a neural code. Using this database of videos and coded responses, the scientists eventually put a new set of students into the fMRI scanners and showed them a different set of YouTube video clips. Using the previously created dictionaries, the researchers were able to grossly decode the images that the subjects were seeing, even though they were "blinded" or unaware of the video clips being shown.[51] A few years later, Japanese researchers in Kyoto accomplished a similar feat, this time by identifying the visual content of subjects' dreams.[52] In fairness, the algorithms did not actually reconstruct subjects' dreams as the Berkeley group had been able to do for subjects viewing natural images. But dream content is still a step forward. Though in terms of privacy:

In the years since, the Gallant Lab has created a number of interactive viewers[53] that have explored how the brain represents and encodes semantic data, including its response to storytelling, one of the most natural things we do as social animals.

There are multiple modalities of non-invasive brain reading. Gallant's work is based on the changes in blood flow in the brain measured in a magnet, functional magnetic resonance imaging (fMRI). Other forms of non-invasive brain mapping include the electroencephalogram (EEG), the magnetoencephalogram (MEG), and near-infrared spectroscopy (NIRS). While fMRI and MEG are currently bulky and obvious, the EEG is being progressively made more accessible and portable (see companies like Emotiv, Neuroelectrics, Neurosky, and open-source initiatives like Open-BCI). Openwater (Mary-Lou Jepsen, Founder-CEO) and Kernel (Bryan Johnson, Founder-CEO) are attempting to make smaller and more powerful non-invasive imaging in the infrared (NIRS) and using MEG to see into the brain and map its functionality. Their devices are initially intended for a medical and research community, but they plan to make them ultimately available to consumers.

The main uses for brain decoding have been their applications for understanding the neural correlates of behavior and perception, diagnosing and performing biomarker discovery for neurological disease (e.g., Alzheimer's, schizophrenia, addiction), and creating closed-loop systems for enabling people with functional limitations to interact with the outside world. Acoustic decoding enabled one of the earliest brain-computer interfaces to emerge—the cochlear implant. By understanding how the brain decodes sound waves of different frequencies, a decoder plus electrical stimulator device can bypass a damaged or non-functional hearing apparatus in the periphery, and convert sound waves to electrical signals that stimulate the cochlear nerve, thus providing a rough way of bringing sound into the brain for those who cannot hear. Similarly, for people who have limitations in sight, understanding the neural code for vision, as early as nerve cells ("neurons") in the retina at the back of the eye is an important step (the retina is a piece of the brain sticking out beyond the skull that binds visual information, or photons of different wavelengths, from the outside world). Understanding how neurons encode, filter, and compute information forms the basis for creating retinal and visual prosthetics that can bypass damaged or incompletely formed areas of the eye, transmitting light and form to places in the brain that can make sense of it. As we speak, bionic eyes and other visual prosthetics are taking off.[54][55][56] In addition to supplementing vision for those with retinal damage like macular degeneration, a group in Hong Kong recently published a study in which they created a curved visual prosthetic, with nanowires functioning much the same way as optic nerve fibers do (the highway on which information bits travel from the eye to the brain).[57] The prosthetic's resolution is currently significantly inferior to the human eye, but the researchers anticipate this will improve with time. Their goal—ultimately, to make bionic eyes for robots that can see better than human eyes, yet make the robots themselves appear to be more human. Recently, high-functioning robots are turning out to be quite creepy (for reference, see the Headless Boston Dynamics Dog).[58][59]

Despite early work in sensory systems, the majority of the exceptionally highly visible/profile advances have taken place in the space of movement. For brain-machine interfaces to work, brain mapping has to be of sufficient accuracy to understand how the brain is perceiving (sensory), planning, or creating intention to do things (motor). Because planning motor activities, like the trajectory of movement of one's limbs (How would I throw a baseball with my right hand? How would I pick up the orange with my left? How do I move my feet to tango?) is highly mathematical, this code is easier to understand, and to translate into electrical signals that can drive computer monitors, mice, and other actuators outside the brain like robotic arms[60] and exoskeletons.[16]

Another general principle—non-invasive brain readers have less fidelity and accuracy than invasive ones. That is why the potential for closed-loop systems built with invasive interfaces (i.e., electrodes touching the brain) is higher than for non-invasive ones. The Braingate2 Consortium,[61] an academic group of researchers mostly working with tetraplegics (patients paralyzed from the neck down) has shown amazing promise. An array of 96 metal electrodes can be implanted into the motor cortex of these patients, which receives signals for planning motion from upstream parts of the brain. Over time and multiple trials, the chip learns what the intended motion is (much like the algorithms in the Gallant Lab learned to make sense of what subjects were seeing). The decoder can then bypass the damaged motor tracts in the brain, spinal cord, or muscles and direct an actuator outside the subject to perform the intended movement (like a robotic arm bringing a water bottle to a subject's mouth, or using a keyboard to type onto a screen). New advances have been made by the consortium in terms of wireless interfaces to the skull,[62] and the ability to decode imagined handwriting, and turn that into typed words.[63] These connections to computers outside the brain can even enable one to surf the internet with one's mind.[64] Elon Musk's Neuralink has gained a lot of social media exposure for taking this technology to the next level, by reducing the diameter of the electrodes, increasing the packing density, decreasing the heat generated and decreasing the power requirements of these invasive brain-machine interfaces.[65] Despite talk of wanting to create humans that can outcompete AI,

Neuralink's first target, like Braingate's, is also people with paralysis to restore movement to them. The value that Neuralink brings to this endeavor is that Musk can fund rapid technological break-throughs at a rate that it is hard for government-funded projects and academic centers to match.

YOUR BRAIN WAVES CAN UNIQUELY IDENTIFY YOU

Reading brainwaves provides some additional surprises. Non-invasive EEG and fMRI patterns can identify certain kinds of neurological diseases, or even tendencies. In other words, they can serve as a biomarker for a disease state. Several studies have shown that EEG can pick up alcohol addiction tendencies or schizophrenia by looking at brainwave patterns. Could future employers or health and life insurance companies make using a brain-reading device mandatory, just as some do for urine drug screenings, height, weight, and blood draws? Could this be made a condition of employment? To determine if you are insurable? Even more interesting, Dr. Sarah Laszlo's lab found that using non-invasive EEG caps enabled her to read the summed electrical potentials on the surface of the skull evoked by looking at images—and that the shapes of these potentials were so unique to the individual, they could identify them with 100% accuracy—a *brainprint*.[66] This use of brainprinting could be mandated by organizations, employers, or even financial institutions in the near future, to authenticate an individual. What if large tech companies started to require this to unlock your smartphone, or activate Alexa? Would they then own your brainprint? Could that be combined with a number of other biometrics to create a deep fake of you?

YOUR BRAIN WAVES AND YOUR BODY CAN
BE HACKED, LIKE A SMARTPHONE

In 2017, an interesting study was published in Financial Cryptography by Neupane, Rahman, and Saxena, at the University of Alabama.[67] The researchers were looking at commercially available EEG headsets that could be used for mind control during gaming. They found that if the subject paused a video game and logged into a bank account while wearing an EEG headset, they were at risk of having that password stolen. They tested this in 12 subjects, by asking them to type a series of randomly generated PINs and passwords into a text box as if they were logging into an online account while wearing the EEG headset. The act of typing in a password into a screen-based login involves visual processing, and motor movements. If a malicious program had gained access to the device's software and was training itself on the subject's typing and brainwaves (much as algorithms were trained during Dr. Gallant's experiments in visual mind reading), that program might be able to "read" the password. It turns out that just 200 characters were enough for the algorithm to train on a user's unique brain wave response to visualizing and typing in keystrokes corresponding to those PINs. The algorithms decreased the odds of a hacker's guessing of a four-digit PIN from 1 in 10,000 to 1 in 20; the odds of guessing a 6-letter password decreased from about 1 in 500,000 to approximately 1 in 500. And the only solution to protect ones' brainwaves from being hacked was to introduce noise. One scenario that Dr. Saxena painted was "in a real-world attack, a hacker could facilitate the training step required for the malicious program to be most accurate, by requesting that the user enter a predefined set of numbers in order to restart the game after pausing it to take a break, similar to the way CAPTCHA is used to verify users when logging onto websites."[68]

How many enthusiastic gamers would recognize this risk while playing video or virtual reality games? Many of them are already actively "contributing" their brainwave data to the refinement of algorithms that make mind control of avatars, controllers, and video actuators more precise. Oculus is now requiring that its users log in with their Facebook accounts. Currently, data breaches and ransomware attacks are prevalent. A hacked Facebook account could be used to gain illegal access to one's headset, and therefore, an individual's biometrics and brainwaves. That is in addition to the risk of Facebook owning all that neural data.

Medtronic was the subject of a "white hacker" break into some of their best-known, life-saving medical devices.[69] Both their pacemakers, and mini-insulin pumps, when connected to the outside world for software updates, device programming, and interrogation, could be controlled by outside (good) hackers to either deliver aberrant shocks or electrical signals to the heart, or abnormal doses of insulin to the bloodstream. Both shocking the heart or over/underdosing someone with insulin could be fatal. This prompted a 2019 FDA recall of the remote controllers for Medtronic's mini-insulin pumps,[70] and a reworking of their cybersecurity. Other companies creating implantables, like Abbott and Boston Scientific, are now similarly invested in cybersecurity.[71]

WRITING TO THE BRAIN'S HARD DISK

In light of this, could writing to the brain be possible? In fact, yes. Medtronic, Boston Scientific, and Abbott make invasive deep-brain stimulating (DBS) electrodes that deliver electrical stimuli to the brain, and rewire brain circuits in order to treat the symptoms of diseases like Parkinson's, epilepsy, and obsessive-compulsive disorder. As an example:

"Abbott DBS operates with Apple iOS software and controllers for a possibly more familiar interface and easier programming experience. Abbott's new technology, the first of its kind in the United States, also allows people with these devices to communicate with their clinician and receive DBS adjustments remotely, from their home or other location with Wi-Fi or cellular access." [Emphasis mine.][72]

The newest DBS device approved by the FDA in 2020, Medtronic's Percept,[73] can both sense and record an individual's unique brain signals, to enable symptom correlation with local electrical field potentials, precisely because these electrodes touch brain tissue. While this might enable more precise DBS adjustments for better control of symptoms and side effects, without the appropriate cyber controls, remote sensing, writing, and machine learning could be used to take invasive control of brain circuits. While they could not write just anything to the brain, they certainly could affect the circuits and resulting behaviors that formed the pathway in which the electrodes were embedded.

For the subjects of the invasive electrode implants, writing to those circuits *remotely* might also be possible in the future, as the electrodes are usually bidirectional (capable of reading neurons as well as stimulating them). That would mean that a population of humans for whom these implants were necessary to overcome disability would be vulnerable, in the same way subjects with pacemaker or insulin pump implants are. More alarming is the possibility of this extending to a larger swath of the population. The hype around companies like Neuralink is partly fueled by people like Elon Musk, implying that individuals might choose to get these minimally invasive implants in the future to enhance themselves, rather than treat dysfunction. If that were to happen, the population of vulnerables open to neural hacking becomes much greater—in cyber terms, the threat radius markedly enlarges to augmented humans.

Others have wondered if non-invasive control is possible. Most of our non-invasive brain rewiring technologies like transcranial electrical and magnetic stimulation, or focused ultrasound, would be near impossible to do without knowledge and consent since they involve an apparatus to be applied to the outside of the skull that is not subtle. (Notably, this does not eliminate the possibility of coercion, i.e., enforced compliance for the sake of employment, money, etc.). But some of the cyberattacks on U.S. embassy officials in places like Cuba and China[74][75] seemed to involve potential microwave, or pulsed RF warfare directed at the brain, causing intolerable pain, headaches, disrupted sleep, mood, and unwanted sensory experiences. To date, there are no declarations on banning the use of this type of warfare using non-invasive energy, though some are suggesting that international guidelines on "biological" warfare be applied to regulating these use cases.

A FEW OTHER SCI-FI POSSIBILITIES – TELEPATHY, THE METAVERSE, AND IMPLANTED MEMORIES

Some other extraordinary examples of brain read-write technology have occurred in recent years. Non-invasive brain reading (EEG) was used to transmit bits of information through the internet to a non-invasive brain-stimulating device (TMS) in 2 or 3-brain networked situations.[76] In one case, the thought of a foot or hand was delivered seemingly "telepathically" by connecting a sender and receiver's brain through the internet.[77] A similar feat was achieved with 3 brains engaged in a social network ("Brainet") that could solve problems and play games together.[78] The most likely scenario is neurogaming enthusiasts who are already trying to connect to the virtual world by connecting their brainwaves to the metaverse. The metaverse is considered a collective virtual shared space, created by the convergence of virtually enhanced physical reality and a physically persistent virtual space, including the sum of all virtual, augmented worlds and the internet. This may form the backbone for a parallel reality for many, just as the internet is for us today. If a user's equipment is hacked, information sent could be either read, or manipulated by brain-writing techniques, for nefarious purposes.

Researchers in Tonegawa's Lab at MIT demonstrated in 2013 that it was possible to record memories from mice that had experienced them in one setting, and use those neural recordings to create false associations that had never been experienced before.[79] They were essentially moving memories within an organic brain, creating new contexts. This is not too different than what the character, Neo, experienced in the film *The Matrix*, when his brain was uploaded with patterns for jiu-jitsu. Later, this memory implanting technology was extended to using optogenetics (light-activated, genetically addressed, ion channels in the brain) to write new engrams to brain circuits that had never experienced a memory.[80] This is quite extraordinary—if memories can be created de novo, just by knowing the neural code, terrible memories and associations that contribute to mental suffering, like PTSD, can be similarly erased. But with coerced access to neural circuits, in the future, an individual wanting to be malevolent could hack those circuits, and rewrite them with specific memories or associations.

NEUROGAMING

We've alluded to gaming in several places. Gaming presents an interesting possibility on both the read-write levels, and interactions with the emerging metaverse. We highlighted how engagement and identity might be read. Based on biomarker discovery using fewer and fewer EEG leads, your brainwaves might give away your addiction potential or predisposition to developing anxiety or depression. Manipulating you to log into sensitive accounts and enter PINs could result in password theft. But the really frightening part of neurogaming is the potential for digitally twinning you.

We've already seen that machine learning coupled with ever more powerful computing chips is enabling intelligent algorithms, with minimal data on your facial expressions or voice, to create a realistic simulacrum of you, a so-called "deep fake." Facebook's CTRL Labs wristbands can use EMG-based (muscle) activity to "read" your limbs' low-energy gestures to do things like control objects in the real world, or in VR, mapping how you move.[81] Biometric data (brain waves, eye-tracking, heart rate, sweating, pupillary dilation, gestures, voice) collected from an individual while responding to natural world simulations in order to improve an avatar's function in the virtual world could enable the ultimate deep fake, a complete digital avatar of you. Some companies like Singularity Studio are already working on 3D avatars, built on DNA Block,[82] to create digital twins that can do your job or train others to, at an enterprise level. In these scenarios, identity theft would be difficult to prove. A near-facsimile of you could fool family members into paying ransom on your behalf, could open bank accounts, impersonate a company CFO to commit wire fraud,[83] or commit federal crimes in your name.

NEUROMARKETING, NEUROCAPITALISM, AND NEUROSURVEILLANCE

The ultimate, seemingly benign use of neural data is to further the cause of capitalism. Neuromarketing has become a field unto itself. It is part of the curricula of business schools, and scores of self-made consultants as well as startups exist in the space to provide neural data to companies looking to sell products and perform customer research. Using increasingly consumerized neurowearable devices, one can use brain waves to measure engagement with a product, or even an idea. Other biometric data collection can also give away the secrets of the nervous system—an excited subject might have dilated pupils, a faster heart rate, or spend more time scanning an object they find interesting with their eyes. They may sweat more, and have a change in their galvanic skin response. They may exhale more CO_2.[84] All these little signals can be a surrogate for interest, sometimes that the subject isn't even consciously aware of. This might enable mass marketing studies, or even rapid brainstorming or prototyping, saving time and money to a company engaged in customer research. However, these signals can be exploited, and also warehoused for future use. For instance, even though you did not provide explicit consent, many stores will use cameras to passively read your interest and engagement with their products and displays. Alexa can listen to changes in your voice, and coupled with AI, detect a change in your health, or engagement with a product, song, or device. As of this writing (June, 2021), a company called Alfi Inc. announced they have forged a deal with Uber and Lyft to provide 10,000 screens to drivers that show ads and other content, while using cameras and facial expression algorithms to determine passenger engagement. These are to be rolled out in Miami, Florida, to start, but will expand to other cities. Consumer choice, consent, or opt-in is not part of the conversation at this moment (for instance, could you specifically request a rideshare car that *does not* have this technology for scanning your face and reactions? Can the screen be turned off at the rider's request? Since drivers make money using them, would that affect the rating they give to riders?). On June 29, 2021, a Silicon Valley startup called Worldcoin, which counts Sam Altman, the Co-Founder of Y

Combinator, as part of its founding team (backed by Andreessen Horowitz, Reid Hoffman, and Day One Ventures) claimed they will be able to provide a Universal Basic Income and democratize access to cryptocurrency by having one exchange it in response to a scan of their iris (part of the eye).[85] This has a number of privacy groups completely concerned[86] —if someone hacks your credit card, or digital account, you can get a new one. You cannot easily get a new eyeball.

In certain countries, these types of data gathering have become more and more commonplace, and the use of that data less regulated, and more obscure to the person from whom the data is being collected.[87] Further, even though certain types of data are protected (e.g., your financial details while you are shopping online at a store), other biometric data are not (e.g., facial recognition within their physical stores). Even worse, if there are regulations in place, these rules regarding your sovereignty do not follow you around, they track and morph with the jurisdiction. Your ultimate self in this scenario is not really sovereign. It depends on how you and your data are viewed across arbitrary lines drawn across the globe. One has to ask how meaningful those geographical lines are given that the data we are speaking of exists in a purely digital form. Soon, humans may as well.

This foretells of an increasing geopolitical versus individual tension regarding neural rights.

DO WE NEED NEW RIGHTS?

If you believe that these things are true:
- Each human being has the right to mental privacy;
- Each human being has the right to own and control their brain's data and identifying features;

- Each human being has the right to freedom from mental manipulation (their free will);
- A person's brain, mind, psyche, and memories are part of one's very Selfhood, and neural rights can be considered human rights...

... then we should be arguing for *a new code of ethics surrounding neural data* and define human rights' principles that will safeguard them. Those principles should be drafted and reinforced by governments of the international community, and followed by independent adjudicators. They should also be willingly undertaken by companies in the private sector, especially as there really are no geographic boundaries any longer within which companies operate.

WHAT SHOULD GOVERNMENTS DO?

There are several ways to protect our neural rights. These might follow one of several models, well described by Rafael Yuste, one of the founders of the NeuroRights Initiative at Columbia University.[88]
Your data could be considered as your:

1. Digital exhaust – these are the breadcrumbs you leave behind on websites and social media platforms you engage with. The most rigorous digital personal rights are the EU's GDPR. Despite the right to privacy being considered a human right under EU law, it doesn't come close to protecting what might be considered the most consequential data you produce.
2. Medical data – in the U.S., medical data is specifically protected by the Health Insurance Portability and Accountability Act (HIPAA), whereas in the EU, it is protected to varying degrees by the local implementation of GDPR. Still, medical

data has fairly strong legal protections around its ownership and sharing.

3. Genetic data – within the EU, genetic data privacy also comes under GDPR, but as with medical data, specific rules are drafted and deployed by country. A law called the Genetic Information Nondiscrimination Act (GINA) in the U.S. prohibits employment and health insurance discrimination on the basis of your genome sequence. But it does not necessarily impact its collection or security, merely its use.

The alternate and most comprehensive viewpoint is that your neural data, given it may be considered to be commensurate with your Selfhood, should enjoy the highest levels of protection. These rights should be considered a territory of Absolute Sovereignty, and should be protected as human rights. Your neural data should also never be used against you—either to discriminate, or to hold you accountable for thoughts you have, even if you have committed no actions (otherwise, we could embark on a Minority Report-like future). And neural writing technologies for forced coercion should not be legal.

Yuste and other scientists and ethicists around the world consider that neural data is commensurate with Selfhood, and should be afforded the highest protections. This is a position I agree with, especially as the unimagined consequences and potential misuse of this data will only increase with time. Chile has written a Neuroprotection Bill of Law into its new Constitution. OECD nations have outlined a privacy framework that touches on ideas such as security, collection and purpose limitations, and consent. For the reasons discussed above, these probably do not go far enough. Even the United Nations High Commission in 2018 defined a Right to Privacy in the Digital Age. From General Comment 16:

"Effective measures have to be taken by States to ensure that information concerning a person's private life does not reach the hands of persons who are not authorized by law to receive, process and use it, and is never used for purposes incompatible with the Covenant."

Others have advocated that a section on neurorights be added to the Universal Declaration of Human Rights. And two existing U.N. treaties, the Biological Weapons Convention (BWC) and Chemical Weapons Convention (CWC), could be updated to limit abuses of brain technologies. These documents did not anticipate future technologies, and weren't written in such a way as to cover all emerging weapons, or misuse of neurotechnology. Because neuroweapons do affect the brain as a biological system, the BWC could be modified to include prohibitions against the use of weapons to target the nervous system.

WHAT SHOULD BUSINESSES DO?

Sell privacy, not people.
The first point of merit is that if your only business model for making money and scaling is predicated upon taking people's data without consent or obfuscating its collection, selling it to the highest bidder, or using this data without the data producers having knowledge about how it is to be used, perhaps your company needs a new business model. In fact, consumers are becoming increasingly concerned about their privacy, data, and how that data is used, and one can make money protecting and securing data, rather than exploiting it. Pavel Durov, CEO of Telegram, noted that in January 2021, when Facebook changed its privacy policies around the supposedly secure WhatsApp platform, the industry noted the largest mass digital migration in history. In 72

hours, Telegram gained 25 million new users, including heads of state. Durov feels that people no longer want to exchange their privacy for free service and "no longer want to be held hostage by tech monopolies that seem to think they can get away with anything as long as their apps have a critical mass of users."[89] Some companies have already built a business model around collecting and selling individuals' data. There are ways to potentially migrate this to privacy-centered models of data protection, by charging a premium for privacy as an upgrade, and using this as an interim business model till such a migration is complete. This also increases transparency for the consumer regarding how their data is used. We don't want this freemium model to be the only ethical business model surrounding data—the risk is that we will create a future in which only the wealthy can purchase their privacy and have security, and that is not the distributed, abundant future we want.

Do not simply exploit addiction centers in people's brains to sell a product.

Marketing can light up reward circuits in the brain.[90][91] Although advertising is a necessary part of the growth of a company, if utilizing knowledge about a person's attention and engagement is solely to engage in neuro-manipulation (as an example, see social media algorithms),[92] by driving the addiction centers in people's brains, then perhaps the company would be better served by a different product or business model.

Security and privacy should never be an afterthought.

In any system in which there is a flow of data, the security and privacy should be included from the ground up. That includes the cryptography used in the application layer (the part that faces the consumer on their edge device), the security of the architecture of the data fabric and network used to store and exchange data, as well as the permissions used to authenticate users that come onto the network. This should hold for both data producers and requestors.

Do not collect or store user data if you do not have to.
This should be self-explanatory. Given the proliferation of cheap computing and chips that outstrip the pace of Moore's Law,[93] AI at the edge (on local devices facing the consumer or user), not just in the cloud, is being enabled. Do your intelligence and sense-making at the edge when possible, so you decrease the risk of a consumer's data being exploited or hacked.

Incentivize people not to give up their neural data and be transparent when they are.
Many consumers are unaware of the consequences of giving up their data. For example, gamers using neurowearables in the AR/VR/XR (mixed reality) spaces believe that sharing these datas might aid in developing neural signal-based control devices or more realistic avatars, creating more authentic gaming experiences. But these things could be accomplished at the edge, without giving up control over this sensitive biometric data. Other consumers may participate in neuromarketing schemes. If there is good reason to share their neural data (e.g., with pharma companies for biomarker research), then:

1. Build in guardrails for transparency (what am I giving up, how will it be used?);
2. Make a user's data rights easy to understand, and not embedded in 5-point font legalese;
3. Use systems that enable the consumer to transact with their data (e.g., give them the means to sell their data to requestors they think may use their data for a legitimate cause), and
4. Provide a system for expiring authorization, or the means for actively revoking authorization to use that data.

There is another real concern for consumers that are incentivized to sell their data. Are we creating a two-tiered market system in which those who have less power or means are incentivized to sell their data while those who can afford privacy do not? If you liken your biometric data to one of your organs, you can see the parallel. There are people without means who feel pressured to sell a kidney. What about their brain's data? We do not want to find ourselves in a world in which neural privacy and security are only the right of the wealthy.

Erase people's data if they revoke consent.
It is possible that a user may consent to data collection or data use and then change their minds. A mechanism for deleting their neural data, along with their memories and any downstream constructs such as a simulacrum or data-based avatar, should be built into the system and easy to activate.

Define your ethics early.
Create ethical frameworks as soon as you create your company. Draw your lines in the sand. Every time you create a new product or service, use that framework as a barometer. Does your product and updated business model comport with the guidelines you originally set? Or is there the potential for misuse, which would violate your ethics? If so, don't do it. Or find ways to build in the protections.

Constantly assess whether your incentives align with your ethical principles.
As your company scales, is your growth strategy consistent with your ethos? Is it consistent with the principles of doing no harm? Of not violating a person's Selfhood and right to mental privacy? Find ways to reward others in the system for doing the right thing,

and form alliances with other companies that maintain this ethos. Create an ecosystem that is aligned with this vision.

Constantly pressure-test your system.
Get periodic feedback from neutral third parties, cybersecurity professionals, and consumer groups to see if you are meeting your security and neural protection goals.

CONCLUSION

"Nothing was your own except the few cubic
centimeters inside your skull."
– GEORGE ORWELL, 1984 (1949)

In 1949, even in the dystopic world of George Orwell, he conceived of a world in which your brain and your thoughts were the last bastion of personal privacy. But the idea that your thoughts are yours may be a passe phenomenon in today's technological landscape.

We live in a world full of enormous possibility thanks to advances in technologies to read and write to the brain. We have also created systems in which the brain can connect to computers, machines, robots, and other actuators outside itself, giving function back to those who have lost it. There is also an entire augmentation movement in which brain-to-machine interfaces are being used to confer new senses and capabilities to humans—superpowers, if you will, forcing the brain to evolve under this new pressure. It is therefore incumbent upon us to anticipate the other edge of the sword of technology, its potential for dual use. Unlike many other kinds of tech, the brain and its neural code go to the very fabric of who we are. It is integrally associated with our Selfhood and autonomy. This makes it deeply important and timely to consider the ethical ramifications of this technology now. While we are already having conversations around technology companies tracking our digital breadcrumbs and where our attention goes, data generated by the nervous system and read by passive systems, including neurowearable devices and cameras, might easily capture unconscious thoughts and feelings. This makes this data especially vulnerable to violations of principles of consent and privacy. Already, algorithms are being deployed to influence our thoughts, behavior and attention. Neurotechnology is more insidious and more powerfully invasive, potentially altering free will. In the face of this, principles of transparency, autonomy, privacy, consent, self-determinism, and free will become extremely important. The right, also, to mental augmentation and cognitive enhancement also becomes a concern—if only the wealthy and powerful have access to it, it will further accelerate a process of human-directed evolution that we are already seeing, one that exacerbates the fracture lines between the haves and have-nots. Privacy and freedom from manipulation might also become the purview of the rich. I propose some methods by which governments and businesses might consider the implications of this technology so they can anticipate them and act within strong ethical frameworks. We are only as strong as the most vulnerable amongst us.

DIVYA CHANDER

Divya is an anesthesiologist and neuroscientist who also works at the intersection of human health, data, technology, and data security. She is a practicing physician, Singularity University Chair of Neuroscience (and Faculty of Medicine), and Senior Nonresident Fellow at the Atlantic Council GeoTech Center. She leads two companies she cofounded during the pandemic—Lucidify, a remote brain monitoring platform for the detection of delirium, and Plexxus, a company building the platform to support telehealth and the world's connected global immune system.

Divya also served on a NASA task force for COVID-19 and has co-chaired and directed the post-pandemic global health initiative for OneShared.World. Her research interests center around mapping consciousness, how consciousness will be altered by human augmentation, and how mapping consciousness in humans may enable us to recognize it in nonhuman, intelligent beings (both on and off-planet, e.g., through initiatives like SETI, where she joins the newly formed SETI Complexity Group). She also works in space life sciences and medicine.

HUMAN RELATIONSHIPS: THE ETHICAL HEART OF RESILIENT ORGANIZATIONS AND COMMUNITIES

MEI LIN FUNG

To write about ethics at work creates a dilemma for me—company "ethics" triggers an unhelpful reaction for an out-of-the-box, intuition-driven digital pioneer like me. Ethics has a bit of a scolding judgmental quality... as if lawyers bring out the "ethical contract" you have to sign as you join an organization, and human resource specialists insist you attend boring, preachy and totally forgettable "trainings" so they can tick off their compliance check boxes. The dilemma is reflected in this question: should we only be concerned about ethics at work?

Or might we abandon the old-timey preachy judgmental attempts at claiming authority through pronouncements by a nameless person from "Department X." Come fly off the page with me to examine ethics (and work) starting from multi-millennial western and eastern foundations.

Ethics, by Aristotle,[94] is practical rather than theoretical... it is not only a contemplation about good living, because it also aims to create good living. It's therefore connected to Aristotle's other practical work, the Politics[95], which similarly aims at people becoming good.

The study of ethics is about how individuals should best live, while the study of politics is from the perspective of a law-giver, looking at the good of a whole community.

Confucianism[96] transcends the dichotomy between religion and humanism, considering the ordinary activities of human life—and especially human relationships—as a manifestation of the sacred, because they are the expression of humanity's moral nature (xìng 性)... Confucianism rests upon the belief that human beings are fundamentally good and teachable, improvable, and perfectible through personal and communal endeavor, especially self-cultivation and self-creation. Confucian thought focuses on the cultivation of virtue in a morally organized world.

I live the confluence of these as an ethnic Chinese born in Singapore who learned English in the UK as a child, grew up in Singapore, and went to college and worked in Australia before the US where, after an MBA at MIT, I worked at Intel in the heart of Silicon Valley, California where I've lived ever since, building relationships in the technology world over the past three decades.

In 1988, I joined Oracle Corporation, the fast-growing relational database company, at the invitation of Tom Siebel who went from being Oracle's top salesperson to head of product marketing, and then started a Direct Marketing Division because he had a vision. He'd talked with businesses about how to use a relational database (preferably Oracle's) to improve their relationships with customers. Oracle's customers were business-to-business, selling to other businesses, not consumers. Back then, over 30 years ago, technology was extremely expensive—just as electricity was when introduced 100 years ago. Companies hired VPs of electricity to work out how the company's functions could be transformed by the use of electricity.

Similarly, in the 20th century, technology was not part of the lives of ordinary people, before the Internet had brought it into people's homes, schools, and libraries. It was a tool for Fortune 500 companies to automate functions like banking, oil production, manufacturing high ticket items like planes, cars, heavy duty machinery and goods involving high volume unit production.

Oracle had already signed up most of the Fortune 500 companies, a sales cycle of 12–18 months from first contact to shipment of Oracle software and signing the technical support contract. Oracle had been growing revenue at 100% a year, and to continue to double, had to learn how to shorten the sales cycle to close deals with 10's of 1,000's of small and medium-sized enterprises (SMEs). Tom Siebel decided that, as no Oracle client had yet managed to use our relational database competence to improve customer relationships and grow sales, Oracle itself would have to be the guinea pig. This was the genesis, over 30 years ago, of Customer Relationship Management software, now the fastest growing category at 14% a year and expected to reach $80B annually by 2025, with 91% of companies over 10 employees using a customer relationship management system.

WHAT HAPPENED TO RELATIONSHIPS THOUGH, AS CUSTOMERS WERE "MANAGED" BY BUSINESSES?

Technology is obedient—doing only what you program it to do. When we incentivize CEOs to increase the stock price, to grow profits, they no longer prioritize measuring what matters to humans. Should we be surprised to suffer deteriorating customer relationships, employee relationships, community relationships, neighborhood relationships and family relationships?

This systemic disconnect cannot be solved by an ethics "rule-book" or "compliance police" because people do what they are paid to do. Seventy thousand Wells Fargo employees were ordered to disobey

US and California laws and sign customers up for new accounts without the customer's consent, or face being fired. Should we be surprised that the rate of suicide among middle-aged men has been rising and that political polarization linked to income inequality has also been rising for years? When businesses ignore human relationships and treat people like "widgets," it becomes natural to evolve from a world in which "fairness" requires that CEOs look their employees in the eyes and see them as full human beings, to one where "fairness" is dismissed as "socialism" as if it's a dirty word. A few behind the tech curtain get to set the rules, the rest fume.

In the past 20 years, it's been acknowledged that we need to satisfy "our customers," even while technology has been misused to generate unwarranted bonuses for managers in the following way. How do we know we're satisfying our customers? Commission a customer satisfaction survey? Who will write the survey? Well, the Customer Service Manager of course. But if many customers give a high score, the Customer Service Manager gets a bonus, and probably many others also, all the way up to the CEO.

So, what are the obvious incentives? Write a customer satisfaction survey that generates a high score!

Only ask questions that customers will answer positively. My husband was very angry at a home appliance warranty service, having stayed home from work for 14 separate visits before the appliance was finally replaced. Two months later, he was called by a third party interviewer to ask some questions about whether he was satisfied. Eager to tell what went wrong, he waited for the right question—it never came. He asked the person doing the survey—how can I tell you what went wrong? I am so angry I'm cancelling the service, but you have no place for me to give you this information. The third party surveyor said, "I am sorry there is no place in this survey for me to input this information about your dissatisfaction, and that you are canceling the service because of it." From the point of view of those who would earn bonuses, this was a great survey. From the point of view of the shareholders and the people making the products and doing the services, nothing had gone wrong. Oh, you've fixed that problem? Bonus-hunters will find other ways to game the system, and blame the technology, scapegoat those who cannot defend themselves.

This is corporate death by a thousand cuts, technology is being misused in ways that are killing companies and destroying people by allowing individual greed to thrive without being balanced by corporate objectives—where the personal incentives override organizational and relationship priorities.

I worked with Oklahoma State University on a leadership program for a Cash Collections group situated in Oklahoma City. Their problem was $1B in past due accounts receivables which they just couldn't collect. The low-level collectors were easy to scapegoat—high school educated, with no reporting mechanisms for them to explain the failures to executives so eager to blame them as lazy and incompetent.

No collector, no matter how hardworking or competent, would be able to collect on invoices for which:
- The contract was not signed;
- The purchase order had not been issued by the customer;
- The product had not worked as promised;
- The services had not been delivered.

The collection company's top executives threatened that, if the $1B was not collected, they would all lose their jobs and the entire cash collections department would be outsourced to India. No manager had asked, as I did, what are the causes of non-collection which are the responsibility of other departments like Legal, Accounting, Product Marketing, Sales, Product Development, Customer Services and Technical Support?

There was no way within the company to surface the ignorance of its CEO and management team who allowed prejudice, blame, and incompetence to flourish amongst lawyers, MBAs and career managers. For a major corporation's top management to see that they are being misdirected to scapegoat a group powerless to defend themselves, in order for managers to justify bonuses earned when "technology" presents only the data that gives the managers their bonuses and none of the data that shows the full picture of what's going on.

Income inequality is not just unfair, it's made possible by leadership tolerance of operational incompetence and prejudice, whether conscious or not.[97]

Digital trails and forensic audits today could expose these pathetic episodes of small-scale corruption which can be found in dark corners of many a company to justify bonuses to people who either don't know what they're doing wrong, or know it's wrong and do it so they can keep their jobs. Unfairness and inequality results in part when in a networked world where the information management and executives' need is available, but they don't know how to ask for it, nor even what to ask for. New leadership competencies for a networked world must be practiced, with focus on the skills that work, emphasized and highlighted to be learned by others.

It might seem easy to blame individuals—why would you do that: issue an invoice when you know the sale has not closed, when a contract is not signed? But each individual must pay their mortgage, keep food on the table for their families, and when everyone around you is doing it—then it seems ok. I would be stupid not to do it—this is how the company works.

Working on ethics at work is like trying to address climate change by going to a rally. It makes you feel you are doing something, but real change requires new approaches.

In 2009, the US Department of Defense perceived the

partisanship surrounding the implementation of the US Afford-able Care Act and wanted to look at the future of health from a long-term perspective. The US Air Force Surgeon General Bruce Green initiated the Federal Health Futures project for which I served as Socio-Technical Lead. In that project, we looked at what had changed with networks and what new models of leadership are needed. We developed "Networked Leadership Competencies," which, if they had been applied, could have helped reduce the sys-temic risks to project implementations.

NETWORKED LEADERSHIP COMPETENCIES

Competency	Illustrative Characteristics
Ability to Develop Trust	Establishing rapport and building relatonships to culti-vate a culture of trust.
Active Listening	Suspending judgement to hear and understand the thoughts, ideas, emotions and perspectives of others.
Agile Thinking	Thinking systematically with the ability to shift para-digms and perspective, with the capacity to incorporate and appreciate multiple viewpoints.
Aspirational Future-based Leadership	Leveraging strategy, operations, tactics, to harness the collective wisdom with an inspiring vision of the future to help realize a shared vision of a desired future state.
Building Partnerships	Ability to form and sustain effective relationships across organizational boundaries in pursuit of mutual interest.
Creating Learning Networks	Curious and open to new ideas and information with a willingness to share and reflect systematically on the insights arising and the ability to cultivate, encourage and sustain these behaviors with others.
Creating Conditions for Success	Offering resources, building capacity, anticipating and removing obstacles, to provide clear strategic intent and sustained focus.
Developing Present Moment Awareness	The ability to see everything as new; including mature self-awareness and freedom from the fog of preconcep-tions and groupthink.

Net Centric Communication	Smart and progressive use of information technology to optimize resource use in a complex and rapidly evolving environment.
Network Goal Setting	Ability to see and shape the combined results of multiple objectives pursued by multiple stakeholders and the capacity to define and negotiate coherent action plans.
Network Leadership	Vision and ability to reach across traditional organizational boundaries and to engage through collaboration and mutual interests.
Resilience	Ability to bounce back from adversity. Patience and will power to persevere in the face of setbacks.
Thriving in Complex and Ambiguous Environments	Ability to tolerate ambiguity and act effectively under conditions of uncertainty, able to recognize patterns and adapt quickly and iteratively as new signals emerge.

These competencies build on human relationships and help us realize that networks are very powerful, but only if built upon an underlying foundation of trust. And trust requires human relationships to be built, where trust is earned and kept and, if damaged, is repaired.

In the end, how we set up incentives in our society drives behavior. If the incentives are set so that people earn huge amounts of money by "gaming the system", manipulating technology and creating progress reports where there has been no progress, then we have exactly the system we live in. The foundations need to be changed, and leaders are calling for systemic change around the world.

Rarely do such imperatives motivate global practices, except when recovering from global conflict and the fog of war.

On October 15, 2020, Kristalina Georgieva, Managing Director of the International Monetary Fund and recently President of the World Bank Group said:

"Reflecting on the dramatic change in the world over the last year, I paid a visit to Bretton Woods, New Hampshire, where 44 men signed our Articles of Agreement in 1944. Our founders faced two massive tasks: to deal with the immediate devastation caused by the War; and to lay the foundation for a more peaceful and prosperous postwar world."

"At the conclusion of the conference John Maynard Keynes captured the significance of international cooperation as hope for the world. "If we can continue... The brotherhood of man will have become more than a phrase," he said.

"As we look forward to welcoming Andorra as our 190th member, the work of the IMF is testament to the values of cooperation and solidarity on which a sisterhood and brotherhood of humanity is built."

"Today we face a new Bretton Woods "moment." A pandemic that has already cost more than a million lives. An economic calamity that will make the world economy 4.4 % smaller this year and strip an estimated $11 trillion of output by next year. And untold human desperation in the face of huge disruption and rising poverty for the first time in decades."

"Once again, we face two massive tasks: to fight the crisis today—and build a better tomorrow."

We know what action must be taken right now. Develop resilient organizations and communities, built on human relationships.[98] The future we need must be fueled by friendship, founded on trust, and fueled by institutional transformation. Otherwise, our future will be "gamed to death" by the fog of technology.

MEI LIN FUNG

Mei Lin is Chair and Co-Founder with Vint Cerf of People-Centered Internet and an early pioneer of customer relationship management (CRM). She keynoted on Decade of Digital Transformation at the World Bank IFC Global SME Financing Forum, presented at the World

Economic Forum Digital Economics 2017, was the socio-technical lead for US Federal Health Futures initiative and convenes Digital Cooperation and Diplomacy network. Mei Lin is also Chair of IEEE Industry Connections Social Impact Measurement committee and founder of the Global Help Desk.

She has worked at Intel & Oracle, then as Douglas Engelbart's business partner and organized the 2008 Program for the Future. Mei Lin was on the 2016–2018 WEF's Global Future Council on Digital Economy and Society and a member of the Precision Medicine and Digital ASEAN working groups. She holds a BSc in Math ANU and MBA in Finance MIT.

BUSINESS ETHICS:
ALL EMPLOYEES, EVERY QUARTER

NATHANIEL CALHOUN

The phrase "business ethics" is uncomfortably similar to "office party," "friend from work" or "corporate culture." In each case, the thing of value (the friend, the party, the culture or the ethics) is devalued by its association with work and business. Depending on your cultural background, it may be common to evoke business as a valid excuse for unethical behavior. After someone betrays you or causes harm, they might say, "It's just business" or "Don't hate the player, hate the game."

For some businesses, it is sufficient to work within the bounds of the law. This, however, can create an appetite for locating jurisdictions where the law may be flexible, out-of-date or little enforced. Equating "law-abiding" with "ethical" doesn't leave much room for ethical thinking—especially at the frontiers of social and technological progress. It's common for people to criticize government for being slow, out-of-date or inefficient. This criticism runs loudest around matters of technology, especially when public servants are uninformed about how fast growing or newly popular technologies work.

Businesses frequently operate in spaces not yet anticipated or covered by regulation—creating things not yet understood by the law or causing types of social and ecological harm that are not yet regulated, measured or even visible. Because of this, business ethics ought to be one of the most fascinating and relevant arenas of ethical thought. The potential for business ethics is extraordinary. The potential to show leadership in society by developing and honoring business ethics is limitless.

That potential will not be realized within a given business unless the business undertakes a deliberate effort to create and protect its own ethical culture. Often, raising ethical concerns can feel unsafe for employees around the world. Employees who raise ethical concerns may find themselves painted as traitors, persecuted as whistleblowers or prosecuted to the full extent of the law. This holds true for the those who clean the office or those who close the deals.

Many business cultures ensure that it feels uncomfortable to swim against the stream of profit maximization or to raise complex concerns that might force a costly shift in strategy. A first pass at improving this situation might prompt a search for a quick or easy fix: would an anonymous suggestion box do the trick? A corporate retreat? How about an external ethics consultant or a new partnership?

Cultivating an ethical culture is like cultivating any other skill—it takes practice, and the benefits from coaching and success really become visible only after new habits are created and become dependable.

From 2013 through 2017, I helped to launch and mentor more than a hundred different startups in Silicon Valley in a program focused on creating solutions to large global problems. A primary goal within this program was creating a safe space for ethical concerns to be raised while holding an expectation that these concerns be factored into the design of products and business strategies.

At this program, we convened innovation specialists from

organizations like UNICEF and Amnesty International, monetary theorists and currency designers, experts in the cooperative and circular economies, race and gender activists and scores of investors, designers, engineers and businesspeople.

Our support to the startups was contingent upon their willingness to rise to the ethical level that was set, collaboratively, by this richly experienced community of practice. We did everything in our power to mitigate against the possibility that a well-intentioned team would cause harm or damage to society or the planet. This meant invalidating the idea of "accidental" harm or "externalities."

We also made sure that individuals were celebrated and appreciated for sharing ethical concerns, even when those concerns resulted in delay or the "failure" of a popular idea. Within our culture, it was better to have people leave the program after 10 weeks with no viable company, than to leave the program with viable companies that would be neutrally beneficial or net harmful. However, spotting potential future harms is not easy.

The fastest way to create safety for employees to identify potential harms and to address the difficulty of the exercise is to make the spotting of potential future harms into a team sport. It's not realistic to ask an individual leader or employee to anticipate and avoid all the harmful ramifications of her product or company.

Digital and global products and companies, by their nature, impact numerous cultures, economies and ecosystems—many of which will be unfamiliar to individual decision makers. But, when teams of employees are held accountable, together, (and recognized together) for their ability to avoid negative impacts on society and the planet, then individuals want to do their best and simultaneously benefit from the diverse perspectives and synergies that come from team discussion.

Design thinking has taken some steps towards avoiding harmful outcomes—but it often focuses so closely on the customer or the user, that it crowds out other groups who might be impacted by the product (or indeed impacted by the users of the product). So, for example, design thinking is great for determining how to make a smart surveillance doorbell irresistibly purchasable. But it doesn't ask itself: how does this impact the neighbors, the homeless, or the power balance around law enforcement and human rights?

Fortunately, the skill required to spot the risk of future harm is beneficial to strategy and operations in general: complex systems thinking. Unsurprisingly, complex systems thinking is hard to describe with a checklist or a short essay. Instead, new books and research are emerging that help to address some of the economic blind spots that are most predictive of unethical behavior.

CREATING AN ETHICAL CULTURE

Step One: Create a cadence of regular (quarterly?) harm-spotting meetings across all levels of the company.
To escape a business culture that normalizes silences about ethical concerns will require sustained commitment. For ethical thinking to become a part of workplace culture, it must be incorporated into the regular quarterly rhythms of the business and throughout all layers. This institutionalizes the commitment and signals to employees that it is not a one-off initiative. In many companies, it will take time for employees to believe that such initiatives are not covert and potentially dangerous loyalty tests.

These meetings convene small groups of employees who would be reasonably comfortable in discussion together, based on their levels of authority. Meetings can be brief (45 minutes or less) and focus on topics that help to: underscore the reasoning behind the company's effort to involve more people in setting ethical culture, raise employee awareness of known ethical concerns and then open space for new observations and thoughts.

Step Two: Create and announce appropriate incentives and recognition for employees who make strong contributions within the meetings.

The goal is to become aware, as a company, of potential harms before committing them in the normal course of doing business. When employees successfully help the business to avoid or minimize such harms, it needs to be recognized throughout the meeting structure and with other incentives. Scheduling meetings is not enough to break down the usual secrecy around harms and potential harms. Where harm-spotters previously feared to speak out, or hid behind anonymity, strong ethical culture rewards and promotes them for speaking up.

Step Three: Meeting groups can introduce background reading and concepts where educational levels permit.

For workforces comfortable with economics and finance, it may help to read recent works on complexity economics—a new evolution within economics that is influenced by today's breakthrough mathematical concepts. This discipline starts from the reasonable assumption that economics should not continue to rest on mathematical formulas and conceptions that are out-of-date and no longer fit for purpose.

For a general audience, a better starting place would be Kate Raworth's Doughnut Economics, which is both eye-opening and accessible. Like complexity economists, Raworth sees cause for concern in typical "intro to economics" textbooks; but her set of solutions is wider and embraces complexity economics within itself. Doughnut economics is a great starting point because governments and businesses around the world are beginning to adopt its frameworks as a means of improving policy decisions and long-term goal setting.

Doughnut economics will gather more momentum because of the way that it conjoins leading environmental science (as represented by the planetary boundaries concept created at the Stockholm Resilience Center) and consensus-based social science, governance and public health policy as represented by the Sustainable Development Goals.

Step Four: Create rigor and structure around ethical discussions so that teams improve upon their own method.

In the following pages, I'll introduce a simple framework that can help during these meetings. It's adapted and simplified from a framework that I used in Silicon Valley with startups that spanned many industries. The framework itself draws upon hard won lessons from the international aid and development community—especially the digital development community—where in spite of clear good intentions, poor planning or poor risk mitigation can result in embarrassing failures. When used most effectively, this framework helps a team to clean up their business plan before they need to pitch to management, investors or the public. It's discrediting to be oblivious about the harmful consequences of a team's idea. Using this framework carefully can help a team to keep their credibility and to keep their impact positive.

This framework is built around three filters. Imagine each filter is a mesh of questions and considerations that help to catch certain categories of harm. A proper water filtration system has different layers, like charcoal, ceramic plates and mineral sands, which catch and remove bacteria, heavy metals or other contaminants. The filters below have a similar ability to catch and remove harms such as reinforcing corruption, discriminating against people with physical disabilities or polluting rivers.

Each filter is described below along with a few conversation starters to help groups get started. Your company, or teams within your company, can easily modify the filters and questions below. These are by no means exhaustive or complete, but many teams have found them a helpful starting point. The goal is to encourage close observation and careful conversation—if a team focuses on just one question for an entire meeting, it's safe to assume they're embracing the spirit of the exercise.

ECO-PLANETARY FILTER

It is not easy to be a business with a net positive impact on the health of the planet. The more that scientists study our smallest ecosystems or our largest planetary systems, the more we find that they are impacted by human behavior and industry. For businesses striving to be part of the planet's healing and thriving, it helps to answer questions like these:

    a. What are the waste products that result from your way of doing business and how are they disposed of?

    b. For companies that manufacture physical goods: what are the end-of-life options for your products? Is it possible, easy or desirable for them to be entirely recycled or re-used? (Consider introducing "cradle to grave" or "life cycle assessment" practices.)

    c. Many companies are one or two steps removed from bigger environmental polluters, such as companies within their supply. When you look at your supply chains (upstream or downstream), where do you see the greatest concentrations of environmental harm?

    d. Are there certain species, ecosystems or habitats that are stressed, harmed, depleted or destroyed by the way your company operates? If there were just two or three species that would have a big problem with your company, what would they be and why? If there was one ecosystem or body of water that would have a big problem with your company, which would they be and why?

e. Which of your business practices contribute the most to the rising temperatures of the planet and how are these practices correlated with the growth and success of your business?

SOCIO-CULTURAL FILTER

Sometimes the way that a business operates contributes to the suffering, exploitation or exclusion of certain groups of people. This goes beyond simply beating the competition in a fair fight—it involves the risk of discriminating against or disadvantaging groups of people in ways that are unhealthy for society. The questions below can help to prevent such impacts:

a. Are there any groups of people that typically oppose or object to your way of doing business? If so, what are their concerns and are these being addressed over time?

b. Many companies depend upon partners, suppliers or customers who create considerable social harm, perhaps in another country or region. When you look at your supply chains and larger business ecosystem, where do you see business practices that are increasing conflict between people or the suffering of particular groups?

c. Does your company or your company's advertising or your company policies make people feel inadequate or angry? How could your company have a more unifying or connective impact on society?

d. How inclusive is your business culture and how inclusive are your business products and services? In what ways does your business ignore or even devalue the cultural experience of different races, genders or cultures?

e. What future of work is your business involved in creating? When is it creating good jobs and when is it creating jobs that are unreliable, dangerous, degrading or low paying?

TECHNO-REGULATORY FILTER

As technologies develop, new forms of harm become possible. As regulations fail to keep pace, new forms of harm emerge that are technically legal. The questions below help teams think about cutting edge issues at the intersection of technology, law and commerce.

a. How does your business engage with surveillance technologies in the workplace and with regards to your customers? Where does your business remove or compromise privacy?

b. What does your business do with the different data and information that it gathers about customers, employees and partners? How easily understood are your company's data policies and who is least likely to understand them?

c. Are there any parts of your business, your supply chain or your partner ecosystem that benefit from looser regulation in different countries? Under what circumstances does your business consider it necessary to take advantage of places with different labor laws, environmental laws or tax codes?

d. How is your business using or planning to use artificial intelligence? Under what circumstances does your company use or plan to use "predictive" algorithms? What is your company's approach to replacing existing jobs and functions, customs or practices with AI-driven or automated systems?

CONCLUSION

To become an ethical company requires the creation and maintenance of an ethical culture. This, in turn, requires staying up-to-date about the areas of harm and exploitation that accompany new technological developments, shifts in labor market dynamics or larger cultural issues. There's no reason to wait for these conversations to happen externally amongst your competitors, critics or customers. When the harm is incipient or apparent, when emotions and the reputational stakes are high, you've already missed the opportunity to lead well.

If all layers of a company build the habit of scrutinizing operations on a quarterly basis, harms can be reduced while motivation and worker empowerment may rise. A thorough, persistent approach to cultivating business ethics may even become an avenue for making corporate culture more meaningful and engaging—even if the risk mitigation discussions outlined above aren't particularly well suited to office parties.

NATHANIEL CALHOUN

Nathaniel is the Co-Chair of Impact Faculty at Singularity University, where he helps to guide strategy and messaging around using technology to solve the world's biggest problems. He has guided hundreds of impact-driven start-ups and specializes in technologies that help in low-income countries or challenging environments. He formally advises several start-ups in the space of AI, blockchain, big data and community currencies. His company, Code Innovation, works with INGOs and government agencies to use digital technologies for productive conservation and biodiversity preservation. He speaks publicly and consults to private sector actors on technology trends as well as strategies for using digital democracy tools for improving corporate culture.

Photo Credit: Nick Otto

EFFECTIVELY MANAGING A DIVERSE ORGANIZATION RELIES ON ETHICAL LEADERSHIP

ISABELLE RINGNES

The corona crisis threw leaders across the globe to their ultimate test. Suddenly we skyrocketed into a future we thought we had years to plan for. But amidst the chaos, it presented an opportunity to start thinking about what leadership means as the world becomes ever more volatile, uncertain, complex, and interconnected.

The companies that emerge from a crisis with stronger teams and revived business models are the ones whose leaders' decisions have been guided by their values and their actions inspired by their ethics. The kind of leadership that sets a new standard for the future.

At Equality Check, our mission is to drive equality in the workplace through transparency. We empower people to support their employers in becoming more diverse, equal and including. Diverse companies are highlighted time and time again as businesses that generate more innovation, increase profits, and are considered to be more likely to become successful in an exponential, convergent future.

Effectively leading a diverse workforce relies on ethical

leadership. The following core values prove as important when leading through a crisis as they do when managing a heterogeneous workforce. Being open and transparent, inspiring by leading by example, treating everyone with fairness, and displaying empathy.

BEING TRANSPARENT AND LEADING BY EXAMPLE

When COVID-19 hit, leaders around the world stood in awe watching as a wave of disruption flooded their core business. First, survival instinct spilled into every boardroom and executive group. Second, tough decisions had to be made at speed while struggling to stay afloat. Third, as the wave started regressing and we started seeing clearly again, the ones who survived stood looking at what remained. What they saw spoke volumes to the core ethics of their leadership. In the worst of cases they saw a battered organization, distressed employees and the remains of short-sighted decisions. What went wrong?

When a crisis occurs, the hunger for information is nearly insatiable. A leader's priority should be to communicate frequently, openly, and clearly to every stakeholder about how the crisis is developing and how it affects their personal situation. People follow and believe in leaders who are honest with them, who extend trust and take responsibility.

A few weeks into the corona crisis, a friend called me and told me she had just received a notice from her employer to go on temporary leave. Her employer, a prestigious consulting firm, also required the entire company to take a 25% pay cut. Because they had been transparent about the situation and communicated daily updates on how it affected each individual's work, most of their employees were understanding of the tough decisions that had to be made. However, a few weeks later employees learned that the company's leadership and investors had been paid sizable dividends, without informing them. Employees immediately felt deceived that they were left to take the hit alone. My friend told me that shortly after she noticed a shift in the company culture. From having been a company where everyone felt like a team, employees had started to disrespect one another, take credit for other people's work, and ultimately had started looking for other jobs.

As a leader, employees will look to and emulate your behavior, choices, and values. A leader should be transparent also when it feels uncomfortable. If they want to build an ethical company with trust and respect, they need to lead by example. A leader's actions communicate her priorities, and employees need to feel that they are valued.

BEING FAIR AND CHECKING YOUR BIAS

Ethical leadership entails designing for fairness. Being fair means seeing and treating every employee with respect, dignity, and ensuring that one provides equal opportunity for growth. It means impartial and just treatment, without discrimination. Fair leaders stimulate cultures where every employee feels safe, included, and valued. This may sound like corporate jargon, but because we're often unfamiliar or oblivious to the dynamics of different cultures, leaders frequently fail at instilling a culture of fairness. Not necessarily by intention, but as a result of unconscious bias.

We all have biases. We're born into a world in which bias and stereotypes are deeply embedded in society, which results in unconscious decisions that may present disadvantages for certain groups of people, often minorities in a company.

During the corona crisis, it was brought to attention following a conversation with the head of the Norwegian Gender Equality and Anti-Discrimination Ombud that pregnant women and older people were more at risk for being laid off than others. Employers unconsciously considered them susceptible to getting sick from COVID-19, and thus wanted to ensure their safety. The intention was most likely good, but it is not a leader's decision to decide one's destiny at work when the foundation of the decision is guided by an individual's physique. Equality Check launched a survey showing that at least 20% of respondents felt they had been discriminated against when they were laid off. Women cited gender as the most common reason, while men cited age. Several parents told us how they had been laid off with the reasoning that "because you have kids, you'll not be able to work as much as others without kids."

Leaders may make tough decisions with a strong intention to act in accordance with what is best from a business perspective. But this behavior is often short-sighted. Once they emerge from the crisis and are ready to welcome their employees back, guess what? They'll remember them as the leader who let them go because of their personal situations and individual traits and they'll be left with employees whose loyalty and trust passed together with the crisis.

Checking your bias is increasingly important as the workforce gradually becomes more diverse.

Leaders need to admit to their flaws and become self-aware of their thoughts and actions.

Before a leader makes decisions, they must ask themselves why they are making this exact decision and whether bias may be at play. A frequent everyday example could be that a manager tends to give women tasks that are more like support functions such as designing presentations or taking notes, while they hand men more visible and challenging tasks that in time may lead to leadership roles. They may not think twice about this in a given situation, it's just their unconscious mind guided by gender stereotypes assuming a woman is more esthetically gifted for creating presentations or attentive in a meeting to take notes, and perhaps they assume a man is open to take on risk and more prone to handle attention. The result of this biased treatment over time is that women and men aren't met with equal opportunity for growth under his or her leadership. Bias has largely contributed to and continues to maintain predominantly white and male executive teams across the globe.

Ethical leaders are inherently including and supportive of all their employees. Leaders who ensure everyone has equal opportunities to grow are the leaders who are able to tap into the potential of each employee and build resilient teams.

A resilient team is able to productively adapt to disruption and change, such as during the corona crisis. Building a resilient team means that all team members feel like they have a shared sense of purpose, direction and that they have a strong relationship to each other. Apart from just baring competence, a resilient team is also highly committed to protecting each other and to solving the problem at hand. In order to do that they need clear and transparent communication all the while feeling safe to provide their honest opinion and critical feedback.

CONCERN FOR OTHERS

Diverse organizations may present friction. This is a natural state as multiple cultures, perspectives, and backgrounds consolidate. It's a leader's responsibility to ensure the friction results in a productive dynamic as opposed to a hostile and siloed environment. This happens by enforcing a culture of mutual respect, empathy, and open-mindedness. This means encouraging and valuing differences in opinion, establishing effective ways of communication, and making sure everyone is heard.

A former colleague of mine had built an impressive career

despite her young age. As a result, she found herself being invited into boardrooms on the premise that she would contribute with her insights from her unique background. What she experienced is very common, especially for a young woman with a minority background. She found herself in a room with six middle-aged white men competing to dominate the conversation. She felt like her ideas were ignored, but once the same ideas surfaced by someone else at a later point, they were praised. When she read the formal reference from the meetings, she found that her contributions had been left out. She told me that she did not believe this was intentional, this behavior was the result of the established culture. Making sure everyone felt encouraged to voice their opinions was not a high priority. They were used to a culture in which the ones who spoke the most and the loudest were the ones worth listening to. They did not share her background, and lacked empathy for how she felt as the only young female minority in a loud room. An ethical leader makes sure everyone is heard and encourages differing opinions. But valuing a contribution is more than just letting someone speak. It means asking why and how and distributing credit where credit is due.

An ethical leader shows empathy for her employees and makes sure everyone is accounted for, regardless of the situation. A mundane example from a company I've worked at was how we would celebrate success. Our boss would plan a company party, and without thinking twice she had ordered hot dogs and beer for everyone. After the party, several employees left hungry because their religious beliefs, allergies, and personal dietary choices hadn't been considered. While relatively small, these decisions witness a lack of concern for the many people who don't fit the norm.

As our workforce becomes ever more global, diverse and interconnected, so will the demand for ethical leadership and diversity. We're heading into a world in which decisions will impact humanity for hundreds of years to come. In a technological future in which decisions are determined by seemingly invisible artificial intelligence built on biased, historical data, diversity and ethics are essential to avoid reinforcing our biases, flawed decision-making and worst tendencies overall. Consider the failures of unethical leadership and imagine how they will scale as we hand over our authority to AI systems in everything from our insurance, loans, hiring practices and even our self-driving cars. The way in which we govern and act in accordance to organizational values, doing the right thing even when it may stifle short-term results, and tapping into the potential of your diverse workforce through fairness and empathy are just a few of the things you should be designing for as a leader in the years to come.

ISABELLE RINGNES

Isabelle is the Co-Founder and Chief Evangelist of Equality Check. It is a platform for anonymous reviews about equality and diversity in the workplace, which supports organizations to improve diversity through a data-driven and evidence-based approach. In 2015 she founded TENK: a technology network for women aiming to inspire women and girls to lean in and contribute to shaping our world's future with technology. She has established two-yearly tech camps for young girls and spoken to thousands of girls around Norway to inspire them to choose technology.

In 2014 Isabelle cofounded #Hunspanderer, a social movement addressing unconscious bias and gender stereotypes reaching millions of people and engaging CEOs across Norway's most influential companies to champion the issue. In 2016 she won a national competition granting her a scholarship to attend Singularity University where she is currently faculty on diversity. Isabelle has been named one of the 100 most influential people in Nordic Tech, one of the 50 leading women in Tech in Norway, and top Inspiring Fifty women in tech in 2016 & 2019. Isabelle also produces a podcast called Future Forecast and wrote the best-selling book *Hvem Spanderer* about unconscious bias.

EMBODYING ANTI-RACISM
WORK IN BUSINESS

ROGER COURAGE MATTHISEN

This essay aims to deliver tools and habits to take ownership of your own personal leadership and to embody your anti-racism work regardless of your organization's willingness to commit to this essential agenda or not. You can still create and inspire change yourself.

The killing of George Floyd in Minneapolis sparked a global protest movement, not just against the tyranny and brutality of the police in the United States against Black people but also against the inherent and unjust racial structures in the American society as a whole. And the global uprising is also a loud and clear NO to oppression and equality worldwide—a clear call to action to dismantle racism on all continents and in all societies. We see the same call to action regarding #StopAsianHate. The United Nations has also adopted a resolution to make 2015–2025 the international decade for people of African descent to strengthen economic, social, cultural, civil and political rights for people of African descent and their full and equal participation in all aspects of society. Thus, the awareness regarding anti-racism work is growing and there are clear call to actions from civil society, business and the political sphere.

The face and appearance of racism have shifted throughout history. Although it doesn't look the same as it did 200 years ago the dynamics and mechanisms of inequality and oppression are the same. An example of this is how debates about immigration, assimilation, and multiculturalism tend to seem respectful but often serve to preserve the pillars of racial segregation both ideologically and practically—also known as neo-racism; where the construct of racism used to be premised in biology it has shifted to focus on culture or 'cultural differences.'

Lastly, we have to remember that when we're working with conscious and unconscious bias in anti-racism work, we can act on this change work from a personal as well as a systemic approach. Which approach is more fitting depends on the situation and circumstances. But regardless of approach, it is seldom fruitful nor correct to call people out as racists and sexists because this is rarely the case. Committing sexist and racist actions does not make our identity racist. We are not our actions; we are much more than that. And the conversation about race is hard enough as it is without it being derailed by people fleeing from the fear of being identified as a racist or sexist instead of them accepting responsibility for their conscious or unconscious racist or sexist actions and joining in taking action against these unfair norms and behaviors.

PERSONAL LEADERSHIP

Working with the human potential in diversity and inclusion work is an ongoing process encompassing the fact that people are dynamic and in constant change. To gain the highest effect of our investments and efforts against anti-discrimination in organizations several important factors which have gradually been uncovered through research and evidence on a global level must be included in our work with diversity, inclusion and anti-racism.

To mention a few, these factors include getting numbers on the table—measurements of progress and effect, ensuring real equality in the recruitment process, staff retention, talent management, involvement of underrepresented groups throughout the process of creating a level playing field, as well as one of the most important aspects, holding management and boards accountable.

Although I only mention a few factors you probably already sense that it will require massive efforts to just getting to the finish line within these areas. But there is a number of habits and actions that we as practitioners can use systematically. Habits and actions that will help us in reaching our goals faster and that no matter how long the road is or may seem in reaching our subsidiary goals, will have a great impact on our change efforts, strengthen our credibility and furthermore support us in our work processes when it becomes difficult or when we encounter resistance.

Leading the fight against racism is for you who wishes to strengthen your anti-racism work through personal leadership, regardless of if you are self-employed, work in management, do volunteer work, are a government employee, or work in the private sector. It is always possible for us to step into character and lead the way forward, also when we make mistakes.

SETTING YOUR OWN STANDARDS FOR ANTI-RACISM AND ANTI-DISCRIMINATION WORK

Combatting discrimination is at the core of diversity and inclusion work. So put it on the agenda as an independent development process and goal in your work with KPIs, performance appraisals, and annual performance reviews. Several analyses show, that when we put equal treatment as an independent point of attention with our union representatives and managers, in our performance appraisals and staff development interviews, we strengthen several important factors simultaneously such as employee retention, anchoring of feedback loops and involvement of underrepresented groups.

HOLDING MANAGEMENT ACCOUNTABLE FOR REPORTING BACK ON PROGRESS AND DELIVERING ON COMPANY OBJECTIVES

Not delivering on diversity also means missing out on a stronger profit for your company. Among much research in the last decade a report from McKinsey shows us that "In the case of ethnic and cultural diversity in 2019, top-quartile companies outperformed those in the fourth one by 36 percent in profitability." If diversity has the potential of delivering such a significant boost in the annual revenue, in addition to higher innovation and employee satisfaction rates, there really cannot be found any excuses not to deliver on diversity. If management has not built in diversity in the KPIs of your organization there are several approaches to nudging them to do so. Start by building a library of statistics showcasing companies whose revenue and innovation increase when diversity is at the core of their business strategy. The correlation between these factors across the globe cannot be denied and will serve as evidence in your pursuit of implementing diversity as a part of corporate strategy itself. I will also go further into the approach of building this library in a later chapter.

You can also focus on bringing in experts in the field of diversity for short seminars, workshops or choose the more diverse partner when collaborating with external teams or companies. This will help you start the conversation and build a base of peers who will stand by you in demanding accountability from management in delivering on diversity.

Even if your organization is dragging its feet in establishing a Diversity, Equity and Inclusion (DEI) strategy, you can still choose to do so yourself. Besides personally leading the way by holding yourself accountable and taking action, you will also be able to showcase what the process means for you, and what the greatest impacts are. Hereby, you will be a source of both empirical knowledge, as well as an inspiration for others regarding what personal leadership means to you when it comes to anchoring change in your organization.

SHOWCASE YOUR MISTAKES. AN INCLUSIVE WORK ENVIRONMENT IS ALSO A VIVACIOUS LEARNING ENVIRONMENT THAT PROVIDES SPACE FOR MISTAKES

Discrimination manifests itself as inequality. Differential treatment means unequal access to power, influence, opportunities and decision-making. Structural discrimination is the reproduction and reinforcement of the differential treatment through cultural norms, codes, and learned behavior in society and within the system structure. Behavior, particularly, is central in working with anti-racism because discrimination occurs and develops through action—or lack thereof, whether consciously or unconsciously. In this way, we all adopt the behavior. This is inevitable as we are all a product of the society we live in. When it happens to you show the way forward by what we at Courage Institute call "common humanity." Meaning, that through our mistakes we discover and acknowledge our own and common humanity.

So be brave enough in showcasing your mistakes and use them as part of the learning process for you and your network. It does not have to be a serious error but could just as well be an email where you by mistake excluded someone through choice of language, or maybe you made a decision where those affected by the decision were excluded from the decision-making process and didn't get the chance to be seen and heard.

When you dare to showcase your mistakes you tell a story to other employees within your company. You tell a story, that we, as humans are not perfect. You also create a work environment where others dare to open up and share their experiences regarding discrimination. As managers and role models this practice will have a major impact because only when there is a general perception that inequality is being acted on, will the most vulnerable and marginalized employees feel safe and confident enough in sharing their experiences.

ACQUIRE FURTHER EDUCATION

If all of us already possessed the skills and knowledge necessary in combatting discrimination and creating an equal and just society, you would not be reading this contribution. In addition, language and the international community are experiencing rapid change due to globalization and the development of technology. Algorithmic bias is a factor that we to a greater extent have to be aware of and take into account. From a European perspective, the free movement of workers in Europe in addition to these challenges all require improved cultural understanding within business. This factor will be a challenging task for Europe moving forward towards 2050 because European societies to a high degree are dependent on the ability to attract and create bright minds and qualified labor. Just as we across the planet have gradually recognized that we must listen to and involve science and research in relation to the climate crisis, it is also imperative that we to a higher degree recognize and involve science and research in combatting discrimination and racism. With relevant education within DEI, you will stand strong and on firm ground in this field.

CULTIVATE YOUR COACHING SKILLS
AND PROVIDE MORE USEFUL FEEDBACK

A big part of anti-racism work is preparing people to willfully adopt the agenda and act on it. However, motivation and willingness are qualities that mature differently from person to person. Your ability to play others well and equip them in taking a larger personal leadership responsibility is crucial for a high success rate in working with anti-racism. This pertains to your collaboration with management and the board, current employees as well as new employees, who have to learn to be part of your organization's culture and norms. Practice with someone with whom you feel safe. A good practice is the "first, second and third position exercise": imagine a dilemma you have been dealing with, or an issue you will be exposed to through your work with diversity and inclusion and anti-racism. Imagine the person who you have been—or will be in dialogue with. Reflect on the conversation. First from your own perspective—this is the first position. The second position is from the person with whom you are conversing. The third position is the detached perspective, also called the helicopter perspective. When you allow yourself to be in the first and second position first, then the third position will give you insights into how you can improve your coaching skills by asking the right questions at the right time.

BE CURIOUS ABOUT THE PEOPLE WITH WHOM YOU DISAGREE WITH

We so often land in the trenches and deadlock situations and debates when the topic is anti-racism. Prevent and avoid the traps by being curious about the people with whom you disagree. This practice necessitates insight, empathy and understanding for both yourself and for the person (second position) you are in dialogue with. Try asking yourself these self-reflective and honest questions to retain dignity and worthiness for both parties: "Is this helpful? I might be in the right, but is my way of communicating the message helpful in this moment in reaching common ground?" If your answer is no, consider if dialogue right now is even necessary—and if so, how do you retain dignity and worthiness for the other person? With that said, be aware of your own personal limitations. If you experience that your opponent or counterpart is not sincere in having a genuine and honest dialogue, and the person is not able to retain your dignity and worthiness, stop and respect your own personal boundaries. Invite for dialogue at a later time when you have been introduced to more facts and knowledge on the subject. The most immense and powerful changes come about through a surplus of energy and willingness, not through coercion and penalty.

BUILD A LIBRARY OF STATISTICS AND KNOWLEDGE

In Diversity, Equity and Inclusion we work with social and human values in organizational development both on a personal and structural level. Resistance to this work is often to dismiss initiatives on the topic by highlighting assumptions of the insignificance or the unmeasurable aspect of the value created even though these assumptions often tend to be based on anecdotes, assumptions and biases. E.g., in retail where you have some parts, you put them together and sell the product and the output is clear. It can be a challenge to measure what the concepts of belonging and inclusion delivers to a company if you do not have the tools or know what indicators could be valuable to examine.

However, there are massive research, empirical knowledge and data worldwide, which present hardcore numbers underlining the advantages of working with inclusion, diversity and anti-racism.

Getting used to maintaining a library full of statistics and knowledge can be very beneficial to the work. Use either digital notes you share across devices, or an online project management software such as Trello or Podio. Remember to make a short description of the sources filed or highlight numbers and knowledge from the source you particularly want to pay attention to. This makes it easier to look up the needed information the next time you want to make use of a certain quote or result of a particular analysis. To navigate by norms and assumptions instead of seeking more knowledge is natural to humans when we act or choose a certain behavior. Therefore, it is important for us who work with anti-racism that we credibly and factually are able to present new knowledge that contributes to expanding the perspective and bring about change to our old norms and presumptions. Last but not least, remember to be generous with your sources i.e., sharing these with your colleagues. When you play others well alongside presenting new knowledge you increase the probability of recognition and acceptance of this new knowledge.

TAKE GOOD CARE OF YOURSELF

Working for equality and equal opportunity and treatment of others, can at times feel and be overwhelming because in some areas the journey is still very long. This is partly also because some myths and assumptions are more persistent than others. Resistance to DEI initiatives may be expressed as anger, aggressions, irritability or carelessness on the receiving end and prompt attacks on your work or character.

It is very beneficial to make use of qualified sparring, coaching or supervision in your work and also to combine it with the practice of mindfulness. Mindfulness is a method consciously used to gain control over the quality of your life. One fundamental principle of mindfulness is that we try not to run from unpleasant emotions but that we instead practice being with our emotions attentively, self-lovingly and present. This will to a great extent often contribute to us being able to calm our minds to a place where we feel connected and grounded in ourselves. Both, when things are going well, when things are difficult, and at times where we have to take a stand and draw a clear line. And perhaps most importantly—that when we practice being present with ourselves and in the present moment, we cultivate a greater awareness and sense of self. This becomes a positive and personal feedback loop that strengthens our ability to cope with our circumstances and act in accordance with our needs.

I wish you a good fight and meaningful change work.

In solidarity, Roger

 ROGER COURAGE MATTHISEN

Roger has more than 16 years of experience teaching, coaching and mentoring in interpersonal communication, diversity management, inclusion and anti-racism. Roger is the Director of the Courage Institute and former member of Parliament in Denmark. He launched the first anti-racism action plan for a political party in Danish history in May 2019. He is educated as an MBSR instructor (Mindfulness Based Stress Reduction) at master's level and holds a bachelor's degree from CBS in business economics, communication and English and a profession bachelor's degree from the Danish National Theatre School in acting, theatre history and communication.

He is a boardmember of European Network Against Racism Denmark, Chair of the board of ECO 6 Nordics, Boardmember of African Chamber of Commerce Scandinavia and a Member of Parliament for SOAD, State of The African Diaspora.

WE OWE IT TO OUR GRANDCHILDREN TO FIX THE BUGS IN THE HUMAN ALGORITHM

YNGVAR UGLAND

We are at a second beginning. We have created algorithms, and we have told them to be fruitful and multiply. As a result, they have filled the earth.

Do you catch the similarities in the wording with Genesis, the opening of the Bible? Then you might have guessed that the question at hand is whether the algorithms will "subdue earth and rule every creature that crawls upon it." That remains to be seen. Also in Genesis, it is said that God created man in His own image. Shouldn't we make sure that algorithms, similarly, are created in our image? I think so. I think we need to create algorithms in the image of humanity.

Algorithms are the foundations of logical computer programs. Artificial intelligence (AI) is the phenomenon when algorithms can learn based on the data we keep feeding them. As these self-learning algorithms make more and more decisions for us, it is of utmost importance that we feed them with the right data. The right data isn't necessarily historically "correct data." Keep in mind, for example, that historical data shows that most CEOs are men, as are Presidents of the United States of America. And this is reflected in datasets. In order to change datasets to the right ones, we need to identify our own "right." This is what I like to think of as our "human algorithms." We need to develop those human algorithms before we pass on the data to the machine algorithms.

I would like to tell two stories. The first one is about how a human algorithm with a bug led a person towards the wrong goal, due to a failure to capture his inner core. In the other one, an inner core and a true purpose of a team made the difference between extinction and survival during times of crisis. These stories are highly relevant because the latter is from the trenches of the pandemic but also because we live in a world where algorithms—which run all the apps in our lives from social media to work software and entertainment—make up a threat to our minds.

Why do these topics occupy me, you might ask? Well, I am a technologist by trade, and I spend a lot of time exploring which opportunities tech gives us and how we can use that to shape a better future. I am also a human being. And I am a technology optimist. I am a technology optimist for the sole reason that I am a humanity optimist, i.e., I am optimistic about the future of our human algorithms, which is the condition for my optimism in technology (machine algorithms).

However, a few years ago, I had to make a confession to myself. I had become an addict. I was powerless. I was addicted to my phone. I brought my phone from one room to another, even if it wasn't in my pocket. If I didn't know where it was or how I could get a hold of it, I got really anxious. I also slept with my phone. And, if you can believe it, more often than not, I checked my phone before I said good morning to my own kids. But admitting this to myself was the first step. Now I have been on rehab. I started with phone-free hours, then phone-free days. I don't know if I will ever have a phone-free life. But now I control it rather than it controls me.

Addiction is good business. Tech companies have engineers working entirely on one purpose: to make us addicted. The measure for success is dopamine released in our brains. We live in a world where search engines make us dumber. A world where image-sharing apps make us feel uglier. We live in a world where, in truth, it only takes 144 characters a time to make up a perfect platform for mockery and harassment. Are we about to become "enslaved by our own minds" through technology?

To not become enslaved by our own minds, we need to take our minds back. Which brings us to the question: what does it constitute to be a human being? For one, it is our ability for meta-cognition, an ability unprecedented by any other species throughout time. Computers don't possess this ability either. It is the ability to have a thought process about our own thought processes. To see ourselves from the outside. Secondly, it is imagination. This ability to see things before we do them. To envision paths for the future as well as for simple actions before we actually take action. Thirdly, it is our conscience. Our inner compass for distinguishing right from wrong. These three things are core to being human. We can see ourselves before we act, compare the scenarios against desired outcomes we have already imagined, and have our conscience confirm whether it is good or bad. This ability comes with a responsibility. It is up to us not to blame conditions, but to make decisions. Responsibility is a wonderful word: response-ability. Even despite unfavorable conditions or ungrateful circumstances, we have the ability to choose our own response. We can pause and reflect on our response. To put it in the lingo of a tech person: in the program of your life, YOU are the programmer. Thus, we can search inside ourselves to find out: who is it that I truly am and what is it that I truly want to become? My true self, my purpose, my why—my reason to exist.

Have you ever done the gravestone test? Using your imagination to envision your own funeral. Many years from now, what is it that people will say when they share their memories of you? What you were like? What you were really about? And ultimately, what is it that is written on your gravestone? Most likely you would want something deeper than "she was a diligent technologist" or "he was an early-bird fisherman." Let me exemplify by telling one of the stories I promised. This one is about Batman. I had a coach at the time. I knew I was a good performer in my job, but I wanted to become a top performer like I had been in a previous job. I asked my coach for advice. She listened and asked me to take a piece of paper and make a drawing. I am not good at drawing, but it was our eyes only. "Now draw yourself as you are today in the lower left corner, and then draw yourself as a superhero." I drew myself as Batman. "Also draw an arrow from the lower left to the upper right, and in between draw all the obstacles, the things that impede you from becoming the superhero." So I did (see drawing in the figure below. So much for "for your eyes only"). I was excited to get her input on how to remove those obstacles. But instead, she said "Yngvar, when I hear you talk about those obstacles, I can see how your eyes sparkle, how your energy rises. They are not obstacles. They are your genuine passions. You should find a job where the obstacles are an essential part of the job. Maybe that is the only thing you should do, if such a job exists, from the way I hear you describe the obstacles."

So, I had to change jobs. I had to become Batman. It wasn't as easy as I make it sound right now, but it was the right thing to do. I had to do the right thing, not strive to do the wrong things right. I also did the gravestone test. Typically, a person has many roles, and you can do the gravestone test for each one of them. I am a single parent, and that is my most important role. But for now, let's focus on my professional imaginary gravestone where it would say something along the lines of: "a technology dreamer" or "a crusader of always changing the game." And although this may change over the course of a lifetime, my gravestone test from that time still stands. I am still "a technology dreamer and a crusader of always changing the game." The process helped me capture my inner core, eliminate the bug in my human algorithm and allowed me to become Batman.

My other story starts on March 26th in the year 2020. Norway had shut down due to COVID-19. Restaurants, bars, hairdressers, retail shops, almost all companies that depend on customers coming physically into their premises, except shops defined as "essential," lost all revenue overnight. The Norwegian Minister of Finance had just received the answer to an important calculation: How long will it take for shops to go bankrupt? The answer was despairing: for many of them, it would be a matter of only three to four weeks. Tens of thousands of Norwegian companies needed cash support from the government, and they needed it fast if they were to avoid bankruptcy. We are talking about the transfer of billions of Norwegian kroner, every month. The Minister had the cash for *Kompensasjonsordningen*, or the Norwegian Compensation Scheme, but he had no means to identify the companies in need and distribute the cash to the right beneficiaries. Money transfers between governments and private companies are typically handled by government administrations, such as the tax administration or the labor and welfare administration. But modifying their existing computer systems for this task would have been a complex and time-consuming task. It simply could not be done fast enough. In Norway, there is a long tradition for collaboration between the public and private sector, and hence a circle of trust between the parties. And since banks do the actual payments on behalf of government administrations, banks were the natural parties within the private sector to ask for help. The banks optimized their computer systems in order to help companies with loans, but not for government cash support. However, in one of the banks, there was a small, different team. You might have understood by now, that this is the team that I am fortunate to be leading now—after changing jobs to become Batman. We are kind of a SWAT team, almost like an odd little Silicon Valley startup within this circle of public/private trust. My team's usual (or maybe rather "unusual") job is to build new digital solutions from scratch. We used to do this through experimentation and rapid cycles of trial and error, trying and failing in the lab, before bringing it out in the real world. We like to say that "nobody fails as fast as we do." In this precarious situation, the government's attitude was to "heal the patient first and fill in the papers later." The detailed criteria of who could get support and how much, were not ready, and hence not passed in Parliament either. Although the details were not in, although it was said to be impossible to carry out in this short timeframe and although this was not really our job, we decided to give it a try. This was not an experiment, but we truly thought it was possible. It simply had to be. Failure was not an option this time.

If money sent to the correct accounts in three weeks was the necessary outcome (oh, and by the way: without getting hacked because this was the mother of all honey pots for malicious minds), we asked ourselves: which truths would have to be realized? Which conditions and circumstances would we have to create for ourselves in order to make this happen? Because clearly, normal rules, and normal conditions did not apply. One such truth was: this must be the simplest, but convincingly secure version of all possible solutions to this particular problem. Despite attacking the problem in a radically untraditional way, we immediately realized that we had to keep an enormous pace. Working around the clock became almost literal. Twenty-hour working days became the standard rather than the exception during the project.

Personally, I lost perception of time until my 12-year-old daughter asked me if I was still in a meeting, politely reminding me that it was almost midnight and that it was Easter Eve. That immediate feeling of not being present tore my daddy heart apart. Not that she minded staying up late. But three weeks later, the minister could go on TV and announce that money was on its way. There were many parties involved but all of them were very satisfied. Perhaps the most satisfied were my kids who got their dad back. But at the core of it all was this one small team, that through a deep sense of purpose redefined their circumstances, mobilized the finest in humanity, made the impossible possible and helped cause survival rather than extinction for thousands of companies, their employees, and their families. They showed that in the program of their lives, they were the programmers. And because circumstances were different than normal, they reprogrammed to avoid bugs. During this urgent project, we lived by that.

So, what is our purpose? Our purpose, our why, is that in everything we do we believe in creating a future where people have more peace of mind and where people and companies can do more of what really matters to them. Our WHY.

The way we do this is by fearlessly exploring how new technologies can create a portfolio of options for what might become this future. Our HOW.

We do this by building and breaking things in the lab. Our WHAT.

But neither WHAT we do nor HOW we do it was checked off this time. It was the essence of our WHY, the "peace of mind," the "sleep well at night" and the "what really matters" to people that were checked off. Because if companies went bankrupt, we would not create "peace of mind for the employees and their families," and not at all allow people to "do what really matters to them." During the chaotic and confusing times of the corona crisis, our purpose was our guide. Our purpose was our driver to embark on this trip through dire straits and stormy waters. And our purpose kept us fighting when there were not enough hours in the day and when it felt like the ground was dissolving underneath our feet. Our purpose made us dry our tears and go where our hearts truly lie. In a world where computer algorithms make more and more decisions for us and become better than us at a lot of things, we need to capture what is genuinely human, capture our inner core, our reason to exist—our purpose. As individuals, as teams, as communities and ultimately as humanity. This has changed the way I look at myself, how I look at human beings and how I look at what is possible.

I make no claim of being the discoverer of this. But through my stories I experienced it and I firmly believe this to be a universal law that should apply to everyone, at all times and under all conditions. And this is why I want to share my stories. The universal law should go like this: *We need to nurture our human qualities which computers don't have: meta-cognition, imagination, and conscience, and use that to find our true purpose, choose our own conditions and be the programmers of our own lives.* When that force awakens, it creates hearts of lightness. It mobilizes the finest in humanity. It shows the power of purpose. Just like our dearest child mobilizes an unconditional power in us and a devotion to doing almost anything for it, just like that: the dearest child of humanity is purpose, and that makes the impossible possible.

The bug in the human algorithm can be fixed, by finding our purpose and driving our own circumstances—being the programmers in the program of our lives. And the bugs in the human algorithm need to be fixed. If we don't fix them, we will get regression bugs. That means that the bugs in our human algorithm will be passed on to computer algorithms. A bug-free human algorithm is the foundation for creating the right dataset. This is the way to teach computers about humanity, to create algorithms "in our own image," by passing on such a dataset and let computers learn from that. We owe it to our grandchildren not to let them be born into a world where our minds are already enslaved.

YNGVAR UGLAND

Yngvar is an adventurer at heart. In his day job, as EVP of New-TechLab at Norwegian bank DNB, he loves to boldly go where no banker has ever gone before. Off-work he is a saxophone player, soccer coach and enthusiast, chopper rider, university lecturer, sailor, and aspiring author. But first and foremost: a single-parent to his wonderful children. Yngvar gets inspired by ambition and courage and by leaders that live ambition and courage. He holds teamwork and trust close to his heart. He loves to build teams that dream of shaping a better future. He is on a life mission to always change the game.

WHY COMPANIES SHOULD CARE ABOUT EVERYONE'S LOVE LIFE

DAISY LØVENDAHL

Before reading this essay, I want to invite you to do a small thing for me. Can you give me two minutes extra of your time?

Close your eyes. Take a deep breath. Allow yourself to inhale and exhale for a minute where you completely engage in the simple yet powerful action of breathing. One of the amazing things about your breath is that you do it 20,000 times a day without thinking about it. Just do it three times now while appreciating that you can.

Then think back of a time in your life where you really struggled. Where life was giving you sorrow, your career was falling apart, or you dealt with loss. What kept you going?

For the last ten years I have been the trusted advisor to many companies and people. I have held a confidential room for personal development, leadership coaching, couples therapy and the human need to understand oneself and live a good life. My experience tells me that what keeps people going in times of trouble is one thing. Love.

They say: my children keep me going. My wife. My husband. The responsibility for my great team and my wish to create positive impact. My sister who died and my promise to her that I will embrace life even deeper, because she is not here to do so.

Let me ask you another question. Think back on an amazing day in your life. A day full of joy, happiness and meaning. What happened on that day?

The stories people share when asked this question are beautiful. They talk about a day on the beach with their family. Their kids playing in the sand, grandmother on a chair in the shadow, and a salty kiss from their loved one. They talk about the feeling of making a difference and share memories of when someone said: "Thank you. I could not have done this without you"—whether that is a dyslexic child who read her first book or a grateful family who just moved into the house you designed and built. They talk about weddings and births and celebrations where "everyone I loved was gathered." They talk about long days with no plans with their best friend drinking coffee and listening to music. They talk about laughing with their team and going home to their family. They talk about love.

We talk about love, when life is hard, and we talk about love, when life is sweet, because love is fundamentally important for us. Research from Barbara Fredrickson shows that love and moments of connection create more happiness, more meaning in life and more psychological resilience as well as better health and improved longevity. Love is not just a nice feeling. It is essential to every aspect of a good life and being in good health. We might not think much about it on a normal weekday where we are busy at work, but we do, when life invites us to ask the bigger questions. Because humans are wired for love and connection. Wealth, entertainment, random sex, great colleagues, lots of amazing experiences are nice. But not essential. To love and be loved is just as essential as clean water, food and fresh air. So, when I talk about love, I talk about one of the most powerful feelings humans have. Maybe the feeling that defines us the most.

Love is a deep feeling that reaches from the generous love to the world and its people to the intimate love between a couple and the loving bond between parents and children. It is not a feeling reserved for the special few when we look at it from a scientific point of view. New science tells us love can change the way our DNA gets expressed within our cells and affects our health, vitality, and well-being. Our bodies can experience the emotion love even from a brief meeting with a stranger.

So, I am asking you to set aside whatever cultural messages you grew up with about love being only for family, only romantic or mostly sexual and reserved for your special someone and open up to the fact that love is also a supreme emotion happening in moments of connection. That feeling is the remedy for much depression, loneliness, and pain. It is that feeling that makes people survive wars and invent ways to clean the ocean and marry someone and give them half of what they own and their whole heart. Because love is what ultimately makes life worth living. Just like in the pop songs.

When we are out of connection and we do not experience love, we become more depressed, more stressed and more vulnerable to getting sick. We also do worse work. During the COVID-19 lock-down in the spring of 2020 I had so many people reaching out to me. They were desperately lonely and feeling like they were losing their minds at the same time. As one of them said: "My life is empty. It is just work stripped from every cup of coffee, smile and sense of belonging, and I feel like I can't think." I share this with you, because I want to make it clear that feeling love is not something private apart from your professional life. That is like saying the Sun has no relation to the Moon. Or the body no relation to the mind. That idea of dividing life up in two parts, work life and private life, is basically putting an unsolvable burden on us. From the day we formulated those two areas of life as separate, men and women have struggled to find balance and stress has become a challenge for many people that yearly costs billions in lost productivity and treatment. The more I have worked with people and seen the inside of people's lives, the more I am aware that it is time to acknowledge that life is a whole. People can handle a lot of work pressure, when they know the kids are doing good and their partner is happy. On the other hand, people fall hard, when they can't be everything they need to be.

At the same time as we know this, we act like we are completely unaware of it. We work until we break down from stress and our families break. We prioritize getting the next assignment ticked off and ignore our basic needs for activity and connection. We are too busy.

We need to create a new way, where people are being supported in living a good life as part of their work life. That means that companies and both private and governmental workforces must work from a completely different philosophy. That is the call to all ethical leaders.

Not just because it is good. Also, because it makes sense. Because people who experience love, who take care of their needs and dedicate themselves to their community and loved ones, do better work. Maybe not at the factory where work was just about moving things from a to b, but in a more technological world where thinking, creativity and dealing with complex situations is needed. It is time to act on a knowledge that has been described by the ancient philosophers of Greece who believed the good life "Eudaimonia" was a life with both purpose and happiness. A life that cultivated both the experience of meaning and pleasure, beauty, wealth, health and engagement in the society and political development of the country. The philosopher Aristotle argued that Eudaimonia was the goal for ethical behavior and all political philosophy. I am deeply fascinated by that idea because it links together all-important aspects of life and argues that ethics is living the good life.

That also means that it cannot be ethical to sacrifice work for love or the other way around. We must cultivate all of it. In the way we organize our society and in our individual lives. I find it worth adding to this that present day leading psychologist Martin Seligman who has made ground-breaking research on happiness concludes that there are five important factors to happiness. Positive emotions, engagement in something, relations, meaning in life and achievement. This means we should stop living a dilemma where we struggle all the time and start creating companies that don't just accept but reward a thriving love life with time for people they care about and engagement in their community. This also means it is time to take a bigger responsibility for what goes on outside of work. Or even better—kill the old idea that it makes sense to talk about work and private life as two different things. We could maintain that idea in the last century, but the technological development has placed a computer in the pocket of approximately every third person worldwide. That means there is no longer a border between being at work and being off work. We can work everywhere all the time. We can work without ever meeting our co-workers or even being in the same country or speak the same language. This completely changes our ways of being connected. Connecting is no longer bound to one place in time and space. It can happen on many different levels at the same time. Just like I talked to both my daughter sitting one meter across from me at the same table and my friend in Mexico while writing this.

This is both a gift and a burden. A burden when we deal with it without thinking about what kind of world we want to create. A gift when we use the technology to create even better lives for everyone. It all comes down to what the philosopher Sartre wrote about as a problem of the free will. We are free to make choices and that leaves us with a responsibility. Technology can empower relations, just as it can ruin them.

The problem is not technology. It is the lack of understanding how important love and relations are. It is the lack of willingness to take responsibility for what is "outside" work. But ethics is not about rules for how to do this or that at work. It is not about saying "what happens after work is not my responsibility."

Ethics in philosophy deals with the basic question: what is a good life? Ethics is about daring to try to answer that question and act accordingly. It is about taking responsibility that goes beyond you.

We need to free ourselves from the old paradigm of going to work eight hours a day and then having eight hours off before we sleep eight hours. We must understand that the freedom to do anything anywhere at any hour comes with the responsibility for then using our time wisely. In that statement I have a question for you. What does it mean to use your time wisely? I ask you this question because we all have a say in the answer. It is not already given. It is ours to create.

Personally, I believe that we need to be better at dedicating ourselves to one thing at the time. Work when we work. Be fully present when we are social. Take time daily to self-care, reflect and exercise. We need to acknowledge the value in spending time with people. Serving our community. Enjoying nature. Making love. Breathe. I believe we need to build an everyday life where there is time for all these things. It is not enough to be with the people we love in the weekends or go for a walk twice a week. We need to find ways to integrate all important aspects of the good life every day. When we do that and see life as one thing, where nothing is sacrificed for another thing—we become better at everything.

Love is a foundation for community and relations. We all want love, but we are not all particularly willing to create a nourishing culture for it. Therefore, I also believe we need to be more ded- icated to our relations. We talk about connection as something our phones create when a phone can merely create a platform for communication. We design robots that can act like lovers, so we do not have to deal with the difficulties of real people and take a step further into a world of convenience and a step further away from connection, because one thing is true. Connection, deep relations and lasting love is not convenient and easy.

Particularly not in our time, where both men and women in our part of the world can have sex without producing children, can make their own money and have all the partners they want. We no longer need relations or a village to have a life. For the first time in history, we have freed ourselves from needing other people to the extent where we can have sex, children and care without having relations. But we can't have love without engaging fully in someone else. So, we need to choose love. All of it. Also, the messy, difficult and demanding parts where people get sick, are unreasonable or we disagree. Even there we must choose to stay connected. Not because it is easy or satisfying or we can't get away, but because we choose to be there. With someone we love.

Taking this aspect of life into how we create our business and set up our life is radical. Not making a distinction between work and life and professional and private is daring. It invites us to create a work culture that is driven from values of love, community and positive impact. I think it is possible. Not by applying three specific things or making a hundred rules, but by embracing the value of love and connection. Rules can tell us when to shut down the computer or how many zeroes we must add to our calculations this month, but rules can't lead. And what we need is ethical leaders, that dare to act from these values and investigate in every single company how they can begin supporting people in being both dedicated to their work and dedicated to a good life.

Do you remember I wrote in the beginning of this essay that you breathe 20,000 times a day without thinking about it? Love works in a similar way. We love because we are human. We don't have to think about it. Love can happen to everyone. Every teenager on earth full of hormones is capable of falling in love. Every random wonderful meeting can create connection and the feeling of love. But building lasting, deep, intimate relations that will nourish your soul, make your body tremble with joy and fill your heart requires decisions.

And I wish for all of us that we invite in both the fleeting gifts of love that we can pick up along the way like flowers in the forest and that we cultivate the most amazing green houses with deep and loving relations. That requires one thing. The simple decision to create great circumstances for love to grow. Just like your breath will feel better, when you slow down and breathe all the way down into your lungs, your overall health, happiness and quality of your relations will unfold when you decide to give it a proper space to grow in your life. I can't think of anything more important to grow than love.

I would like to invite you to begin answering the ethical call for a good life in your company by thinking in three dimensions.

FOR LOVE OF THE WORLD

Whenever we as companies create something, whether it is a small gadget or a new marketing strategy, we should ask ourselves: how is this an act of love for our world and its people? By connecting the idea of purpose to love and the individual feeling of being a whole human living one life, we strengthen the ethical perspective and create companies that don't sacrifice people for achieving their big why. When we feel the love in what we do, we also dedicate ourselves deeper. That is why the most passionate people work without looking at the clock or thinking about the paycheck. That kind of work is ever rewarding and should be nourished.

FOR LOVE OF YOUR COMMUNITY

Our way of working is radically changing, and we need to be absolutely clear on which values we want to guide this transformation. From an ethical point of view creating a good life for everyone is essential and therefore we need to think companies more as communities with a social responsibility. We need to create a culture where connection can happen, where everyone is respected and cared for. Where community among co-workers, the possibility for being parents as well as achievers and time for taking care of the body are valued. Where we set aside rigid rules and instead use our creativity and wisdom to create individually adjusted ways to set up life so everyone can both dedicate themselves to doing their work and having a rich personal life. Without the old entrapment of being professional and private as two different things, but with a deep understanding of how to use technology to support whole lives. Not just because it is good and ethical but because it is also better business in the long run, where we avoid much stress and instead create happiness.

FOR LOVE OF YOUR SELF

In the center of your life, you always find you. Better make that a lovely meeting. If you live in a way where you are stressed out, unhappy and unwell you might think you are the only one who suffers, but you are not. Your lack of self-care becomes a lack of connection to others that decreases your capacity for love—and that spreads like rings in the water to the people around you. So, take care of you. Spend time every day on the most important things in your life. On being dedicated to what you do for a living and contribute to in the world. Take care of your body with deep breaths and activity. Spend time with people that you connect to. Make love when someone wants to share pleasure with you. Share a meal with a friend. Love.

DAISY LØVENDAHL

Daisy is a personal consultant, couples therapist, author and speaker. She is a columnist, podcaster, coach and trusted adviser to leaders, families, couples and companies. Daisy holds a Master's in Philosophy and Communication and is author of the trilogy *LIVE, LOVE and DIE*, which examines the existential questions in modern life. She is deeply interested in applied ethics and questions regarding exponential technology and how to create healthy relations, love, and connections in a world where intimacy and deep relations are more and more under pressure. She works to enrich the quality of life and relations, so everyone can lead a happy life.

Photo Credit: Rune Lundø

REHUMANIZE - THE MORE TECHNOLOGICAL WE BECOME THE MORE HUMAN WE NEED TO BECOME

LAILA PAWLAK

WE'VE GOT THE POWER

Imagine living centuries ago. In many parts of the world your future would have been predetermined at birth and your chances of impacting the outcome of your destiny very limited. Even less so your chances of changing the order of things in your community, country, or the world. People died from simple diseases, and many watched their children starve and lived in unimaginable poverty. The "good old days" weren't actually that good for the majority of people.

Today billions of people can make their voices heard in a global setting, protest on the streets with global media coverage and in virtual spaces without borders. Some of the most recognizable messages even come from children or young adults. Millions are cured from complex diseases and the average age is continuing to rise. You and I might very likely live to be 100 – or older.[99] We don't worry about food on the table, if our kids can go to school, or whether we have a place to sleep. Advances in technology and globalization have created possibilities for abundant innovation and we have taken advantage of that. Succeeded beyond any imagination of our forefathers – sometimes even ourselves. We have changed the world!

While this is true, it is only true for some.

You and I are privileged.

We know that. Or should know that. If and when we think about it, it's easy to feel guilty or give up before even starting anything, because what does it matter anyway? We likely can't make the world a better place all by ourselves because the challenges are simply too big to overcome.

That's where we're wrong.

Sure, we're not all going to invent the cheap water purifier that's going to allow the last 2 billion[100] people to also get clean water. Or cure the millions of people who are dying from preventable diseases. Or find a way to make the more than 4 billion people still living under authoritarian regimes[101] freely speak their minds. Or feed the last 10% of the world's population who are undernourished.[102] That however doesn't mean that we are powerless.

We have far more power than we think. Or dare to think.

You and I *can* change the world! One could even argue that we have a responsibility to do so. We impact the world and hence the future of the next generations every day by the choices we make. We do that by deciding how to spend our human currencies: attention, time, and money.

What and who do we grant our attention to? Our attention through (social) media, entertainment, education, reading, watching, and listening?

What do we spend our time on – both when we work and when we are off?

How do we spend and invest our money - both our own and those we are trusted by others?[103]

Which challenges we decide to take on and how we combined spend our *attention*, *time*, and *money* decide the future. This goes for us as private individuals, employees, leaders, and citizens.

DEHUMANIZATION

Let's be real: humans were not built for the lives most of us live today. We are adaptive yes, but fundamentally our brains and general physiques were not built for modern life.

Two main drivers have massively influenced the way we live today: technology and globalization. Neither is slowing down. On the contrary. Today is the slowest it will ever be. And it's making the tectonic plates of our lives move. All of them. Fast.

How we live, work, play, grow, explore, and evolve – individually and as a species – is changing faster than ever.

It seems like for every blink of an eye complexity has increased. And it has. As we develop our organizations and the systems of our world, we continuously increase complexity (and it wasn't that simple to begin with). Even what it means to be human is being challenged.

Technology has enabled us to explore the world – both digitally and physically – 24 hours a day. We can get pretty much what we want, when we want it.

And we want.

A lot.

Technology has accelerated global trade that would have made the Vikings green of envy. This growing globalization has allowed for us to get anything we can imagine we would ever want at cheap, convenient stores or delivered directly to our doorsteps. For businesses it has provided a global workforce at their constant disposal and a competitive landscape in which there is always somewhere to get production cheaper and more efficient. It has also created a flipside to our consumer-driven culture, where discounts and low prices have taken precedence over what goes on behind the scenes.

While it is relatively easy to highlight all of the areas where technology is improving and even saving our lives, we have a moral obligation to also explore the flipside of the coin. We've used technology with immense success in many ways, but we have not yet found the recipe to design a modern life where technology fully supports the human in us.

In our strive for growth we've allowed ourselves too often to take the human out of the equation. We've created jobs that are not fit for humans – psychically or mentally. We've made humans crave things that are not good for them, and we've created an insurmountable garbage patch of psychical and mental junk. We're on the path to forever ruining the ground we walk on, the air we breathe, and the water we live from.

For far too long we've spent our attention, time, and money on dehumanization.

EXPLORING THE DARK SIDE

Dehumanization is about disregarding or disrespecting humans. It's the undermining of positive human qualities, removing people's dignity, or subject them to inhumane or degrading conditions or treatment.

While it's uncomfortable (likely why most people prefer not to do it), let's investigate this dehumanizing flipside of modern life. We can do so through a generic model roughly dividing our lives into work time and personal time (i.e. the time where we are not working professionally) on the horizontal axis and low to high technology foundation on the other, i.e. if the time we spend is enabled by a lower or higher degree of technology. This model makes up for 4 different realms:

- Processed labor (high tech foundation, work time)
- Filtered living (high tech foundation, personal time)
- Manual labor (low tech foundation, work time)
- Raw living (low tech foundation, personal time)

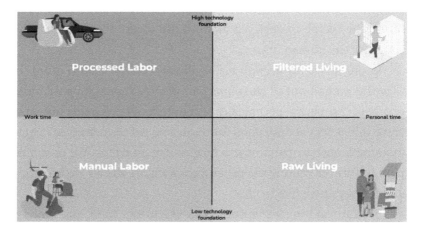

Take two different means of transportation as an example to explain the model: Catching an Uber in your personal time would fall into *filtered living* as the platform enabling your ride is based on a high technology foundation. The driver of the Uber would be performing *processed labor* as he receives his work – your ride – through an algorithm (high technology foundation). In other words, his or her work can be manual, but the anchoring of the job – what brings the job to life so to speak – is technology. Now imagine instead of an Uber you took your bike for a spin in your free time. This would fall into *raw living* as the technology foundation is relatively low. If your bike got a punctured tire and was taken to the bike shop the staff there would be performing *manual labor* as the technology foundation for them to fix your tire would be low.

With these four realms in mind let's allow ourselves for a while to explore the dehumanizing dark side we often tend to ignore. The first step towards more ethical lives is to sharpen our awareness – also when it's uncomfortable.

PROCESSED LABOR (HIGH TECH FOUNDATION, WORK TIME)

Most of us who will be reading this book rely on a lot of technology in our work every day. Meetings, platforms, systems, and most communication are anchored in technology. The pandemic accelerated this virtualization across the entire value chain and has forever changed how many people work.

Processed work is all of the work that is dependent on a high degree of technology and wouldn't likely be there without it. As we digitize more and more, we are transferring a lot of – what used to be - manual anchored labor towards processed labor. Think of take away food where restaurants rely solely on orders through larger platforms. Or online shopping where orders come though platforms and not from people walking into stores. From a dehumanizing perspective there are a number of red flags to raise from this development.

Besides the obvious reduction in human contact this development is largely favoring the large platforms and, in some cases, creates monopoly-like conditions which reduce customer sovereignty and leave little power to suppliers. Large corporations have been found to take advantage of their positions to avoid taxes, undercut the privacy of their users, exploit their suppliers, and create questionable work conditions where delivery drivers have to pee in bottles because they can't take breaks (not even sure how that works for female drivers?), work repetitive tasks under constant surveillance, and get fired by algorithms just to name a few.

Based on the rise of technology anchored work we've also seen an explosion of gig workers – an army of freelancers, who are not unionized or protected from poor working conditions, underpayment or loss of working capabilities. Big tech is even known to fight unionization among workers and freelancers. While some gig workers enjoy the freedom and opportunity to self-employ based on their unique skills many gig workers are not doing it because they want to, but rather because they need to. Their financial stability is low and many work far more to earn a living wage than what is recommended.

From the COVID-19 pandemic we know now that it is possible for many people to work remote in terms of effectiveness and a lot of companies are making remote and hybrid options permanent in line with the majority of workers' wishes (it is also saving companies a lot of costs on expensive office space, furniture, lunches, transportation, etc.). However, we need to prepare for new conversations in relation to working environments in people's private homes and make sure they are adequate. Working from literal closets, in rooms with no daylight, from beds and living rooms, and with interrupting children and animals are rarely ideal for deep thinking or in compliance with most work environment regulations.

Human bodies are designed to be moving around and not to sit in front of a screen all day. Sitting is meant for resting. The rise of obesity, loss of muscle strength and weaker bones as well as weakened immune systems can all be results from being inactive and sitting too much.[104] Digital eye strain is now an actual condition[105] and according to WEF all that time in front of computers, phones and tablets is affecting people's health. The majority of Americans now report symptoms of digital eye strain, neck, shoulder and back pain (36%), headaches (25%), blurred vision (25%) and dry eyes (24%). Worryingly, the percentage of sufferers is greater among young people. Some 73% of adults under 30 now experience these symptoms, suggesting a generational trend.[106]

As more work will inevitably be technology anchored in the future, we'll need to enhance our focus on personal thriving and social relationships as well as physical and mental health. We'll start to see companies moving closer into people's personal spheres and new conversations around human flourishing and organizations' responsibility for that will arise.

In short: Processed labor is on the rise and affecting all industries. A look at this development from a dehumanization perspective shows work that often includes repetitive movements or straining work positions with tasks delivered by algorithms. Often leaving little salary for the job done. It also enables massive players to earn a near monopoly status, and use this position to exploit workers and suppliers, avoid taxes, and undermine privacy.

FILTERED LIVING (HIGH TECH FOUNDATION, PERSONAL TIME)

When we look at filtered living, i.e. our personal time based off a high-tech foundation, we know now that many of the devices, algorithms, and platforms used by billions of people every day are addictive – and designed that way. We are always on. Phones, email, social media, whatever the digital drug of choice might be. While the percentage of smartphone users who would actually be classified as addicted is "only" estimated between 10-12%, around 90% in an American study fall in the category of overusing, misusing or abusing their devices. A recent study also found that 50% of teens feel that they are addicted to their devices.[107] Smartphones are even referred to by addiction experts as "the world's smallest slot machine."[108]

Every time we get a new notification, it triggers a dopamine release and gives us a mini "high" that is similar to our brain being on cocaine. The link to actual drugs might be more accurate than we would like to think.[109] For example, it looks like technology can also worsen memory. Studies show that the level of social media use on a given day is linked to a significant correlated increase in memory failure the next day.[110]

Preschoolers who use screen-based media for more than 1 hour each day have been shown to have significantly less development in core brain regions involved in language and literacy. Brain scans indicate that the more time spent on screens, the lower the child's language skills, and the less structural integrity in key brain areas responsible for language.[111] 9 out of 10 teens go as far as to say that spending too much time with technology is a serious problem facing their generation.[112]

Not only our brains are challenged because of our filtered living. The medical industry now mentions a term called "tech neck", which comes from sitting with our heads down putting stress and pressure on the back and spine, which is bad for posture and increases the risk of neck and back issues.[113]

The increased use of phones alongside the increase in stress (fun fact 2: those two statistics correlate) are also being blamed for the surge in sleep problems. Roughly 62% of adults worldwide feel that they don't sleep well when they go to bed. The CEO of Netflix once mentioned in an interview that Netflix' biggest competitor is not another streaming service – it is sleep. While we enjoy the entertainment and services of big tech we need to be aware that some are consciously competing against our basic human needs. No matter how evolved we have become, humans so far still need to sleep to function optimally. A staggering 80% of us would like to improve our sleep.[114]

We know New York City as the city that never sleeps, but actually most big cities never sleep and research is telling us that might not be so great for humans after all. 24 hour artificial light and constant noise is negatively affecting our well-being.[115] As we move into the cities for work and entertainment and with now more than half of the world's population living in cities (54%) up from 39% in 1980 (expected to rise to 68% in 2050) this is something to pay attention to.[116]

To add an economic perspective, people living in cities have more debt and spend more money. With money worries being one of the main sources of stress[117] it might not be surprising that city populations also have higher rates of mental illness than rural ones.

While we're living closer in cities, you're never lonelier than in a crowd as the saying goes. Loneliness is not unique to cities, but it is increasingly becoming more of an urban phenomenon contributing to the rising rates of chronic physical and mental health problems.[118] In countries like the UK and US they are even speaking of a loneliness "epidemic"[119] and globally a third of adults are feeling lonely.[120] Here are the devastating scienctific facts of why that is a problem: Loneliness and weak social connections are associated with a reduction in lifespan similar to that caused by smoking 15 cigarettes a day and even greater than that associated with obesity. Loneliness is also associated with a greater risk of cardiovascular disease, dementia, depression, and anxiety.[121]

With the increased urbanization we've also doubled down on eliminating space for nature. That too is challenging for humans (and obviously to other creatures living in and from nature). Science is clear on the positive impact of nature on humans – from positive impact on memory, decrease of stress and attention fatigue to increase of creativity and even generosity.[122] The loss of nature plays an important part in the dehumanization of people living in cities.[123]

In short: A look at the *filtered living* realm through dehumanization glasses portrays a modern civilization living - lonely and mentally strained - in mega cities, in nature deserted apartment buildings, behind screens, buying stuff with borrowed money.

MANUAL LABOR (LOW TECH FOUNDATION, WORK TIME)

In our tech-driven society manual labor is often romantizised in the picking-vegetables-on-an-old-farm kind of way. However, the truth is often quite different.

It is more likely than not that some of the food or items in your home today is made by slaves. Yes, you read that correctly. Slaves!

We're in the 21st century and we still need to talk about slaves. Estimates indicate that more than 40 million people live as slaves today – more than ever before in history.[124] That's twice the population of Scandinavia. And almost as many as in all of Spain or Argentina.

Unicef estimates that there are also 160 million children doing child labor - an increase of 8.4 million children over the last four years – with 9 million additional children at risk due to the impact of COVID-19.[125] The Ivory Coast – famous for it's wonderful cocoa beans used for the chocolate we all love - has an estimated 800,000 children working in the cocoa industry alone.[126] The exploitation of child labor and slaves is so bad that some chocolate brands are even starting to position themselves as slave free.[127] Many of us would obviously have thought that all chocolate (and all other products for that matter) were slave free at this point. But the list of products found to be produced leveraging some form of forced labor or child labor is too long: bananas, beans, nuts, palm oil, tea, coffee, sugar, beef, fish, electronics, rugs, furniture, shoes, clothes and the list goes on.[128]

Do you know where and how your purchases are made?

Likely not, but that might not be your fault. Fully understanding the supply chain for the end user is close to impossible. The supply chain of a company like Intel includes around 40,000 suppliers. No ordinary person would have a chance of seeing through that. People and organizations alike unwillingly buy millions of products every day that came about in a dehumanizing manor. As the need for medical gloves surged during the pandemic even a public organization like NHS in the UK came under fire for having purchased gloves from a Malaysian company under investigation for forced labor.[129]

Moreover, many products might be produced locally and sold as such failing to share their journey. Globalization has made it possible for fish to be caught in Norway just to be shipped to China to be turned into filets and then sent back to Norway and sold as local fish.[130] There are many examples like this where the end customer unknowingly and unwillingly not only supports cheap manually anchored labor (potentially even forced labor), but also adds unnecessary strains on the environment while thinking they're buying local.

Imagine how retail and supply chains would radically change if all products had to include visible labels indicating if any kind of forced labor was used to produce them; "This item is produced using slaves and child labor". For now, it's the other way around: labels telling customers if their products are ethically produced. Shouldn't we expect that to be the default?

Before we point fingers we need to own the fact that dehumanized labor is found all over the world – also in your country! Overworking, underpayment, disgraceful working conditions, trafficked women and children – no country is free from devastating stories.

Countries where wages are relatively low often have a high degree of manual labor. Unfortunately, many of these same countries place little emphasis on working conditions or the exploitation of land, forests, special local environments or cultural heritage.

The production of palm oil, soy, cocoa, pulp, paper, timber, and beef continues to rise, and more land is needed to continue to profit. Large corporations are destroying tropical forests at an unprecedented rate often with human rights violations as a side effect.[131]

More than half the world's tropical forests have been destroyed since the 1960s[132] and in 2019, the world lost an entire soccer field worth of primary rainforest every six seconds.[133]

Harvard's Pulitzer Prize-winning biologist Edward O. Wilson, estimates that we are losing 137 plant, animal, and insect species every single day. That's 50,000 species a year. Deforestation also impacts 1.6 billion rural people worldwide who rely on forests for their livelihoods — most of them live in extreme poverty already.[134]

To add to this devastating picture, you and I might even unwillingly be funding it all! Global banks have been found to invest billions of dollars into cattle ranches directly linked to illegal deforestation in the Amazon and palm oil operations, many of which are known to be involved in human rights abuses and illegal clearing of Indonesia's rainforest, to just name a few examples.[135] How we invest our money is crucial for the future we want!

In short: From a dehumanization perspective much manual labor is a disgrace to human progress. Modern slavery, exploitation of children, destruction of land, and deception of customers. This dehumanization cannot continue to be defended – neither ethically nor from a climate crisis perspective.

RAW LIVING (LOW TECH FOUNDATION, PERSONAL TIME)

When we think of low tech free time many of us would be imagining an off grid country house immersed in nature without the buzzing noise of devices and the city. Glamping (a merge between glamour and camping) is hotter than ever, with costs per night higher than some 5 star hotels. While that might also be *raw living*, from a dehumanization perspective it is not what most people around the world are experiencing.

Almost a billion people do not have access to electricity[136] and hence literally live in the dark. Many of those people are the same people who live in slums - usually informal, poor, overcrowded, and dirty areas of bigger cities. It's estimated that 1.6 billion people live without adequate shelter and that around 900 million live in actual slums and the number for this massive housing and health crisis is rising. 1 in every 4 people on the planet will live in a slum by 2030 according to Habitat for Humanity.[137]

As urbanization continues to grow the need for improved infrastructure is massive and unmet. According to the UN 2 billion people globally are without waste collection services, and 3 billion people lack access to controlled waste disposal facilities.[138] Imagine for a minute living just one week without a functioning toilet.

Raw living will for many people mean a life without proper access to schools, medical support, and basic necessities leaving them in a vicious circle of poverty. Combine that with unstable and unsafe living areas without a proper housing address and you're often also kept out of the formal economy. Approximately 2 billion people are under- or unbanked, leaving them vulnerable to forced labor and exploitation.

In short: From a dehumanization perspective, for billions of people raw living means a life outside of the established society, workforce, and economy. An unsafe life with little perspective of improved health, education or general living conditions.

WHEN THE HAMSTER WHEEL BROKE

While we have harnessed the powers of technology to make unbelievable progress across the globe within areas like healthcare, communication, and production we have also leveraged technology to create scalable digital noise and accelerated global production to a point where we accept inhumane work and general dehumanization.

Humanity is on a path towards immense mental, physical, and emotional stress and vulnerability because we've taken the human out of the equation. It doesn't make technology or globalization the enemies, but they have become the means to a systemic race for scale without much attention to the humans involved. After years of focusing on hardware and software it's time to focus on *humanware*. Bringing the human back into the equation.

We got a wake up call.

The world experienced a global pandemic. Millions have tragically died – many alone. Many more fell ill, lost their jobs and livelihoods as country after country shut down. In some regions opportunities for women and girls went back decades and we are just starting to understand the impact on our children and youth. The stories of individual loss and suffering will haunt us for generations to come.

Amidst all the suffering and individual tragedies, we've also witnessed a global reflection – or Covid-awakening. Many people have stepped out of their hamster wheels, their everyday lives have been turned upside down, and for many it has led to a well needed pause and reflection time: Is my life actually as I'd like it to be? Am I spending enough time with my family? Am I doing what is right for me and for the world? Am I spending my time on the job on the right things? Is my job even right? Do I need and want all the things I buy? A lot of highly relevant questions have arisen during these unprecedented times.

This reflection didn't happen to everyone – in many places people's sole concern was how to keep themselves and their families afloat as everything around them broke. It did however happen to enough people to ignite a shift and allow us to witness interesting signals pointing to the possibility of a rehumanized future. We rewired our attention, time, and money!

During the pandemic we rediscovered our families. Nature.

Biking. Baking. Singing. Spending time with close relations and making our homes a better nest. People moved out of the cities in favor of nature environments, re-boosted local communities, connected stronger with family and close relations, and realized that spending hours commuting every day to an office wasn't actually what they wanted. They wanted something else. [139]

People had a chance to reflect and reconnect to their values and to what is important to them. Some countries experienced up to 85% of the population making sustainable lifestyle changes during the pandemic and WWF is talking about an "eco-awakening" after finding that the surge for sustainable offerings is not only up in the wealthier countries, but also in countries like Ecuador and Indonesia. We saw purchases of local products and services rise dramatically and sustainable brands perform 7x better than conventional ones.[140] Some will also argue that the increased focus on movements like MeToo, BlackLivesMatter, and climate related causes are somewhat due to the fact that people had time to touch base with their values. It became clear to many that they morally didn't align with what they saw in their organizations, communities, and the world when actually looking and stepping out of the hamster wheel.

That was just the beginning. A massive 41% of the global workforce[141] is considering quitting their jobs post-pandemic! The number is even higher among younger professionals.

Recognizing that the above primarily are findings from people who – like you and me – are privileged to have some level of security, jobs, roofs over our heads, and generally enough to survive, it does show signs of a much-needed global reflection. Even if it is only signals from the few - that is how shifts start. The butterfly effect is real.

Let's seize the moment to do better!

REBOOT TO REHUMANIZE

Reflective and future-forward individuals and leaders understand the dehumanization that has taken place globally, in organizations, and our lives. They also understand that they have the power to change that path. They recognize that now – going into a post-pandemic world – it is time to click refresh. It's clearer than ever that the more technological we become the more human we also need to become to not only survive, but truly thrive and flourish. We have been given a unique opportunity to write the history of how we reboot after the pandemic. It is the best chance we get to reflect and do things right for ourselves, our colleagues, our clients, partners, and for the world. Now is the time to leverage our individual and collective power to rehumanize!

Companies that neglect the whole human – humans that flourish in all aspects of life - will be left behind in the war for talent and innovation. They might survive in the short term due to virtual immigration as remote working opens up the talent pool to be truly global, but companies that ultimately don't embrace rehumanization will first loose talented employees. Just look at movements like #TechWontBuildIt where talents and (former) employees take a stand against companies that are considered acting with low morals. Secondly, these companies will lose the support of customers. We're already seeing boycotts of large corporations for not paying taxes, neglecting privacy, selling surveillance technology to authoritarian regimes, leveraging underpaid workers, and other morally questionable actions. Everything in the cards reads this will be a stronger trend going forward and not something companies can (or should) ignore. If companies want to win the future, they need to rehumanize – bring the human into the equation, i.e. their employees, customers, and communities, through their products, services, and offerings as well as their narratives, technologies, and general actions.

Rehumanization is not anti-tech. Technology can – and should – be used to make human lives better. Judging what that specifically means can however be hard and increasingly complex. It is – and will continue to be – a crucial conversation to be had in our lives and organizations to discuss if *what* we do and *how* we do it are making humans and our world better. To guide those important conversations, we need to assess how we leverage technology and a global supply chain, make conscious choices - and continuously re-iterate those as we learn more. We need to leverage a diverse group of people likely in combination with technology to make these assessments – while being mindful of biases. We also need frameworks to guide our conversations and to grow as responsible businesses.

THE FUNDAMENTAL 4s

Let's be honest. There are no easy ways to navigate modern society ethically. It requires research, reflection, courage, and determination. It also requires that we don't give up when we are disappointed. Because we will be. We will be deceived by clever design, shady marketing, or lack of information, but we will need to continue. Just like a child learning to walk and not surrendering by the countless times they fall over before they nail it.

Allow me to offer a framework I hope might serve as an anchor in all of this seeming chaos of exponential technological development and increasing complexity. The foundation comes from all people's desire for becoming better or what we like to call the *Quest for the Better Me*. Becoming better drives us as human beings to continue to develop the world we live in. Invent things. Enhance and improve things. This quest to become better is also what has led us to create the complex world we live in – for better or for worse.

It is also what provides stability in all the complexity and chaos that the world brings. It's something we can rely on and confide in when we make important decisions or develop strategies. Because as humans we all want to honor our fundamental motivations to BE, DO, FEEL and LOOK better.

The model that summarizes these human motivations is called The Fundamental 4s. *Fundamental* because the motivations are basic for all humans, *4* because there are four of them and *4s* (read: force) because the motivations are *forces* that drive humans towards action on their quest towards becoming The Better Me.

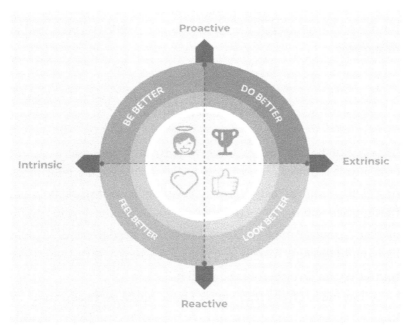

In short the model states this: all people's core motivations are to BE, DO, FEEL and/or LOOK better.

- BE better is about honoring values and moral landscapes, making people feel like a better person.
- DO better is about enhancing results, performance, skills, mastery, making people more successful and capable.

- FEEL better is about triggering senses and emotions leaving people in a better physical and emotional state.
- LOOK better is about improving relations and social status creating sense of belonging and appreciation.

When we are designing, producing, or buying products or services – either as a private person or in duty of work, let's start to ask questions. The Fundamental 4s can help us identify guiding questions like the ones below (feel free to come up with more within each realm) that are helpful to start conversations and take action from:

BE better:
- Is this supporting my own values and moral landscape?
- Is this supporting the values and ethics upon which I think my community / organization / the world should develop?

Think of a company like Patagonia that has taken a clear stand on their values and made their company purpose about being "in business to save our home planet". Relying heavily on manual labor the company has also taken a clear stand on where and how they purchase. They have built a social-responsibility program that analyzes and manages the impacts their business has on the workers and communities in their supply chain. Their goal is not just to minimize harm, but to create a positive benefit for the lives they touch through their business. They are piloting regenerative organic certified™ programs in food and fiber and were part of founding the Fair Labor Association. They have also created Patagonia Action Works that connects skilled volunteers with grassroots groups that are tackling environmental issues.[142]

How might you help yourself and your organization to BE better?

DO better:

The company Be My Eye[143] has more that 5 million volunteers helping blind and visually impaired people "see" through a video-connection anchored in an app. They are getting help from a volunteer with everything from reading a letter to checking a pregnancy test or choosing a shirt in their own time zone and native language. Lately companies are starting to offer help through the app too – like Microsoft help desk and others - providing processed work to benefit blind and visually impaired to DO better.

Asking questions like:
- Is this helping to enhance my own results, performance, skills, or mastery and making me more capable?
- Is this helping other people grow and succeed in a way I think is right?

might be helpful in navigating complexity. And yes, sometimes there will be dilemmas where you might be able to DO better personally on the cost of others. Then you're back to having to check in with your values (BE better). It is not easy, but it's possible. As Christian Erfurt, the CEO of Be My Eyes likes to say: "we're only doing well if no one is doing worse". That philosophy drove them to successfully collaborate with companies on servicing people rather than choosing the easy advertising business model.

FEEL better:

At a program we recently ran at Rehumanize Institute the delegates shared learnings for how they hacked their processed work day with Zoom fatigue and too much sitting down. One person shared how she had started taking "phone walks" – meetings on the phone while walking in nature during Covid. It had completely changed her day, her effectiveness, her mood, and routines for the better and became a change she kept after the pandemic. Interestingly, it also had a contagious effect and phone walks are now a thing in her entire department. Starting small and experimenting for little or no investment can sometimes end up setting new standards and inspire others to change.

Whatever big or small initiative or experiment you engage in, questions like:

- Does this bring me in a better physical or emotional state?
- Does this support people feeling (psychologically) safe and positively impact their psychical and emotional state?

might be helpful to make yourself and others FEEL better.

LOOK better:

Crowdfunding is a way to contribute to and recognize the organizations and products you believe in. Built on that idea, the Danish retail chain COOP – founded more than 150 years ago – decided to create Coop Crowdfunding. A digital platform where they are giving new food vendors the opportunity to get funded and earn space in their store. This has democratized access to their shelves, allowed small vendors a way in, and their customers a say (and a way for themselves to build partnerships with the upcoming, trendy vendors). A relatively simple initiative to allow everyone a way to LOOK better and create a sense of belonging and community.

As we look at ourselves and our business activities let's explore LOOK better questions like:

- Does this improve my relations or sense of belonging?
- Does this reward and recognize the right people?

The more we explore the Fundamental 4s and ask these and similar questions the more transparency we will demand and create. The more we will also develop our own lives and that of our organizations towards a better and more ethical world.

RE-CLAIMING OUR ATTENTION, TIME, AND MONEY

Humans have the unique capability to envision the future. Let's use it. Now. And let's start with ourselves. Just like on the plane where we're told to first put the mask on ourselves before helping others in case of an emergency.

Let's activate the capabilities for reflection we saw surge during the pandemic and turn them into routines. Let's leverage them through The Fundamental 4s to maximize our individual impact towards a better world. Because of the acceleration of technology and complexity we need this global reflection and action to happen sooner rather than later.

Not only do you and I have far more power than we think. We also have a much larger responsibility than we might care to accept. If we are not actively taking a stand to fight dehumanization we are passively defending it. The most important step we can – and need - to take to lead ethical lives is to decide to be bothered. Bothered about the humans that live on this planet with us and those that come after us – our children's children and generations after them. Bothered about the spaceship, that carries all of us humans, called Earth. Bothered about how and why offerings are being developed, produced, and distributed. And bothered about how we use the "currencies" we control; our *attention*, *time*, and *money*. If there was ever a time to re-claim those it is now!

We have been given a chance to reboot. Let's make it right this time!

LAILA PAWLAK

Laila is CEO & Co-Founder of SingularityU Nordic & Rehumanize Institute. She is winner of the Experience Management Achievement Award; named Distinguished Woman Entrepreneur Fellow at the

UN in New York City; nominated twice as Female Entrepreneur of the Year; awarded Investor of the Year; and is on the list of the top 100 female role models, top 50 and 100 people in tech in the Nordics multiple years in a row. Laila is an active angel investor, advisor and board member to startups, politicians and various organizations; she is a global keynote speaker on how to rehumanize our organizations and societies, as well as co-author of *The Fundamental 4s: How to Design Extraordinary Customer Experiences in an Exponential World.*

Photo Credit: Georgi Radevs

ACKNOWLEDGEMENTS

As anyone who has every published a book can attest to, it takes a village. That is particularly true when it comes to non-profit projects and anthologies, which are completely dependent on the generosity of many involved parties.

First off, I need to thank Daisy Løvendahl for sowing the seed that led me to kickstart this project.

All my appreciation and gratitude goes to the essayists who shared their most valuable currencies – time and brainpower – to bring this project to life (in alphabetical order): Adam Pantanowitz, Alex Gladstein, Anna Felländer, Arash Aazami, Benjamin Rosman, Brian David Johnson, Carin Ism, Christian Bason, Christian Villum, Daisy Løvendahl, David Bray, Divya Chander, Elaine Weidman-Grunewald, Evelyn Doyle, Guendalina Dondé, Isabelle Ringnes, Jaya Baloo, Laila Pawlak, Margarita Quihuis, Mei Lin Fung, Mic Mann, Nathaniel Calhoun, Nell Watson, Nille Skalts, Ray Eitel-Porter, Roger Courage Matthisen, Sheila Jasanoff, Tiffany Vora, Valter Adão, and Yngvar Ugland.

Also, a huge amount of appreciation to those behind the scenes who have made the book look far better than I could have imagined, corrected spelling errors and ensured that people can actually get their hands and eyes on it: Nicolette Tham (my wing-person throughout the process), Dania Zafar, and Johanna Petronella Leigh.

Finally, a very special shout out to the one who is always there, my partner in everything, and reason why it all makes more sense, Laila Pawlak.

This has truly been a labor of love. As I wrote in the dedication to my children, they need an ethics revolution. I hope this anthology can play a small part in making that happen!

All the best,
Kris
Præstø, December 2021

ABOUT REHUMANIZE INSTITUTE

Rehumanize Institute is an innovation and knowledge community with the purpose of bringing the human back into the equation to enable everyone to flourish and thrive for the future.

Learn more and how to get involved at rehumanizeinstitute.org.

ENDNOTES

1 https://docs.microsoft.com/en-us/azure/architecture/guide/responsible-innovation/harms-modeling/

2 https://ethicalos.org/wp-content/uploads/2018/08/Ethical-OS-Toolkit.pdf

3 Richard Florida, The Rise of the Creative Class (New York: Basic Books, 2002).

4 Sheila Jasanoff, "In a Constitutional Moment: Science and Social Order at the Millennium," in Bernward Joerges and Helga Nowotny, eds., *Social Studies of Science and Technology: Looking Back, Ahead*, Yearbook of the Sociology of the Sciences (Dordrecht: Kluwer, 2003), pp. 155-180.

5 John Perry Barlow, "A Declaration of the Independence of Cyberspace," https://www.eff.org/cyberspace-independence (accessed August 2020).

6 Kara Swisher, "Hitting the Glass Ceiling, Suddenly, at Pinterest," New York Times, August 14, 2020, https://www.nytimes.com/2020/08/14/opinion/pinterest-discrimination-women.html (accessed August 2020).

7 "Congress Versus the 'Emperors'," New York Times, July 30, 2020, https://www.nytimes.com/2020/07/30/business/dealbook/tech-hearing-highlights.html (accessed August 2020).

8 Marsh v. Alabama, 326 US 501 (1945).

9 https://newsroom.cisco.com/feature-content?type=webcontent&articleId=1815348

10 https://spectrum.ieee.org/transportation/self-driving/accelerating-autonomous-vehicle-technology

11 https://www.forbes.com/sites/bernardmarr/2019/06/05/the-incredible-autonomous-ships-of-the-future-run-by-artificial-intelligence-rather-than-a-crew/?sh=2a335c2b6fbf

12 https://www.theatlantic.com/technology/archive/2016/08/how-artificial-intelligence-got-its-name/495050/

13 https://ieeexplore.ieee.org/document/8746946.

14 https://languages.oup.com/google-dictionary-en/.

15 https://www.reuters.com/article/us-amazon-com-jobs-automation-insight/amazon-scraps-secret-ai-recruiting-tool-that-showed-bias-against-women-idUSKCN1MK08G

16 https://hbr.org/2020/10/a-practical-guide-to-building-ethical-ai

17 https://ieeexplore.ieee.org/document/7924227

18 https://www.aapsonline.org/ethics/oaths.htm.

19 https://www.nature.com/articles/d41586-019-03270-4?utm_source=fbk_nnc&utm_medium=social&utm_campaign=naturenews&sf222706592=1

20 https://scholarlykitchen.sspnet.org/2019/11/26/chefs-selections-the-best-books-read-during-2019-part-1/

21 https://global.oup.com/academic/product/the-death-of-expertise-9780190469412?cc=us&lang=en&.

22 https://ieeexplore.ieee.org/document/7924227

23 Guiding Principles on Trusted AI Ethics, Telia Company, January 2019, https://www.teliacompany.com/globalassets/telia-company/documents/about-telia-company/public-policy/2018/guiding-principles-on-trusted-ai-ethics.pdf

24 Telia Company, https://annualreports.teliacompany.com/en/2016/governance/enterprise-risk-management-/, 2019.

25 Megan Sullivan-Jenks, "Digital advertising trends survey," Choozle.com, July 10, 2018, https://choozle.com/blog/digital-advertising-trends-survey/.

26 Floridi, L. Soft Ethics and the Governance of the Digital. Philos. Technol. 31, 1–8 (2018). https://doi.org/10.1007/s13347-018-0303-9

27 Financial Times (5/07/2019) Are tech companies Africa's new colonialists? https://www.ft.com/content/4625d9b8-9c16-11e9-b8ce-8b459ed04726

28 IBE (2018) The ARTIFICIAL Intelligence Framework https://www.ibe.org.uk/resource/ibe-ai-diagram-int-brefing-final-pdf.html

29 HOUSE OF LORDS, Select Committee on Artificial Intelligenc, Report of Session 2017–19, AI in the UK: ready, willing and able? https://publications.parliament.uk/pa/ld201719/ldselect/ldai/100/100.pdf

30 Grandviewresearch.com. 2020. Artificial Intelligence Market Size Worth $733.7 Billion By 2027. [online] Available at: <https://www.grandviewresearch.com/press-release/global-artificial-intelligence-ai-market> [Accessed 28 January 2021].

31 Colback, L., 2020. The impact of AI on business and society. [online] Ft.com. Available at: <https://www.ft.com/content/e082b01d-fbd6-4ea5-a0d2-05bc5ad7176c> [Accessed 28 January 2021].

32 Gow, G., 2020. Environmental Sustainability And AI. [online] Forbes. Available at: <https://www.forbes.com/sites/glenngow/2020/08/21/environmental-sustainability-and-ai/?sh=13c734d47db3> [Accessed 28 January 2021].

33 See Colson, E., 2019. What AI-Driven Decision Making Looks Like. [online] Harvard Business Review. Available at: <https://hbr.org/2019/07/what-ai-driven-decision-making-looks-like> [Accessed 28 January 2021].

34 See Allyn, B., 2020. NPR Cookie Consent and Choices. [online] Npr.org. Available at: <https://www.npr.org/2020/06/24/882683463/the-computer-got-it-wrong-how-facial-recognition-led-to-a-false-arrest-in-michig?t=161161507751 0&t=1611829043314> [Accessed 28 January 2021].

35 Knight, W., 2019. The Apple Card Didn't 'See' Gender—and That's the Problem. [online] Wired. Available at: <https://www.wired.com/story/the-apple-card-didnt-see-genderand-thats-the-problem/> [Accessed 28 January 2021].

36 Also see View.pagetiger.com. 2019. Responsible AI: Governance Guidebook - 1. [online] Available at: <https://view.pagetiger.com/aigovernanceguide> [Accessed 28 January 2021].

37 Leslie, D., 2019. [online] Turing.ac.uk. Available at: <https://www.turing.ac.uk/sites/default/files/2019-06/understanding_artificial_intelligence_ethics_and_safety.pdf> [Accessed 28 January 2021].

38 West, S., Whittaker, M. and Crawford, k., 2019. [online] Ainowinstitute.org. Available at: <https://ainowinstitute.org/discriminatingsystems.pdf> [Accessed 28 January 2021].

39 Also see Accenture.com. 2020. Professionalization of Artificial Intelligence (AI) | Accenture. [online] Available at: <https://www.accenture.com/us-en/insights/applied-intelligence/professionalization-ai> [Accessed 28 January 2021].

40 Welsh, J., 2019. How Leaders In High Growth Companies Use AI To Accelerate Their Competitive Advantage. [online] Forbes. Available at: <https://www.forbes.com/sites/johnwelsheurope/2019/03/20/how-leaders-in-high-growth-companies-use-ai-to-accelerate-their-competitive-advantage/?sh=4a240f9a369b> [Accessed 28 January 2021].

41 https://en.wikipedia.org/wiki/Distributed.net

42 https://en.wikipedia.org/wiki/Electronic_Frontier_Foundation

43 https://en.wikipedia.org/wiki/Murder_of_George_Floyd

44 https://en.wikipedia.org/wiki/Killing_of_Ahmaud_Arbery

45 https://en.wikipedia.org/wiki/Shooting_of_Breonna_Taylor

46 Collingridge, David (1980). Social Control of Technology.

47 Goering, S., Klein, E., Specker Sullivan, L. et al. (2021). Recommendations for Responsible Development and Application of Neurotechnologies. Neuroethics. https://doi.org/10.1007/s12152-021-09468-6.

48 Cutler, Adam, Milena Pribić, and Lawrence Humphrey (2019). "Everyday ethics for artificial intelligence." PDF, IBM Corporation.

49 https://about.facebook.com/realitylabs/responsible-innovation-principles/.

50 Nishimoto S, Vu AT, Naselaris T, Benjamini Y, Yu B, Gallant JL (2011). Reconstructing visual experiences from brain activity evoked by natural movies. *Curr*

Biol. Oct 11;21(19):1641-6. doi: 10.1016/j.cub.2011.08.031.

51 https://www.youtube.com/watch?v=0017Zwzam1g.

52 Horikawa T. *et al.* (2013). Neural decoding of visual imagery during sleep. *Science 340*(6132): 639-642.

53 https://gallantlab.org/brain-viewers/.

54 https://web.stanford.edu/~palanker/lab/retinalpros.html.

55 https://med.stanford.edu/artificial-retina/research.html.

56 https://secondsight.com/discover-argus/.

57 https://www.sciencealert.com/scientists-reveal-a-marvellous-proof-of-concept-bionic-human-eye.

58 https://www.cnet.com/news/nypd-terminates-robot-police-dog-contract-with-boston-dynamics/.

59 https://www.bostondynamics.com/spot.

60 Hochberg *et al.* 2012, Nature: https://www.youtube.com/watch?v=cg5RO8Qv6mc.

61 https://www.braingate.org/research-areas/neuroscience/.

62 https://ieeexplore.ieee.org/document/9390339.

63 https://www.nature.com/articles/s41586-021-03506-2.

64 Nuyujukian *et al.* (2018) Cortical control of a tablet computer by people with paralysis. PLoS ONE 13(11): e0204566. https://journals.plos.org/plosone/article?id=10.1371/journal.pone.0204566; https://www.braingate.org/publication-videos/.

65 https://pubmed.ncbi.nlm.nih.gov/31642810/; https://neuralink.com.

66 https://ieeexplore.ieee.org/document/7435286?reload=true&arnumber=7435286; M. V. Ruiz-Blondet, Z. Jin and S. Laszlo, "CEREBRE: A Novel Method for Very High Accuracy Event-Related Potential Biometric Identification," in *IEEE Transactions on Information Forensics and Security*, vol. 11, no. 7, pp. 1618-1629, July 2016, doi: 10.1109/TIFS.2016.2543524.

67 https://www.semanticscholar.org/paper/PEEP%3A-Passively-Eavesdropping-Private-Input-via-Neupane-Rahman/893c03f28dfe4d0c7999b0e97744a0df0ca6a7a2.

68 https://www.uab.edu/news/research/item/8454-study-finds-hackers-could-use-brainwaves-to-steal-passwords.

69 https://www.wired.com/story/pacemaker-hack-malware-black-hat/.

70 https://www.fda.gov/medical-devices/medical-device-recalls/medtronic-recalls-remote-controllers-minimed-insulin-pumps-potential-cybersecurity-risks; https://us-cert.cisa.gov/ics/advisories/ICSMA-18-219-02.

71 https://www.mddionline.com/digital-health/how-medtronics-pacemakers-are-now-harder-hack.

[72] https://www.michaeljfox.org/news/
currently-available-deep-brain-stimulation-devices.

[73] https://www.medtronic.com/us-en/healthcare-professionals/products/neuro-logical/deep-brain-stimulation-systems/percept-pc.html.

[74] https://www.nap.edu/catalog/25889/an-assessment-of-illness-in-us-govern-ment-employees-and-their-families-at-overseas-embassies?utm_source=feed-burner&utm_medium=feed&utm_campaign=Feed%3A+nap%2Fnew+%28New+-from+the+National+Academies+Press%29.

[75] https://www.cnn.com/2020/12/05/health/head-injuries-us-diplomats-govern-ment-study/index.html.

[76] https://www.smithsonianmag.com/innovation/
why-brain-brain-communication-no-longer-unthinkable-180954948/.

[77] https://journals.plos.org/plosone/article?id=10.1371/journal.pone.0105225.

[78] https://www.nature.com/articles/s41598-019-41895-7.

[79] Ramirez et al. (2013). Creating a false memory in the hippocampus. Science. Jul 26;341(6144):387-91. doi: 10.1126/science.1239073l; https://pubmed.ncbi.nlm.nih.gov/23888038/.

[80] Vetere G et al. (2019) Memory formation in the absence of experience. Nat Neurosci. Jun;22(6):933-940. doi: 10.1038/s41593-019-0389-0.

[81] Zhao W et al. (2019). Inception of memories that guide vocal learning in the songbird. Science. Oct 4;366(6461):83-89. doi: 10.1126/science.aaw4226.

[82] https://tech.fb.com/inside-facebook-reality-labs-wrist-based-interaction-for-the-next-computing-platform/.

[83] MIT Technology Review In Machines We Trust podcast, 2021-04-28; "What's in a Voice?" https://podcasts.apple.com/us/podcast/whats-in-a-voice/id1523584878?i=1000518953755.

[84] https://www.wired.co.uk/article/breath-analysis-dolby-owlstone.

[85] https://www.worldcoin.global/#news.

[86] https://dogecoincryptonews.com/2021/07/worldcoin-the-eye-scanning-cryp-tocurrency-project-backed-by-sam-altman-and-reid-hoffman/.

[87] https://www.privacypolicies.com/blog/privacy-law-by-country/.

[88] https://nri.ntc.columbia.edu/projects.

[89] https://www.techradar.com/news/
whatsapp-exodus-was-largest-digital-migration-in-history-says-telegram-boss.

[90] Babiloni F et al. (2006) Neural basis for the brain responses to the market-ing messages: a high resolution EEG study. Conf Proc IEEE Eng Med Biol Soc. 3676-9.

[91] Schaefer M, Rotte M (2007). Favorite brands as cultural objects modulate reward circuit. Neuroreport. Jan 22;18(2):141-5.

[92] https://www.thesocialdilemma.com/.

[93] https://medium.com/technicity/ibms-2-nanometer-chip-technology-is-the-world-s-first dcbc56aec416?_branch_match_id=890893649801314751; https://medium.com/technicity/intels-most-powerful-neuromorphic-chips-use-the-human-brain-as-a-model-913acf4b57cc.

[94] https://plato.stanford.edu/entries/aristotle-ethics/

[95] en.wikipedia.org/Politics_(Aristotle)

[96] https://en.wikipedia.org/wiki/Confucianism

[97] Networked Competencies developed by the US Dept of Defense for Health leaders in a Networked world - https://drive.google.com/file/d/0BxWhDjUmHhD6QUdFUDFycDFveFU/view?usp=sharing

[98] https://docs.google.com/document/d/1BBz5lLZ1yL-VSIROWeMAEDHp_SNu-seEmG2wbSj2Rqrw/edit?usp=sharing

[99] https://www.scientificamerican.com/article/humans-could-live-up-to-150-years-new-research-suggests/ https://www.nytimes.com/2021/04/28/magazine/human-lifespan.html

[100] https://www.cdc.gov/healthywater/global/wash_statistics.html

[101] https://hrf.org/presenting-hrfs-2020-annual-report/

[102] https://www.weforum.org/agenda/2021/07/world-hunger-undernourished-food-security/

[103] Shout out to good friend, mentor, and world renowned author and speaker Joe Pine for introducing me to the currencies of time, attention, and money through his pioneering work in 'The Experience Economy'

[104] https://www.gethealthystayhealthy.com/articles/is-sitting-behind-your-desk-bad-for-your-health

[105] https://www.weforum.org/agenda/2016/09/staring-down-the-dangers-of-the-digital-workplace/

[106] https://www.thevisioncouncil.org/media-room

[107] https://www.psychalive.org/cell-phone-addiction/

[108] Technology addiction expert, Dr. David Greenfield

[109] https://destinationhope.com/the-effects-of-drug-abuse-on-memory-and-concentration/

[110] https://www.researchgate.net/publication/339290745_Social_Media_Bytes_Daily_Associations_Between_Social_Media_Use_and_Everyday_Memory_Failures_Across_the_Adult_Life_Span

[111] https://jamanetwork.com/journals/jamapediatrics/fullarticle/2754101

[112] https://www.embarkbh.com/blog/what-is-technology-addiction/

[113] https://universityurgent.care/blog/were-all-addicted-to-our-phones

114 https://www.weforum.org/agenda/2019/08/we-need-more-sleep

115 https://www.businessinsider.com/ways-city-life-is-bad-for-you-2015-7?r=U-S&IR=T#all-that-polluted-air-may-increase-our-chances-of-getting-asthma-5

116 https://www.un.org/development/desa/en/news/population/2018-revision-of-world-urbanization-prospects.html

117 https://www.healthdirect.gov.au/financial-stress https://www.apa.org/research/action/speaking-of-psychology/financial-stress

118 https://www.ha-asia.com/urban-loneliness-little-understood-life-threatening-public-health-challenge/

119 https://www.ruralsussex.org.uk/opinions/only-the-lonely-britains-loneliness-crisis-and-the-urbanrural-divide/ https://time.com/5833681/loneliness-covid-19/

120 https://www.statista.com/statistics/1222815/loneliness-among-adults-by-country/

121 https://hbr.org/2017/09/work-and-the-loneliness-epidemic

122 https://www.nature.com/articles/s41598-019-44097-3 https://selecthealth.org/blog/2019/07/10-reasons-why-being-in-nature-is-good-for-you https://positive-psychology.com/positive-effects-of-nature/ https://greatergood.berkeley.edu/article/item/how_nature_makes_you_kinder_happier_more_creative

123 https://news.mongabay.com/2021/02/as-nature-declines-so-does-human-quality-of-life-study-finds/

124 https://www.globalslaveryindex.org/ https://www.antislavery.org/slavery-today/modern-slavery/ https://www.globalcitizen.org/en/content/9-modern-slavery-items-made-by-slaves-internationa/ https://world-populationreview.com/country-rankings/countries-that-still-have-slavery

125 https://www.unicef.org/protection/child-labour

126 https://www.africanews.com/2021/05/19/ivory-coast-22-people-convicted-of-child-trafficking-on-cocoa-farms//

127 https://www.slavefreechocolate.org/ethical-chocolate-companies

128 https://www.dol.gov/sites/dolgov/files/ILAB/child_labor_reports/tda2019/2020_TVPRA_List_Online_Final.pdfhttps://www.freedomunited.org/freedom-university/products-of-slavery/

129 https://www.freedomunited.org/news/uk-knowingly-sourcing-gloves-company-modern-slavery/

130 Helena Norberg-Hodge, The Future is Local

131 https://www.ran.org/issue/forests/

132 https://www.conservation.org/

133 Weisse, M. and Goldman, E.D. (2020, June 2). We Lost a Football Pitch of Primary Rainforest Every 6 Seconds in 2019. World Resources Institute. https://www.wri.org/blog/2020/06/global-tree-cover-loss-data-2019

[134] International Union for Conservation of Nature. (2021, February). Defor-estation and forest degradation. https://www.iucn.org/resources/issues-briefs/deforestation-and-forest-degradation

[135] https://www.ran.org/issue/whos-funding-forest-destruction/

[136] https://ourworldindata.org/energy-access#:~:text=work%20on%20Energy-,Summary,not%20have%20access%20to%20electricity.

[137] https://www.habitatforhumanity.org.uk/what-we-do/slum-rehabilitation/what-is-a-slum/

[138] https://unstats.un.org/sdgs/report/2019/goal-11/

[139] https://www2.deloitte.com/uk/en/pages/press-releases/articles/four-out-of-five-uk-consumers-adopt-more-sustainable-lifestyle-choices-during-covid-19-pandemic.html https://www.bbc.com/news/business-55630144 https://www.climateaction.org/news/wwf-huge-rise-in-demand-for-sustainable-goods-during-pandemic https://www.reuters.com/article/us-yearahead-europe-coronavirus-sustaina-idUSKBN2950OL

[140] https://unstats.un.org/sdgs/report/2019/goal-11/

[141] https://www.microsoft.com/en-us/worklab/work-trend-index/hybrid-work & https://www.bbc.com/worklife/article/20210629-the-great-resignation-how-employers-drove-workers-to-quit

[142] https://www.patagonia.com/home/

[143] Full disclosure from the author: I met Be My Eyes in their very early days and invited them to be part of an accelerator-program I initiated. I have since joined their board and personally invested in their organization and journey. I have proudly followed them positively impact thousands of people - blind and volunteers alike - around the world since.